面向"十二五"应用型高校国际经贸系列规划教材

国际商务沟通

口语·读写·综合模块

International Business Communication
Oral·Written·Comprehensive model

孙蕊　张鹏　主编

南开大学出版社

天　津

图书在版编目(CIP)数据

国际商务沟通：口语·读写·综合模块 / 孙蕊，张鹏主编. —天津：南开大学出版社，2014.2（2018.8重印）
ISBN 978-7-310-04408-5

Ⅰ.①国… Ⅱ.①孙…②张… Ⅲ.①国际商务—英语—高等学校—教材 Ⅳ.①H31

中国版本图书馆CIP数据核字(2014)第005026号

版权所有　侵权必究

南开大学出版社出版发行
出版人：刘运峰
地址：天津市南开区卫津路94号　邮政编码：300071
营销部电话：(022)23508339　23500755
营销部传真：(022)23508542　邮购部电话：(022)23502200

＊

天津泰宇印务有限公司印刷
全国各地新华书店经销

＊

2014年2月第1版　2018年8月第2次印刷
230×170毫米　16开本　16.25印张　292千字
定价：35.00元

如遇图书印装质量问题，请与本社营销部联系调换，电话：(022)23507125

面向"十二五"应用型高校国际经贸系列规划教材编委会名单

顾　　问：张仁德　纪益员

主 任 委 员：杨灿英

副主任委员：王文治　王乃合

编委会委员：（以姓氏笔画为序）

　　　　　　于志达　王昭凤　刘　琳　孙　蕊　宋春丽　李　菁

　　　　　　张世荣　崔　彤　韩德昌　扈　涛　臧文平

面向"十二五"应用型高校国际经贸系列规划教材

总　序

　　高校教学质量保障体系建设中的教材建设很重要，对于应用型高校来说尤其重要。这是因为：第一，教学需要教材，教材建设需要与时俱进。加强立体化教材建设，教师编写适应网络共享、满足学生自主学习需要、开放式立体化的教材，是适应先进教学理念的需要。第二，改变应用型高校教材建设相对滞后的局面。现行研究型高校本科教材不能适应应用型高校的教学需要，与应用型高校以社会需求为导向、培养高素质应用型人才的教育定位之间存在较大差距。主要表现为：教学内容应试性较强，选择性较弱，与实际需求不相适应，与科学创新不相适应。

　　鉴于此，我们在编写本套规划教材时特别注意了这些问题，并与实务部门及有关教育主管部门沟通、交流意见，力争建立起与应用型高校国际经贸专业外向应用型人才目标管理培养相适应的教材模式和品牌教材。在这个基础上，进一步实施应用型高校的质量管理工程和"本科教学工程"。而着力点是学以致知、学以致用，即以知识和技能的传授、创新、应用为重点，以教学过程管理为主要的工作方法，注意实施形成性评估、养成性教育，而非一次性的终结式评估和终结式教育。这样做的终极目标是突出应用型高校办学最美质量特色，不断提升人才培养质量这条高教生命线的认知水平，更好地满足经济社会发展对应用型、复合型、创新型人才的需要。

　　本套教材规划出版多部书，"十二五"期间将出版10部，它们是：《涉外企业管理》（第五版）、《国际贸易实务操作流程与实训设计》、《创业教育指导教程》、《实用国际经贸地理》、《涉外会计实务》、《国际商务沟通》、《现代商务日语初级教程》（非日语专业教材）、《西方经济学学习指导书》、《企业文化教程》等。此前已出版《中国商务法律》。

　　本套教材涉及面广，受水平和时间所限，内容上难免存在缺点和错误，恳切期望广大读者批评指正。最后以宋·陆游两句诗作结尾："纸上得来终觉浅，绝知此事要躬行。"大意是说，书本上得到的知识终究很肤浅，真正弄懂还要在读书之后亲历实践。

编委会
2012 年 7 月于南开大学滨海学院

前　言

根据当前本科教学的实际情况，结合外向型、应用型人才培养目标，基于课堂教学模式改革及实践型教学方法的驱动，我们组织编写了《国际商务沟通》一书。本书内容设计不同于涵盖商务知识和英语语言学习的商务英语，而是突出了在实际商务环境中应用最广的口头与书面的沟通能力，弱化了一般商务沟通教材中的理论问题部分。因此在全书的结构上，大致可分为以下三个部分：

第一部分为口语部分，由简入繁依次为电话沟通、主持会议、讨论与陈述观点、访谈、工作面试、宣讲技巧和谈判等单元。

第二部分为读写部分，包括电子邮件、备忘录、会议记录、简历与求职信、商务书信、图表应用、（图表）趋势描述、商务报告和跨文化商务沟通等单元。其中，每一单元都包含简介、课文、注释、练习和词汇五大部分。简介部分为中文形式，主要是为了帮助学习者明确每一单元的学习目的和相应沟通技巧的应用方向。课文数量为两到三篇，比较全面地展现了相应沟通技巧的情景模式，是每一单元的学习重点。注释部分是对课文内容的必要补充与精练化总结，强调每种沟通技巧的基本原则、规律与方法。课后练习是针对单个单元的初级训练，建议学习者和教师全面执行并认真修改，为最后的综合模块练习打下良好的基础。词汇部分供学习者和老师参考使用。

第三部分为综合模块，编写这部分的目的是将第一、二部分中的各个单元内容有机地结合在一起，组成较大的学习任务模块，使学习者能够具备将所学知识相互联系，在商务环境中灵活运用以应对实际商务问题的能力。建议利用一定的课时，提供比较真实的场所，指导学习者完成和展示各个模块的任务。

本教材具有注重商务业务模拟和技能训练的特征，适用于以应用型人才为培养目标的高等院校商务英语、国际经济与贸易、国际商务及文秘英语专业的学生，同时也可供企事业单位的相关工作人员作为培训用书与参考资料使用。

本教材由孙蕊、张鹏主编，河南财政税务高等专科学校的赵巍巍参与了第二部分7、8、9单元的编写工作。本教材的编写是建立在实际商务英语教学经验的基础上的，其中的很多注解与练习是通过对多届学生的教学而提炼总结出来的。这样的一个阶段性成果离不开专业主任杨灿英教授对于教学改革的深刻理解与坚持不懈的研究与创新，更离不开经管系各位教授与老师对于教学过程的信任与支持。南开大学的师英副教授、天津理工大学的包延军教授、常海潮副教授等提出了宝贵的修改意见。南开大学出版社协助出版了此书，在此一并表示由衷的感谢！

在本书编写过程中参考了相关的文献，在此向相关作者表示衷心的感谢。由于编写时间仓促及编者水平有限，书中不妥之处在所难免，敬请广大读者和同仁批评指正。

编　者

2013 年 6 月

Contents

Unit 1   TELEPHONE CALL ·· 1
Unit 2   CHAIRING MEETING ·· 13
Unit 3   DISCUSSION AND OPINIONS ·· 25
Unit 4   INTERVIEW ·· 33
Unit 5   JOB INTERVIEW ··· 43
Unit 6   PRESENTATION SKILLS: Organizing the presentation ····················· 50
Unit 7   PRESENTATION SKILLS: Visual aids ··· 66
Unit 8   NEGOTIATION ·· 83
Unit 9   E-MAIL ·· 99
Unit 10 MEMOS ·· 104
Unit 11 MINUTES ·· 110
Unit 12 RESUME AND JOB-APPLICATION LETTERS ································ 121
Unit 13 BUSINESS CORRESPONDENCE ··· 129
Unit 14 CHARTS ··· 140
Unit 15 DISCRIPTION OF TRENDS ·· 152
Unit 16 BUSINESS REPORT ··· 165
Unit 17 INTERCULTURAL BUSINESS COMMUNICAITON ······················ 176
Comprehensive Modules ·· 187
课文译文 ··· 192
课后练习参考答案 ··· 235
主要参考文献 ··· 249

Unit 1 TELEPHONE CALL
电话沟通

I. INTRODUCTION

  毫无疑问，随着大量信息交流的需要，有效的电话沟通技巧日益成为了一种重要的管理范畴的技巧。一个工作人员的电话沟通表现可以被接听者视为整个机构的表现。因此，每天都在发生的电话沟通事关重大。除了一般的员工会接听电话以外，还有一些人会负责接听公司主要的几部电话，他们对于公司的公共形象影响很大。这些人必须训练有素，而不能是新人。因为这些人同客户之间的接触所塑造的公司公共形象比任何广告和宣传都有影响力。

  声音的重要性　电话沟通的最大特点就是通话双方不是面对面的，这意味着对方的声音和语言就成为了沟通的主要媒介。也许实际上并非如此，但是你的或刺耳的或嘶哑的或高声的或微弱的声音可能会被对方当成生气、兴奋、抑郁或无精打采的表现。因此，要学会控制你的声音来给对方留下一个友好、积极向上、热情的形象。

  你的声音要尽量清晰，通话时要郑重其事，不可以一边嚼口香糖或吃东西一边通话。如果你是在用头和肩膀夹着电话通话的，那么你的咽喉部分是歪扭的，因此你的发声吐字就会不清楚。

  还要注意的是，你要像当面遇到一样，在电话里同对方微笑着致以问候。当你微笑的时候，你的声音听起来会更使人愉悦。一项实验显示，电话销售员微笑着同客户交谈时的销售业绩是愁眉不展时的两倍。

  何时接电话　接商务电话时需要及时而且礼貌。电话铃声一般不要超过三声，避免让对方等待太久，无论你有多忙，你总不希望给对方留下你所在公司并不看重客户的印象；也不要响一下就立刻去接，这样对方会感觉非常突然，没有心理准备；当电话响至第二声或第三声的时候，通常就是应该接电话的恰当时机了。清楚和缓地的应答电话，报出公司的名字，比如"Hello, this is … company."（"喂，您好，这里是……公司。"）接内线电话应报出部门名称，如果接到打错的电话要礼貌，不能过于粗鲁。

切记，就算一天内你已经向垂询者问候了50次，对于对方来说也是第一次。还有，在接听电话的时候不要分心，特别要留心听好对方的名字，然后在通话中使用这个名字称呼对方来进行有针对性的信息传递。

搁置电话　据估计，大约70%的商务电话在通话中都会被暂时搁置。美国的商务部执行人员平均每年花在这方面的时间是60小时。如果你因其他亟待解决的事情而必须暂时搁下电话，通常应该询问"您可以稍等吗？"（"May I put you on hold?"）或者"过几分钟再给您打电话，可以吗？"然后等待对方的答复。当你返回通话时，不要显得匆忙，要予以耐心等待的对方足够的重视。

II. EXAMPLES

Call 1

A: Krondike Electronics. Can I help you?

B: Yes, I'd like to speak to Mr. Edwards, please.

A: Who's calling, please?

B: John Bird.

A: Just a moment, Mr. Bird. I'll put you through.

C: Miss Taylor speaking.

B: John Bird here. Can I speak to Mr. Edwards?

C: I'm afraid he's out at the moment. Can I take a message?

B: Yes, could you ask him to call me back as soon as possible?

C: Yes, of course. Could I have your number?

B: He's got it, but just in case, it's 071-253 4686.

C: It's 071-253 4686. Thank you, Mr. Bird. I'll make sure he gets the message.

B: Thank you. Bye.

C: Goodbye.

Call 2

S1: System Support.

Bennett: Good morning. Could you put me through to your purchasing department?

S1: What's it in connection with, please?

Bennett: Software development.

S1: And who would you like to speak to?

Bennett: The department manager. By the way, could you give me his name?

S1: Graham Wareham is our software development manager.

Bennett: Could you just spell that, please?

S1: Yes, W-A-R-E-H-A-M.

Bennett: OK, could I speak to him, please?

S1: One moment, please.

S2: Software development, Janet Parks speaking.

Bennett: Good morning. Could I speak to Graham Wareham, please?

S2: Sure.

Wareham: Wareham.

Bennett: Good morning, Mr. Wareham. My name is Alistair Bennett from Access Computers.

Wareham: Good morning, Mr. Bennett.

Bennett: Mr. Wareham, I see from our files that last year you were interested in commissioning some software from us. I was wondering what had happened to that project.

Wareham: Well, in the end we gave the system control software project to one of your competitors.

Bennett: I see. Well, the reason for this call is that I shall be in London on 21st September, and wonder whether it would be useful for us to meet to discuss other projects.

Wareham: I don't see why not, though there's nothing in the pipeline at the moment. But we can certainly discuss things generally.

Bennett: Okay. Can we say 2 o'clock on the 21st?

Wareham: Yes, 2 o'clock on the 21st is fine.

Bennett: I look forward to meeting you then.

Wareham: Bye.

Bennett: Bye.

Call 3

In this conversation, A (Rocky) is the owner of a small company that manufactures recreational speedboats. He is having a telephone conversation with B (Jacques), owner of a seaside resort in another country.

A: Good morning, Jacques. Nice talking to you again. How's the weather in your part of the world?

B: Couldn't be better, Rocky. Sunny, 29℃, light breeze …

A: Stop! I can't take any more. So, what can I do for you, Jacques?

B: I need a couple of your SY2000 speedboats to rent to guests. Can you give me a price quote?

A: Let's see … uh, the list price is ＄6,500. You're a valued customer, so I'll give you a 10% discount.

B: That's very reasonable. Do you have them in stock?

A: Sure do! We set up new inventory controls last year, so we don't have many backlogs any more.

B: That's good. The tourist season is just around the corner, so I need them pretty quick. What's the earliest shipping date you can manage?

A: They can be ready for shipment in 2-3 weeks.

B: Perfect. What's the total CIF price, Rocky?

A: Hang on … the price will be ＄15,230 U.S. to your usual port. Do we have a deal?

B: You bet! Send me a fax with all the information, and I'll send you my order right away. I'll pay by irrevocable letter of credit, as usual. Same terms as always?

A: Of course.

B: Great! Nice doing business with you again, Rocky. Bye for now, and say hello to your family for me.

A: Will do, and the same goes for me. Bye, Jacques.

III. NOTES

A. The telephone conversations include a number of steps, in particular:

1. Identifying yourself/your company

Krondike Electronics. Can I help you? (A typical switchboard response)

John Bird speaking.

This is Pete Edwards.

John here.

2. Asking the caller to identify himself/herself

Who's calling please?

3. Asking for a connection

I'd like to speak to …, please.

Could you put me through to …, please?

I'd like to speak to someone about deliveries, please.

4. Taking/leaving a message

I'm afraid he's out at the moment. Can I take a message?

Can you ask him to call me back?

5. Explaining the reason for the call

The reason I called is …

I am (just) phoning to …

6. Making appointments

Could you manage Tuesday?

What about Friday?

Shall we say two o'clock?

Just a moment, I'll get my diary.

I'm sorry, I'm out all day.

Friday would be fine.

That suits me.

7. Signing off

I look forward to seeing you.

Thanks for calling.

Goodbye.

Bye.

B. In the telephone conversation the speakers followed a number of steps when handling and exchanging information, in particular:

1. Clarifying information

If you feel the speaker is being vague or imprecise, you can use one of the following expressions to ask for more precise information:

Could you tell me exactly what …?

What do you mean, exactly?

What exactly do you mean by "incorrect bank details"?

Could you explain what you mean, please?

2. Asking for repetition

You may need to ask for repetition in two situations: if you didn't hear what was said, or if you didn't understand what was said.

a. If you didn't hear, you can use one of these phrases:

Sorry? (With a rising intonation)

Pardon? (With a rising intonation)

Pardon me? (With a rising intonation) (US)

Excuse me? (With a rising intonation) (US)

Another strategy is to state your problem and then make a request.

Stating your problem:

(I'm) sorry. I didn't hear what you said.

I didn't quite catch what you said.

I didn't quite catch that.

Making your request:

Could you repeat what you said, please?

Could you repeat that / say that again, please?

b. If you didn't understand, you can state your problem and then make a request:

Stating your problem:

(I'm) sorry. I don't quite follow you.

I don't understand what you've just said.

Making your request:

Could you go over that again, please?
3. Asking for spelling
Could you spell that, please?
4. Showing understanding
I see.

I've got that.

Right.
5. Correcting information
It is quite common to soften a correction by using a polite formula before making the correction:

(Excuse me.) Not the 30th, the 13th.

(Sorry, that's not quite right.) It should be the 13th, rather than the 30th.

(Sorry, I think you've made a mistake.) The 13th rather than the 30th.

No, not Seanew, Seaview.

That's not right, it's …
6. Confirming information
If you want to check that you have understood what the speaker has said, you can use one of the following expressions:

Let me just repeat that, …

Did you say *the bank of Scotland?(stressed, to check that it is the correct word)*

Let me just check …
7. Acknowledging
That's right.

C. Communication by phone involves two parties—the caller and the person called. To be effective on the phone, the caller must have:

1. Clear objectives.

2. The relevant information.

3. A clear strategy and structure for the call.

D. Phone communication—caller's steps:

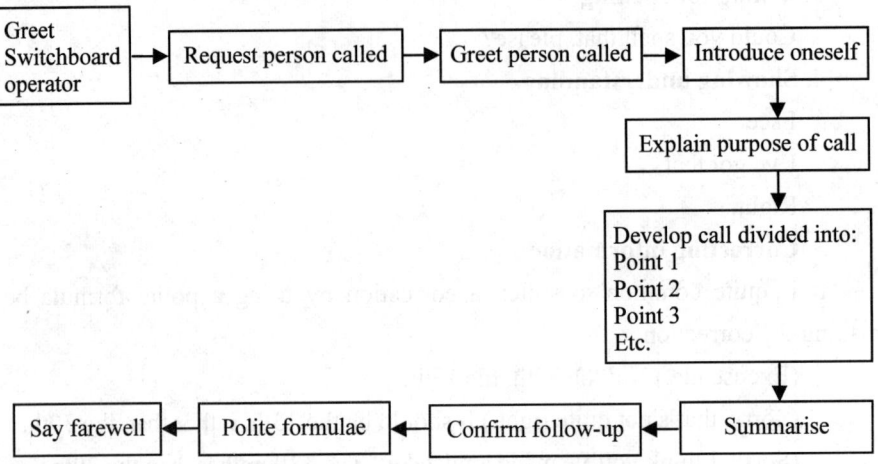

Phone communication—the steps taken by the person called:

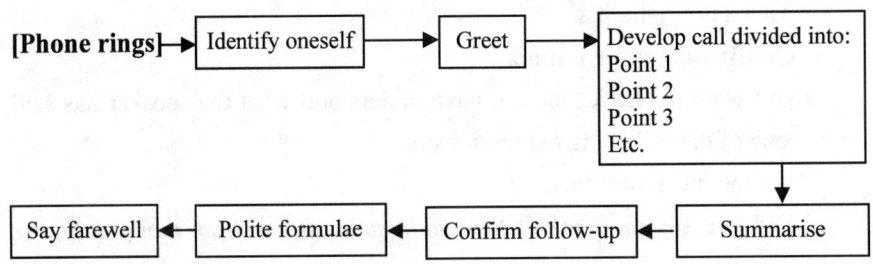

IV. PRACTICE

A. Put the following extracts of telephone calls into the correct order.

1. Just a moment, Mr. Jones, I'll put you through.
   Yes, I'd like to speak to Miss Rathbone.
   Peter Jones.
   Who's calling, please?
   Pan Electronics. Can I help you?

2. She's got it, but just in case, it's 071-253 4686.
   Yes, could you ask her to call me back?
   Mr. Gotman here. Could I speak to Ms Fields?

Yes, of course. Could I have your number?

I'm afraid she's out at the moment. Can I take a message?

3. I'm sorry, I'm out on Wednesday.

Good, that suits me too. Shall we say 11 o'clock?

Just a moment, I'll get my diary … you said next week?

Yes, could you manage Wednesday?

What about Thursday then?

Yes, Thursday morning would suit me fine.

B. Complete these dialogues.

1. My name is Pinkerton.

   _____

   Yes, it's P-I-N-K-E-R-T-O-N.

2. The address is 24 Tunnyside Lane.

   _____

   Yes, of course. 24 Tunnyside Lane.

3. My phone number is 04325686.

   04325688?

   _____ 5686.

   _____ 04325686.

   _____.

4. I'd like an appointment with Mr. Dunn.

   _____

   Yes, I'd like to talk about extending my credit.

5. We would like to visit your factory with a view to buying it.

   _____. When would you like to come?

6. The figure is 3.56 m.

   _____. And what was the other figure?

7. So, an appointment at two would suit you. _____ again please?

   Yes, certainly. It's Macintosh.

   _____?

   Yes, M-A-C-I-N-T-O-S-H.

C. The following sentences (1-16) are taken from a phone call. The purposes of these sentences (a-m) are listed below. Match each sentence with its purpose. The first one has been done for you.

1. Thank for calling. ____l____
2. Can you manage … (day) at … (time)?
3. Yes, that suits me fine.
4. See you soon.
5. I'm afraid I won't be in the office on … (day).
6. My name is …
7. Hilary Beacham.
8. This is … here.
9. Could we meet some time soon?
10. Could you put me through to …, please?
11. Well, thanks for the information.
12. Not at all.
13. I'm phoning to let you know the details of ….
14. Well, I look forward to meeting you next … (day) at … (time), then.
15. Who's calling, please?
16. I'd like to speak to …, please.

a. introduce oneself—first introduction	g. request appointment
b. introduce oneself—second and subsequent introduction	h. suggest time for appointment
	i. confirm details of appointment
c. identify self	j. agree to details of appointment
d. request person called	k. decline appointment
e. ask for caller's identification	l. thank
f. explain purpose of call	m. polite formula

D. Please make use of the following sentences as many as you can and add some necessary supplements to organize a business telephone call and demonstrate it with your partners.

I'm afraid the connection is bad. Would you mind calling back this afternoon?

I'm sorry to interrupt you, but it's urgent.

This is Laura. Sorry to have kept you waiting.

There is much noise here. I'd better hang up and call you in another office.

I think maybe you have dialed the wrong phone number.

His line is still busy. May I take a message or should I tell him to call you back?

Hello, this is Tommy's office. Please leave a message after the beep.

Would you please transfer me to the Sales Department?

Would you connect me with the person in charge of R&D Department?

I am calling to report my progress in project.

It's been a while since we've talked to each other last time. I'm pleased to hear you again.

This is … calling from Guangzhou branch. May I set up an appointment with your manager?

I'm sorry to bother you again. I am calling to check the date of meeting.

I just call for maintenance because my washing machine is not working properly.

I am calling to ask when you will dispatch my order.

Hello! I'm at the intersection of Hugo Street and Chamer Street. Could you tell me how to get to your company?

If there is position in our company that is suitable for you, we'll call you.

Would you be so kind to check my order status?

V. WORDS AND EXPRESSIONS

Put through　接通（电话），通常用作 put sb. through，指的是帮助某人接通他/她呼叫的电话线，常用在总机台的服务语言中。

In case　以免，以防（万一）

　　The meeting will be put off in case it (should) rain.

Purchase　v. 采购

　　相关词汇　purchaser 采购商
　　　　　　　sale 销售

Commission　v. 委托，委任，授予

　　You can commission them to paint something especially for you.

In the pipeline 在酝酿中，在完成中（pipeline 输油管道）
  Important changes are already in the pipeline.
Recreational adj. 消遣的，娱乐的
  The school offers many recreational activities for the students.
Speedboat n. 高速游艇
  What happened when the man tried to swing the speedboat round?
Resort n. 度假村，度假胜地
  The resort is tuned in to the tastes of young and old alike.
Quote n. v. 报价
  Please quote this reference number when reordering stock.
Discount n. v. 折扣
  This has forced airlines to discount fares heavily in order to spur demand.
In stock 有备货，有现货
  We have many patterns in stock for you to choose from.
Inventory n. 存货，盘存
  The inventory situation was righting itself.
Backlog n. 没交付的订货，存货
  We are faced with a backlog of orders we can't deal with.
Around the corner 迫在眉睫的，马上发生的
Shipment n. 装运，载货
  The goods are done up in bundles for shipment.
CIF abbr. Cost Insurance and Freight 到岸价格
  The CIF term requires the seller to clear the goods for export.
Hang on 等候
  Please hang on while I go for some water.
Irrevocable adj. 不可撤销的
  He said the decision was irrevocable.
Letter of credit: 信用证 L/C，是指开证银行应申请人的要求并按其指示向第三方开立的载有一定金额的，在一定的期限内凭符合规定的单据付款的书面保证文件。信用证是国际贸易中最主要、最常用的支付方式。
Term n. 条款，术语
  Myocardial infarction is the medical term for a heart attack.

Unit 2 CHAIRING MEETING
主持会议

I. INTRODUCTION

主持会议的执行者是会议主持人或大会主席，在英语中通常会用 chair/chairperson/chairman 来表示，其中 chairman 一词因为涉及性别区分而常受到女性主义者抨击，所以要慎重使用。

会议主持人是贯穿会议的重要角色，他或她通常会是会议的发起人，因此应该在组织中具有一定的领导力和影响力。会议主持人应该对会议的最终目标非常明确，并尽一切努力引导会议达到预定的目标。这就要求会议主持人在会议的进行过程中展现出强大的控制力。

在会议的开头，会议主持人要根据会议议程陈述会议目标。在会议进行过程中，要注意控制时间，不要让参会人的讨论在一些细枝末节上纠缠不休，使会议进程停滞不前。除非特殊情况，大多数会议主持人会遵循一套既定的程序。

在会议进行过程中，要注意避免参会人说得过多或是偏离主题。在必要的时候作出下列评价："I see your point, and that relates to what we were just discussing."可以帮助会议主持人控制会议而又不会冒犯发言人。会议主持人还需要鼓励那些沉默不发言的人说出自己的观点，例如"Juan, how does this look from the perspective of your department?"

在会议的末尾，会议主持人需要汇总大家的意见，总结会议决议，重申需要布置的任务并确保每一个人都清楚他们的职责。

II. EXAMPLES

MEETING 1

There are three managers discussing some strategic options.

Doug: Look, let's get down to business. We've essentially got two items to cover this afternoon: firstly, the short-term decision about the appointment of a new UK marketing manager and secondly, the longer-term strategic issue—namely developing international managers throughout the group. So, where do we stand on this appointment? Helga?

Helga: If we go for the obvious choice—that's Mary Walters—we'll be making a safe decision. If we went for the other strong candidate—that's George Maxwell—there would be more of a risk, but, as always, perhaps more of an opportunity.

Doug: I know what you mean. What do you think, Wayne?

Wayne: I look at it from the corporate point of view. If we don't appoint from inside—that's Walters—we won't be listened to when we talk about "opportunities within the group". I understand what Helga is saying about George Maxwell—he's a maverick and sometimes organizations need people like him. But if we appointed him, I'd have to resign and you, Doug, would have to as well.

Doug: I think you're overstating the case but I see what you're getting at—so it's going to be Mary Walters. Let's leave that for a moment and move on to the related issue of developing international managers. Wayne, I know you have strong views on this.

Wayne: Dead right. It's vital for the group that we get our act together. There are two major options: either we take the long-term route via internal development—in other words through training—or we go out into the market and start looking for international managers. If we take the first option, it'll be five years before we have a pool of managers with genuine international experience. If we took the second option, we could do it by next year, but I'm not sure at what cost to the morale of our existing staff.

Helga: Quite so. What is an international manager anyway? No, in my opinion, we have no option. We must develop our own people. If we started a system of exchange between sales and production staff from one country to another, it wouldn't take five years. It would also identify those managers with the motivation and the potential.

Doug: Right. I sense you're both in favour of the home-grown option. Wayne, could you put something on paper so we can present it to the board?

Wayne: of course, Doug.

Doug: Right, let's just come back to Mary Walters.

MEETING 2

Mortenson is one of the world's biggest leisure groups. They own and manage a number of theme parks throughout the world. Their European headquarters are based in Amsterdam. The European business coordinator, Jane Newby, has called a meeting to discuss the possible closure of one of their theme parks outside Paris—Megadrome. Attending the meeting are Francois Picard (Manager of Megadrome), Helmut Ritter (Financial Controller—Europe) and Pam Cohen (Marketing Director – Europe).

Jane: Right, you all know why I've called this meeting. The Megadrome Park has had a serious drop in income over the last 6 months. Francois has circulated a report in which he makes it clear that he feels this is only a temporary setback and he expects the park to return to profitability in the first half of next year. Now, we have three options facing us: one is to close the park completely; the second is to keep it open but on a much reduced scale and therefore cost and the third, which is basically Francois's view, is to continue as before. I think we've all had time to analyse the figures so I'd like to confine this meeting to your assessment and conclusions. Helmut, how do you see it?

Helmut: Very dimly, I'm afraid. I see no evidence that the park will return to profitability next year, or for that matter at any time in the foreseeable future ...

Francois: I don't believe you have read a single word ...

Jane: Francois, you'll have a chance to give us your point of view in a second. Let Helmut finish first.

Helmut: Right, as I was saying. I'm afraid Megadrome is a lost cause. We've already lost nearly $400000 in the last 6 months. We can't afford to continue absorbing those sorts of losses. I think we should close it down as soon as possible and liquidize our assets.

Francois: What do you mean by liquidizing our assets? ... We wouldn't be able to sell ...

Jane: Just a moment, Francois, we'll come to you in a moment. So, let me just summarise. Helmut is for closing the park as soon as possible and selling off the land and property. Is that right?

Helmut: Yes, I know we're not likely to get a very good price for the land but I think we're better off selling now rather than waiting another 6 months and finding property prices have fallen even further.

Jane: Thank you, Helmut. Pam, what's your view?

Pam: Helmut's right when he says we've lost an awful lot of money but I think we have to look at in the wider European context. All our European parks are going through hard times and entry numbers are down in all cases ...

Helmut: Maybe, but nothing like ...

Jane: Helmut, let's see what Pam has got to say.

Pam: Yeah, I was saying all the European parks are suffering as a result of the tough economic climate and we've just commissioned an independent survey of the entire theme park business in Europe which indicates that as many as 40% of all parks will have closed by spring next year.

Helmut: Exactly, that's just my point.

Jane: Helmut, we've listened to you. Let's listen to Pam now.

Pam: Right, so we can anticipate a much reduced number of theme park operators next year. At the same time, most economists are forecasting a recovery throughout Europe from about the middle of next year. Now, at the moment, our customers are staying at home and saving their money but I feel we can expect them to start spending again by the middle of next year. There will be fewer parks to visit and I think Megadrome could be very well placed to pick up an increased share of the market.

Jane: So, you're in favour of keeping it open?

Pam: Oh, yes, I am. But at a reduced level through the winter months. I'd like Francois to propose a plan for limited opening for the period November to March and then start again with a bang beginning of April in time to catch the Easter holiday business.

Jane: Right, Pam. So you're in favour of option 2—operating on a much reduced scale—for a 5 month period?

Pam: That's right.

Jane: Francois. You've been very patient. No doubt you see this differently.

Francois: Not really. I agree with everything Pam has said but I'm worried about her conclusions.

Jane: You mean the 5-month reduced operation?

Francois: That's right. I'll look at that option, of course. But you've got to understand that the largest running cost of Megadrome is the depreciation on all the equipment. If we just open at weekends, for example, we've got to offset a reduced gate income against the same level of depreciation.

Helmut: Francois is right. That's why I feel the only option is to close down and sell off the equipment.

Francois: You've heard what Pam was saying about the state of the market. There's no way we would find a buyer for the equipment in the present economic climate ...

Jane: Ok, Francois, I can see what you're worried about. I'd like you to go away and work on a couple of reduced opening options—say, just weekends and a more drastic solution—just over the Christmas period. Right, we'll have another meeting next Monday when you can present the financial implications of the two options and we'll make a decision then. Right, there's just one other point ...

III. NOTES

A. Outline of meeting 1

Jane Newby chaired this meeting quite actively. She controlled the process tightly but gave each individual a chance to express his/her views. Let us look at some of the language she used:

1. Introduction
- Indroducing the subject:

Right, you all know why I've called this meeting. The Megadrome Park has had ...

- Introducing the scope:

Now, we have three options facing us: one is to close the park completely; the second ...

I think we've all had time to analyse the figures so I'd like to confine this meeting to your assessment and conclusions.

2. Controlling the discussion

- Starting:

Helmut, how do you see it?

- Dealing with interruptions:

Francois, you'll have a chance to give us your point of view in a second. Let Helmut finish first ...

Just a moment, Francois, we'll come to you in a moment.

Helmut, we've listened to you. Let's listen to Pam now.

- Summarizing:

So, let me just summarise. Helmut is for closing the park as soon as possible and selling off the land and property. Is that right?

- Concluding:

So, you're in favour of keeping it open?

- Clarifying:

You mean the 5-month reduced operation?

- Sympathizing:

Francois. You've been very patient. No doubt you see this differently.

Francois. I can see what you're worried about.

3. Assigning action points

I'd like you to go away and work on a couple of reduced opening options.

B. More examples

a. Meeting requirement

Good afternoon, everyone. Let's get started. First of all, there will be no cell phones at the meeting, so please turn off your phones now. Second, let's go through the agenda, we have three topics today: (1) Mr. Stone will make a presentation to us; (2) We'll discuss the presentation; (3) We'll discuss the report from account department. Now let's go to the first topic. Henry, please.

b. Opening greetings, address and introduction

Ladies and gentlemen, please take a seat. The meeting is about to start. My name is Mary Ross, and it's my honor to serve as master of ceremonies for the 4th annual meeting. On behalf of our company I would like to give a warm welcome to every distinguished guest. I thank you for having graciously accepted our invitation and truly hope that you feel stimulated by this exchange of ideas. First of all I'd like to introduce our guests present at this meeting ...

c. Announcing objectives

- The purpose of this meeting is to plan ahead for next year's marketing strategy.
- One of the topics for today's meeting is how to increase our market share.
- We're here today to discuss about the interest rate rise.
- Today, I'd like us to consider marketing in general and European marketing in particular.
- I've called this meeting in order to discuss about the interest rate rise.
- At this meeting, we're going to look into the pros and cons of employing immigrant labor.

d. Task assignment

- Kevin, please take notes.
- Mr. Brown, could you please take the role of our timekeeper?
- Susan will lead point 1, Tom point 2.
- Could you send me an email, listing all the support needed for this program?
- Could you provide a program status summary to me?

e. Agendas

- There are four items on the agenda, first ..., second ..., third ..., and last ...
- The game plan for this morning's meeting is to finish ordinary business in the first half hour, then take time out for coffee, so then, in the second half, we can zero in on the all-important question of new product development.

f. Moving forward

- What shall we discuss next? I suggest we have a word about insurance.
- Now I'd like to turn to the possible solutions.

g. Keeping the meeting on time

A: How are doing on time? Do we run out of time?

B: There are only five minutes left. The meeting has to be run behind schedule.

A: Since we are a little short on time, can you please explain it briefly?

B: Sure, because our time is running short, I'm going to skip over the next two points and concentrate on the last point.

h. Keeping to the point

A: How does this point fit in with the issue being considered?

B: Sorry, I'm wandering off the point.

A: But that's interesting. Could we come back to that a little later?

B: OK, thank you.

A: Now let's get back to the subject.

i. Invitation to speak

- We sincerely hope that all present will feel free to speak candidly and exchange their opinions constructively.
- I encourage and hope that everyone participate in today's discussion.
- Mike, can we get your input?
- Before starting this second brainstorming, I would like to give the floor to my colleague George, who, I am sure will be very delighted to brief you about our governance approach.

j. Keeping order

A: What qualifies you to say so? I'm not satisfied with you, too.

B: Let's not get too heated up.

C: He told us completely different things last time and today. What on earth is going here?

A: I think I should clarify that. Last time probably you didn't hear clearly. I'd like to repeat again, please pay more attention.

B: Ok. Everyone, keep quiet!

k. Taking a break

- We don't seem to be making much headway in our discussion. Why don't we call time out for half an hour and then try again?
- So, as we are more or less agreed in general terms, why don't we break off now and come back later to deal with each item in detail?

l. Recapping the meeting

We have covered a lot of points today. First, our designing team has come up with a final version of the product that emphasizes technology. Second, after a long and arduous process, we've made it past the review board and received approval to begin production. Lastly, we have organized a production team to oversee the manufacturing stages.

m. Closing the meeting

- I thank you for your attention and I declare this conference closed.
- That concludes the formal part of our program. Anything you'd like to add?
- I think we've dealt with all the issues on the agenda today. Thank you for coming.

IV. PRACTICE

Divide into groups of five, with each person assuming the role of a chairman at your institution. Draw straws to determine who will be the chairman calling the meeting, and use this person's agenda. Conduct a 15-to-20-minute meeting. Following the meeting, evaluate its effectiveness.

V. WORDS AND EXPRESSIONS

Get down to   开始认真处理
   Okay, that's the broad plan—let's get down to the specifics.
Item   n. 项目条款
   The next item on the agenda is the publicity budget.
Cover   v. 覆盖，涉及，包括
   The book aims to cover all aspects of city life.
Issue   n. 问题
   I want us to play hardball on this issue.
Appointment   n. 任命，委任
   动词形式   appoint
   They made the appointment of Peter as chairman of the union.
Corporate   adj. 法人的，公司的

名词形式　corporation

The owner opened a corporate checking account at the bank.

Maverick　n. 特立独行的人，标新立异的人

He was too much of a maverick ever to hold high office.

Resign　v. 辞职

The President is under intense pressure to resign.

Overstate　v. 夸大，夸张

He tends to overstate his case when talking politics.

Dead　adv. 绝对，极度

Dead stop　急刹车

Dead sleep　沉睡

Get our act together　行动一致

We need to get our act together and come to see you.

Route　n. 路，途径

The plane did not fly the usual commercial route.

Via　prep. 通过，凭借

They have arrived at a solution via scientific investigation.

A pool of　一组，一队，储备的

Genuine　adj. 真正的，纯种的

Is the painting a genuine Picasso?

Morale　n. 士气，斗志

Mail from home is a great morale booster for our soldiers.

Motivation　n. 动机，动力

The motivation for the decision is the desire to improve our service to our customers.

Potential　n. adj. 潜力，潜能

The firm has identified 60 potential customers at home and abroad.

Home-grown　adj. 本地出产的，本国制造的

Also, companies need to have homegrown leaders who are paid as foreigners.

Put something on paper　落在纸面上，整理成书面文件

Board　n. 董事会

The board completely disregarded my recommendations.

Theme park　主题公园

A theme park is differentiated from an amusement park by its various "lands" (sections) devoted to telling a particular story. These lands are characterized by the idea that the immersive environment they create contains architecture, landscaping, stores, rides, and even food that support a specific theme. Visual intrusion from other "lands", or from outside the park, are considered undesirable.

Income　n. 收入

　　Who will be the main beneficiary of the cuts in income tax?

Circulate　v. 分发，传递，传阅

　　Cooking odors can circulate throughout the entire house.

Setback　n. 退步，挫折

　　Since that time there has never been any setback in his career.

Profitability　n. 盈利状况，收益性

　　Low levels of profitability mean there is a lack of incentive to undertake new investment.

Dimly　adv. 昏暗的，隐约的

　　He was only dimly aware that it was raining.

Foreseeable　adj. 可预见的

　　A new world war is unlikely in the foreseeable future.

Absorb　v. 吸收，忍受，承担

　　The country simply cannot absorb this influx of refugees.

Liquidize　v. 使流动

Asset　n. 资产

　　Intelligence was her main asset.

Summarise　v. 总结，综述

　　Five chapters are included except preface and summarise.

Sell off　出售，廉价卖掉

　　Investors are set to make a killing from the sell-off.

Property　n. 财产，所有权

　　The property is the birthright of the eldest child.

Be better off　最好是

　　He'd be better off going to the police about it.

Context　n. 全文，上下文，背景

　　We are doing this work in the context of reforms in the economic, social and cultural spheres.

Economic climate 经济形势，经济气候

Few businesses are flourishing in the present economic climate.

Survey n. 普查，调查

The results of the survey made fascinating reading.

Economist n. 经济学家

He cast a professional economist's eye on the problem.

Recovery n. 复苏，好转

The new policy did not bring the hoped-for economic recovery.

Pick up 重拾，恢复，不费劲的得到

Industrial production is beginning to pick up.

Share n. 份额

They claim to have a 40% worldwide market share.

Propose v. 提议，打算

I suggest to propose a toast to our friendship.

Bang n. 砰的声音，猛击声

The birds flew with a bang of a gun.

Easter 复活节

Easter is celebrated on the first Sunday after vernal equinox（春分）every year. It comes between March 22 and April 25. This year it falls on 16th, April. The word "Easter" is named after Eastre, the Anglo-Saxon goddess of spring.

Entry number 进入的人数或次数

Entry number is not exhausted, but no longer valid, should also re-apply for a visa.

Running cost 运营成本，又称 operating cost

Depreciation n. 折旧

The depreciation of other currencies in Asia has also caused a substantial reduction in tourism.

Offset v. 抵消

Prices have risen in order to offset the increased cost of materials.

Gate income 门票收入

Gate money accounts for only two thirds of the club's income.

Drastic adj. 激烈的，彻底的，严厉的

A drastic reformation of the present housing system has been carried out.

Unit 3 DISCUSSION AND OPINIONS
讨论与陈述观点

I. INTRODUCTION

讨论和陈述观点的技巧会被广泛地用于各种会议之中，是商务沟通中的一个必备的环节。讨论中包含有大量的沟通"回合"，每一个"回合"的开始、进行和结束都涉及在本课所介绍的关于倾听他人、打断他人、有效陈述自己的观点、争辩说服、继续推进后续的讨论等技巧。

商务人士如果能掌握良好的讨论技巧，就能在一些事项的决策过程中发挥自身应有的影响力，展现自我的商业才能，推动商务操作的良性运作。

II. EXAMPLES

TEXT 1

Here is a promotion review committee discussing the strengths and weaknesses of three candidates for promotion.

Joan: Oh I don't know. He's already been with the firm for 20 years. Surely he's not still expecting promotion. Do you agree, peter?

Peter: Well, John Jeffrys has always shown great loyalty to the firm. It's time this was rewarded, in my opinion.

Clive: It's not just a question of loyalty. Would he be any good at the job? He would need to manage a small team—he's got no experience of that yet.

Peter: He never will have any experience unless we give him a chance!

Joan: We can't afford to be sentimental. I don't think he's the man for the job. He's always been a follower, not a leader. Let's move on to the other candidates. Rita Hayden has already shown great personnel management skills, I feel, even if she's …

Peter: Oh, come on, Joan! She's still learning her trade! We can't afford to take a risk with someone so inexperienced.

Clive: I agree with Peter. Rita's not yet ready for the responsibility. I favour Susan Palmer. She's got a lot of experience. She's already worked in the department on other occasions so she knows the ropes and she's …

Joan: But she's always struck me as a bit cautious. We need someone dynamic for this job.

Peter: I'd agree with Clive. I think Susan Palmer would do a good job. Maybe she's a bit cautious but she's solid, reliable … We need those qualities too.

Joan: Well, if you're both so sure, I suppose I'll have to agree …

TEXT 2

This is a discussing among four colleagues about the price strategy for a new product.

Alex: Right, we're here today to discuss the pricing of our new timekeeping product—the latest in the range of electronic desk diaries. We need to look at the various elements which make up the final price—starting with the manufacturing cost, which, as you can see from this chart, we have set at $15.80 per unit.

Helen: Excuse me, can I ask a question?

Alex: Of course. Go ahead.

Helen: Is this manufacturing cost based on production figures at full capacity?

Alex: I think Horst can best answer that question …

Horst: Yes, of course. The simple answer is no. The $15.80 figure is based on 70% capacity—in other words, 30000 units a month.

Helen: So, just to get that clear. That means we're working on annual target sales of 360000?

Horst: That's right—the lower end of your forecast sales.

Helen: Thank you. Please go on.

Alex: So, as I was saying, the manufacturing cost is set at $15.80. We have calculated our distribution costs at $2 per unit, bringing the price up to $17.80.

Helen: Can I interrupt again?

Alex: Go ahead.

Helen: Are we planning to distribute solely through our existing wholesalers?

Alex: I can answer that one. Our present distribution policy, as you know, is to use the wholesalers. We have considered going straight to the retailers but, for the time being, we're working on a single channel.

Helen: I see. Because, of course, pricing will have to change if we go direct to the retailers.

Alex: That's right. But let's leave that option open, shall we?

Helen: Sure.

Alex: Now, the next element is our promotion costs. These we have fixed at $3 per unit—giving us a unit price of $20.80. Are you all happy about that?

Helen: That's what we've agreed.

Alex: That's right. Now a typical mark-up for us—the manufacturer—would be around 20%—let's say $4.20—meaning the cost to the wholesalers will be $25.00.

Deborah: Can I just clarify one point?

Alex: Sure, Deborah.

Deborah: This figure's been discussed with the wholesalers?

Alex: I assume so ... Helen?

Helen: Well, we've had some preliminary discussions and indicated this sort of figure.

Deborah: And what's their response been?

Helen: They seem happy with it.

Deborah: Good. Sorry to interrupt.

Alex: Now, that just leaves the wholesalers' and retailers' mark-ups. Typical figures here would be 10% to the wholesaler and 20% to the retailer.

Helen: So that means ... just a moment ... a wholesale price of around $27.50 and a retail price in the shops of ...$33.00.

Alex: That's right. Helen, what do you think?

Helen: In my opinion, it's too high. We've got to aim for a figure around ...

TEXT 3

A: If you don't want the powder to cost more, we can't add anything. We'll just have to sell it the way it is now, and put a warning on it. Then, if someone uses dirty water, they shoulder the responsibility, not us.

B: I'm sorry, but I have to disagree. There are three very good reasons why it would be the wrong thing to do.

A: You seem very sure of what you are saying. Can you back it up?

B: As I see it, first of all, most people there can't read, so a warning won't help them at all. Second, even if their governments say a warning is enough, other groups won't. They call out the media hounds, and many people will be very, very angry with us. Sales will go down everywhere.

C: You said there were three good reasons, Sara. Is there another reason you want to add?

A: Yes, there is. Third, and most important, it just wouldn't be right if we knew even one person wouldn't listen to the warning, and a child is hurt because of it.

C: I can't argue with that. How could we live with ourselves if we knew we let that happen? And just because we wanted to make more money.

A: It wouldn't be just because of the money. Those people aren't healthy, and our powder is better than mother's milk. Some people might set sick, but isn't it more important that we help so many others?

III. NOTES

1. Statement

   We have set (the cost) at $15.8 per unit.

2. Interruption

   Excuse me, can I ask a question?

   Can/May I interrupt for a moment?

   Can I interrupt again?

   Can I just clarify one point?

   If you don't mind, may I say one word?

   If I can just interrupt for a moment, I'd like to make the point that …

I'm sorry. I don't quite follow you. Could you go over that again, please?

3. Encouragement

   Of course.

   Go ahead.

   Sure.

   Certainly.

4. Question for information/clarification

   Is this manufacturing cost based on ...?

   This figure's been discussed with the wholesalers?

   You suggested that we might be spending too much on advertising. Can you clarify that?

5a. Direct answer

   We've had some preliminary discussions.

   As I understand it, we can look forward to an important policy this year.

   Does that answer your question?

5b. Redirection

   I think Horst can best answer that question.

   That's a tough question to answer; I don't think I'm the right person to answer this question, perhaps our general manager can help to answer it ...

5c. Postponement

   Let's leave that option open, shall we?

   I'd rather comment on this later on. I will pick up where we left off just now.

   I'm sorry I cannot answer your question at this time. I will have an answer ready before the next meeting.

6. Checking/Confirming/Understanding

   So, just to get that clear. That means ...

   That's all right.

7. Giving opinions

   We can express our opinions on a scale from strongly to weakly.

   Strongly—I'm convinced/sure/positive that ...

       I definitely/certainly think that ...

       I really do think that ...

Neutrally—In my opinion, …
　　　　　I think/consider/feel that …
　　　　　As I see it, …
　　　　　From my point of view, …
Weakly—I'm inclined to think that …
　　　　　I tend to think that …

8. Agreeing/Disagreeing

We can use the following scale to show the range from agreement to partial agreement to disagreement.

Agreement—I totally agree/accept …
　　　　　I fully/completely agree …
　　　　　I am in total agreement with …
Partial agreement—up to a point/to a certain extent I'd agree with …, but …
　　　　　You could/may be right, but …
Disagreement—I'm afraid I can't agree with …
　　　　　I don't agree.

9. Likes and preferences

I'd like to look at the arrangement.

I like to start by …

I'd prefer not to run it.

I don't particularly like running interviews.

10. Advising and suggesting

Shall we …?

Let's …

We should … (strong)

The figure shouldn't be changed. (strong)

Production ought to manage with less. (strong)

Why don't you …?

How about …?

I suggest you …

I always advise colleagues to …

I'd also recommend that ….

11. Moving on/Back to the topic
    (Thank you.) Please go on.
    Good. Sorry to interrupt.

IV. PRACTICE

Please compose a group work discussing one of the following topics:
—Reducing inventory levels
—Recruiting a new employee
—Running a marketing campaign

V. WORDS AND EXPRESSIONS

Promotion　n. 促销，推广
　　During 1984, Remington spent a lot of money on advertising and promotion.
Loyalty　n. 忠诚，忠心
　　She told him the truth from a sense of loyalty.
Sentimental　adj. 感情用事的，多愁善感的
　　I realized he accepted my suggestion for purely sentimental reasons.
Inexperienced　adj. 缺乏经验的，不经事的
　　She was inexperienced and needed a guiding hand.
Know the ropes　懂行，老马识途
　　It took me several weeks to know the ropes in this office.
Strike　v. 猛然意识到，突然想起
　　At this point, it suddenly struck me that I was wasting my time.
Dynamic　adj. 有活力的
　　The last decade saw the emergence of a dynamic economy.
Solid　adj. 踏实的，可靠的，可信赖的
　　Mr. Zuma had a solid reputation as a grass roots organiser.
Quality　n. 素质，品质，才能，优点
　　He wanted to introduce mature people with leadership qualities.
Pricing　n. 定价
　　And I could do the selling and the pricing at the boutique.

Manufacturing cost 生产成本
The lower end of 下限，下端
Distribution n. 分销
  He admitted there had been distribution problems.
Wholesaler n. 批发商
  The wholesaler admitted there had been distribution problems.
Channel n. 渠道
  The government will surely use the diplomatic channels available.
Retailer n. 零售商
  Take the goods back to your retailer who will refund you the purchase price.
Leave … open 未解决，悬而未决
  Don't take the job now. Keep your options *open* until you *leave* university.
Unit price 单价
  It is a unit price of ten dollars a ticket.
Mark up n. 利润加成，增加标价
  The local customers could not accept not an average mark-up of 10%.
Preliminary adj. 初级的
  After a few preliminary remarks he announced the winners.
Shoulder v. 承担，担当
  He has had to shoulder the responsibility of his father's mistakes.
Back up 支持，证明
  The girl denied being there, and the man backed her up.
Hound n. 猎犬，卑劣的人

Unit 4   INTERVIEW
访谈

I. BUSINESS KNOWLEDGE

Interview 一词一般有两个含义，即"访谈"和"面试"，在这里主要指"访谈"。在商务沟通中，访谈有何用武之地呢？在大多数情况下，访谈被用于商业咨询、客户访问、商业类座谈、财经类广播电视节目等情景之中。特别是商业咨询和客户访问，是很多公司机构在运营过程中需要频繁进行的沟通工作。

访谈的主要目的是要从受访人那里获取大量的、准确的、最新的信息。基于这种特点，在商务访谈在进行之前需要工作人员进行周密的准备。因为商务领域的访谈具有主题性强和后续应用性强的特点，因此它也比一般的访谈更具有专业性，也更严肃，访谈双方都应该很谨慎地参与其中。

从语言学习的角度来说，访谈是属于对话范畴的，但它是一种比较特殊形式的对话，对话的双方分别为采访人和受访人。这样一来，两者的角色就固定下来了。采访人的任务主要是访谈的开启、介绍、引导、提问以及结束；受访人的任务则主要是回答问题。从双方语言的占比来讲，受访人所占的比重较大而采访人所占的比重较小，否则会有喧宾夺主的感觉。

II. EXAMPLES

INTERVIEW 1

Ten years ago, Pete Jenkins started his own landscape design company. His business grew rapidly as his reputation spread as a first-class landscape designer. Two years ago, as the economic climate worsened, his business started to struggle. He has called in a marketing consultant, Simon Clark, to help him increase business once again.

Simon: Mr. Jankins, I think I know enough about the product now. I can see that you're an excellent landscape designer and very well-thought of in the business. I'd like to turn to some other of what we call the marketing mix. I think the easiest way to do this is to consider firstly, your pricing, secondly, your territory—and in particular, how far afield you operate—and finally, promotion—in other words how you spread the word. So, let's start with pricing. Do you think price is an important factor?

Pete: Yes and no. It depends on what type of contract really. For large landscaping projects—you know, new estates, office blocks—price is critical. On the other hand, for small private contracts, you know, private gardens etc., price is not the main factor.

Simon: And what proportion of your business involves large contract work?

Pete: Less and less. It used to be about 75% of the business 5 years ago. Now, I reckon it's not more than 20%.

Simon: And the private contract side is not price-sensitive.

Pete: I wouldn't say that. Price is important to the customer but, if they like the design and you can do it when they want, they're prepared to pay more.

Simon: I see. Well, let's move on now to what I call place. Basically, where is your market and how big is it?

Pete: I suppose 90% of the work we do is local—you know, within a 50 mile radius of here. Occasionally, we go further afield. We had a job up in Scotland for one of our clients recently.

Simon: Is there any reason you have to limit yourself to this area?

Pete: Well, I suppose landscape design is usually a local service—except for the big boys, of course.

Simon: What do you mean by the big boys?

Pete: Well, there are one or two national design companies who operate all over Britain, even abroad.

Simon: So there's no reason why you shouldn't offer your services further afield?

Pete: No, no, I suppose not. Certainly the pure design side could be offered nationwide.

Simon: Right, well we'll come back to that. Let's turn now to the last point which is promotion. How do you go about promoting your services?

Pete: Well, to be honest, it's largely a question of word of mouth.

Simon: You mean personal recommendations?

Pete: Yes, I suppose I do. Of course it's not enough. That's why I've called you in.

Simon: But surely you must advertise your services?

Pete: Not really, we have an entry in the yellow pages—you know, the trade telephone directory and that's about it.

Simon: And do you think that does any good?

Pete: Difficult to say. We do get enquiries …

Simon: Have you ever considered other forms of promotion?

Pete: Such as what?

Simon: Well, advertising in gardening magazines or some sort of sales promotion?

Pete: No, not really. There's an annual agriculture show and we have a stand at that every year. I can't say it brings in any business but it's a type of PR, I suppose.

Simon: What about actual selling, knocking on doors—do you do any of that?

Pete: Well, I used to get to know the planning officers in the town hall—you know, so that I got to hear of any new contracts coming up. But, to be honest, I've stopped doing that. There's no work anyway.

Simon: I see, so you don't do any direct selling?

Pete: No, no, not really.

Simon: Ok, well, let's come back now to the product and …

INTERVIEW 2

Peter Harrington has been voted the Young Entrepreneur of the Year. His company, PH industries, produces a new generation of voice-activated computers (VACs). In this interview he talks about his work with Samantha Evans, a reporter from *Business World*.

Samantha: Peter, you've been voted Young Entrepreneur of the Year. Now, what does this mean to you?

Peter: Well, obviously I'm very pleased that the work we're doing here at PH industries is getting recognition. And I'm pleased not only for myself, but also for everyone here who's made it possible. But I don't want this award to distract me from my purpose here, which is to make PH a major player in the VACs market.

Samantha: PH has taken off in a big way. Where is it leading to?

Peter: Well, if I look into my diary for the next week, we can get an idea of where the interest in VACs lies. On Monday morning, I'll be looking over our new production site at Hinton. In fact, we needed to move in earlier than planned because demand has been higher than expected. So, we've had to speed up every aspect of the operation. One thing I've learned over the last three years is that you never make up lost time.

Samantha: So, have you closed down the old plant totally now?

Peter: Yes, everything is up and running at Hinton. So, after Hinton, I've got a meeting in Paris with our French team. We need to tie up a deal for the distributing of the VAC2000, which is becoming a business-standard model for many big names.

Samantha: So the VAC2000 is making its mark in France?

Peter: Oh, yes, and faster than I expected. Of course, that's part of the reason for the pressure to get Hinton up and running. So, once I've found out the scale of the immediate French needs, I'm moving on to Zurich for an afternoon meeting with a major software manufacturer.

Samantha: Ah, would that be Visitech?

Peter: You'll find that out very soon! Maybe even next week. But there are still some points to iron out. Um, so, that takes care of Monday.

Samantha: A full day?

Peter: Well, let's say a typical day. From Zurich I'm going on to Budapest on Tuesday. There are some very exciting opportunities in Eastern Europe at the moment.

Samantha: Our information is that the market situation is quite stagnant at present.

Peter: Well, Rome wasn't built in a day. We have to take a medium-term view and look at where they are going to be five years from now. The potential is enormous. My job is to make sure that we're there when the barriers are truly broken down. At the moment, I am talking them round to our way of thinking and way of working. The rest will happen when the time is right.

Samantha: So, is Hungary your only area of interest in East Europe?

Peter: No, not at all. In fact, after Tuesday morning in Budapest, I'm going to Prague, where we already have the seeds of a very successful joint venture. We're planning to open up a major production centre in the north of the Czech Republic. It'll be funded partly by us and partly by a new East Europe technology development fund.

Samantha: That sounds very exciting.

Peter: Yes. On Monday and Tuesday I'll be sowing the seeds for the European operations of PH industries.

Samantha: And Wednesday?

Peter: Wednesday, I'm back in Hinton for a series of internal meetings. I've brought forward our monthly marketing meeting, because of the unexpected sales increases. So, I'll be looking over the figures with the marketing team during the morning. And in the afternoon, there is series of technical meetings to look into the successor to the VAC2500. In fact I only put in a token appearance at technical meetings because that's not my forte. Oh yes, in between I have a lunch invitation in London to address the Anglo-Danish Chamber of Commerce on European Technical Integration.

Samantha: Is that as a result of the new political Europe?

Peter: No, not really, it's just a coincidence. Thursday I'm spending here. From my diary I see that my secretary has set up two meetings for me with visitors from European technologists: one from Germany and the other from Japan. I'm looking forward to that; that should be quite interesting. And between the meetings I have to catch up on matters here in Hinton.

Samantha: And Friday?

Peter: As a rule I keep Friday free to deal with matters that need attention here. With the business moving so quickly, I don't like to take myself away from base more than necessary. And I like to give everyone here an opportunity to talk to me about developments on a regular basis. You see, I'm convinced that we've got the winning team here and I want to make sure that it stays that way.

III. NOTES

A. Questions
The interviewers used a variety of question types.

1. Direct questions

   What sort of public transport do you use?

   Are you happy with the service?

   What do you use your car for at the weekends?

   Do you always take your car?

These questions are effective for seeking fairly neutral information.

2. Indirect questions

   Could I ask you what you think of the fares?

   Do you mind if I ask you whether your car is a company car?

These more polite forms are often used when we seek more delicate or confidential information. They are also useful for structuring the interview:

   Could I start by asking you whether you live in …?

   Can I now move on to ask you some questions about …?

3. Statement questions

   I suppose you drive to work then?

   So you use public transport, is that right?

These are often used when we assume or predict the answer. They are also used in a more conclusive way:

   But you don't actually use it for company business at all?

   So you like the idea of the perk – a sort of status symbol?

B. Answers
The respondent used a variety of ways of answering.

1. Direct

   No, I live just outside in a village.

   Yes, I do.

2. Confirming

   That's right.

3. Contradicting

    No, actually I don't.

    I didn't say that.

4. Time to think

    Let me think … well …

    I suppose to …

    I've never really thought about it …

IV. Practice

You are meeting a new potential supplier. You want to find out whether his company will be a good supplier for you. Use a variety of question types. The first one has been done for you.

    1. Start the questioning by asking about the full company name.

        Could I start by asking you what your full company name is?

Ask some direct questions about:

2. Its location:

3. No. of employees:

4. Limited company or not:

5. Date of foundation:

Ask some check questions based on your assumptions:

6. Its success:

7. Its fast delivery times:

8. Its good after-sales service:

9. Now change the direction of the question to more financial areas:

Ask some delicate questions about confidential information:

10. Its finances in general:

11. Its level of liabilities:

12. The name of its bank:

    13. Complete the interview by asking whether you can contact some other customers:

V. WORDS AND EXPRESSIONS

Landscape　n. 风景
　　The landscape had a stark, unworldly beauty.
Well-thought-of　adj. 声誉良好的，受尊重的
　　Their family has always been well thought of around here.
Marketing mix　营销组
Territory　n. 领土，领域，版图
　　Resources in plenty can be found in this territory.
Afield　adv. 远离着
　　Some villagers have never been further afield than the neighbouring town.
Spread the word　推广，传播
　　We hope college life will help him to spread his wings a bit.
Estate　n. 不动产，房地产
　　His estate was valued at $150,000.
Block　n. 街区
　　She walked four blocks down High Street.
Radius　n. 半径
　　They deliver to within a 5-mile radius of the store.
Word of mouth　口头传述的
　　I have informed him by word of mouth.
Yellow pages　黄页（电话）查号簿（按行业、职业分类的部分常用黄色纸）
PR　public relations　公共关系
Distract … from　转移，分心
　　The noise out of window makes me distract from my reading.
Entrepreneur　n.（法）企业家，承包人
　　The entrepreneur takes business risks in the hope of making a profit.
In a big way　大张旗鼓，大规模
　　The Americans, true to style, went into the business in a big way.
Look over　仔细检查审视，翻阅
　　Look over exercises before handing them in.
Speed up　加速

Once these difficulties were got over, the work would speed up.

Tie up 束紧，包起来

They're negotiating a tie-up with Ford.

Big name 知名人士，众所周知的事情

Saunders handled big-name divorce cases.

Make one's mark 成功，出名

If he wants to make his mark on history, he must move faster than his predecessors.

Get … up 安排

Immediate adj. 当前的，直接的

She felt an immediate attraction for him.

Iron out 熨平，解决，处理

He expects to iron out these difficulties at a special conference next week.

Stagnant adj. 不流动的，不景气的，停滞的

His father sowed the seeds of persuing the truth for the young boy.

Talk around 劝说，间接的谈论

Why did she talk around the subject rather than come to the point?

Sow v. 播种，散布，灌输

Why did she talk around the subject rather than come to the point?

Bring forward 提出

We'll bring forward the matter at the next conference.

Successor n. 继任者，继承人

反义词 predecessor 前任

Who's the likely successor to him as party leader?

Token adj. 象征性的，作为标志的

Black is a token of mourning.

Forte n. 特长，强项

Originality was never his forte.

In between 在中间

I'm very busy but I'll try to sandwich that job in between visitors.

Anglo-Danish Anglo 加在表示国家、民族的形容词之前构成新的形容词，表示"英国的"，"英国和……的"

Danish 丹麦的

Chamber　内庭，议事厅
　　Chamber of commerce　商会
Catch up on　赶完
　　I have to catch up on my work so I can't come out.

Unit 5   JOB INTERVIEW
工作面试

I. INTRODUCTION

　　工作面试是面试官与求职者之间的一次正式会面，这期间可以互相询问问题和充分交换信息。工作面试具有双重目的：一方面，招聘单位的主要目的是寻找可以与单位要求最契合的最佳人才；另一方面，求职者的主要目的是寻找与自身能力和目标相契合的最佳工作岗位。

　　求职者在参加面试之前，应该做好充分的准备。首先要尽量多地了解应聘单位的基本情况，例如运营模式、目标市场、战略目标等。接下来，应预测将会被问到的问题以及准备询问对方的问题。再有，要在服饰、发型、面部化妆等方面设计好适合自己并适合应聘单位的风格，这有利于建立自己的自信心。

　　一般的面试流程会包括热身、问答、结束、询问、信息反馈、答谢等环节。进入面试室后，等面试官告诉你"请坐"时才可坐下，坐下时应道声"谢谢"。热身阶段会涉及一些寒暄性的问题，看似和工作岗位关系不大，但实际上面试官已经开始形成对你的印象。因此你的肢体语言、语音语调、面部表情等方面会显得非常关键。问答阶段一定要注意聆听。礼仪方面要注意，坐椅子时最好坐满三分之二，上身挺直，这样显得精神抖擞；保持轻松自如的姿势，身体要略向前倾，不要弓着腰，也不要把腰挺得笔直，这样反倒会给人留下死板的印象，应该很自然地将腰伸直，并拢双膝，两手自然地放在上面。有两种坐姿不可取：一是紧贴着椅背坐，显得太放松；二是只坐在椅边，显得太紧张。切忌跷二郎腿并不停抖动，两臂不要交叉在胸前，更不能把手放在邻座椅背上，或加些玩笔、摸头、伸舌头等小动作，这些都容易给人一种轻浮傲慢、有失庄重的印象。在结束阶段可以涉及一些薪金水平的询问。面试结束后招聘单位会给出通过或拒绝的信息反馈，无论你收到什么样的回复，都应该寄回答谢信。

II. EXAMPLES

TEXT 1

Common types of interviews

Organizations use various types of interviews to discover as much as possible about you and other applicants.

A structured interview is generally used in the screening stage. The employer controls the interview by asking a series of prepared questions in a set order. Although useful for gathering facts, the structured interview is generally regarded as a poor measure of an applicant's personal qualities. Nevertheless, some companies use structured interviews to create uniformity in their hiring process.

By contrast, the open-ended interview is less formal and unstructured, with a relaxed format. The interviewer poses broad, open-ended questions and encourages you to talk freely. This type of interview is good for bringing out your personality and for testing professional judgment. However, some candidates reveal too much, rambling on about personal or family problems that have nothing to do with their qualifications for employment, their ability to get along with co-workers, or any personal interests that could benefit their performance on the job. So be careful. You need to strike a balance between being friendly and remembering that you're in a business situation.

Some organizations perform group interviews, meeting with several candidates simultaneously to see how they interact. This type of interview is useful for judging interpersonal skills.

Another modern twist is the situational interview or behavioral interview, in which an interviewer may describe how you handled some situation in your past. Many companies have learned that no correlation exists between how well people answer interview questions in a traditional interview and how well they perform on the job. The situational interview is a hands-on, at-work meeting between an employer who needs a job done and a worker who must be fully prepared to do the work.

TEXT 2

To handle the interview effectively, the interviewer will need to call into play a number of key tactics.

(1) Observation. To collect data about dress, appearance, voice, height and weight, if these are going to be relevant. The interviewer can also gauge the candidate's mood and the appropriate response by the non-verbal clues that are provided.

(2) Listening. The remainder of the interviewer's evidence will come from listening to what is said. Not only is he listening to the answers to questions, but also he is listening for changes on inflection and pace, nuances and overtones that provide clues on what to pursue further. The amount of time that the two spend talking is important, as an imbalance in one direction or the other will mean that either the candidate or the interviewer is not having enough opportunity to hear information.

(3) Questioning. In order to have something to listen to, the interviewer will have to direct the candidate. Thus, of course, he does by questioning; his questions should encourage and enable the candidate to speak freely, so that the interviewer can learn. The art of doing this depends on the personality and style of the interviewer, who will develop his personal technique through a sensitive awareness of what is taking place is the interviews he conducts.

(4) Answering questions. This is the other side of the coin, and the interviewer needs to ensure that the candidate is given every opportunity to ask his or her questions and get satisfactory answers.

Before closing the interview it is useful for the interviewer to summarise the key points and issues. The final step is for the interviewer to say what happens next.

III. NOTES

COMMON INTERVIEW QUESTIONS

Questions about college

1. What courses in college did you like most? Least? why?

2. Do you think your extracurricular activities in college were worth the time you spent on them? Why or why not?

3. When did you choose your college major? Did you ever change your major? If so, why?

4. Do you feel you did the best scholastic work you are capable of?

5. Which of your college years was the toughest? Why?

Questions about personal attitudes and preferences

6. Do you prefer to work in any specific geographic location? If so, why?

7. How much money do you hope to be earning in 5 years? In 10 years?

8. What do you think determines as person's progress in a good organization?

9. What personal characteristics do you feel are necessary for success in your chosen field?

10. Tell me a story.

11. Do you like traveling?

12. Do you think grades should be considered by employers? Why or why not?

Questions about work habits

13. Do you prefer working with others or by yourself?

14. What type of boss do you prefer?

15. Have you ever had any difficulty getting along with colleagues or supervisors? With instructors? With other students?

16. Would you prefer to work in a large or a small organization? Why?

17. How do you feel about overtime work?

18. What have you done that shows initiative and willingness to work?

Questions about employers and jobs

19. What jobs have you held? Why did you leave?

20. What percentage of your college expenses did you earn? How?

21. Why did you choose your particular field of work?

22. What are the disadvantages of your chosen field?

23. Have you served in the military? What rank did you achieve? What jobs did you perform?

24. What do you think about how this industry operates today?

25. Why do you think you would like this particular type of job?

QUESTIONS TO ASK THE INTERVIEWER

1. What are the job's major responsibilities?
2. What qualities do you want in the person who fills this position?
3. How do you measure success for someone in this position?
4. What is the first problem that needs the attention on of the person you hire?
5. Would relocation be required now or in the future?
6. Why is this job now vacant?
7. What makes your organization different from others in the industry?
8. How would you define your organization's managerial philosophy?
9. What additional training does your organization provide?
10. Do employees have an opportunity to continue their education with help from the organization?

IV. PRACTICE

A. This is a great opportunity to join the team at Google focusing on enhancing our corporate mission through M&A transaction. We are looking for an associate to join our corporate development team where you will be mentored by some of the best deal people in the business. In this role, you will screen external inquiries for potential acquisition deals, research domestic and international market segments, and participate in deal activities working closely with corporate development managers, principals and the director.

Our ideal candidate is a top performer who brings high levels of energy and enthusiasm; works well with large and diverse teams and has a demonstrated ability to think creatively.

REQUIREMENTS:
- Bachelor's degree required.
- 1~3 years of experience in strategic consulting, investment banking or relevant corporate experience preferred.
- Strong quantitative and qualitative analytical ability required.
- Excellent oral and written communication skills.

- Demonstrated ability to manage multiple projects simultaneously.
- Must be a team player with a sense of humor.

B. Divide the class into two groups. Half the class will be recruiters for a large chain of national department stores looking to fill manager trainee positions. The other half of the class will be candidates for the job. The company is specifically looking for candidates who demonstrate these three qualities: initiative, dependability, and willingness to assume responsibility.

1. Have each recruiter select and interview an applicant for 10 minutes.
2. Have all the recruiters discuss how they assessed the applicant in each of the three desired qualities. What questions did they ask or what did they use as an indicator to determine whether the candidate possessed the quality?
3. Have all the applicants discuss what they said to convince the recruiters that they possessed each of these qualities.

V. WORDS AND EXPRESSIONS

Relevant　adj. 有关联的，中肯的
　　Copies of the relevant documents must be filed at court.
Gauge　v. 测量，评估，判断
　　Can you gauge what her reaction is likely to be?
Non-verbal　adj. 非言语交际的
　　Culture plays a large part in non-verbal communication.
Inflection　n. 变音，转调
　　We usually end questions with a rising inflection.
Nuance　n. 细微差别
　　He watched her face intently to catch every nuance of expression.
Overtone　n. 泛音，言外之意
　　It's a quite profound story, with powerful religious overtones.
Imbalance　n. 不平衡，失调
　　Social imbalance worries him more than inequity of income.
Screen　v. 筛，拍摄
　　The ozone layer screens out dangerous rays from the sun.

Uniformity n. 单调，均匀性

The pressure towards uniformity constantly threatens to erode local traditions.

Format n. 版式，形式

They switched from set speeches to a question-and-answer format.

Pose v. 提出，引起

When I finally posed the question, 'Why?' he merely shrugged.

Ramble v. 漫谈，漫步，漫游

We are alone together, and may ramble where we like.

Co-worker n. 同事，同义词 colleague

Strike a balance 调和折中，冲账

We try to strike a balance between justice and mercy.

Simultaneously adv. 同时的，一齐

The Windows allows a computer user to execute multiple programs simultaneously.

Interact v. 相互作用

Teachers have a limited amount of time to interact with each child.

Interpersonal adj. 人际的

Interpersonal skill 人际交往技巧

Twist n. 揉搓之物

A thin twist of smoke curled from the cottage's single chimney.

Correlation n. 相关性

A high correlation exists in America between education and economic position.

Hands-on adj. 亲自实践的，实际动手操作的

This hands-on management approach often stretches his workday from 6 a.m. to 11 p.m.

Unit 6   PRESENTATION SKILLS
Organizing the presentation
宣讲技巧之构架

I. INTRODUCTION

　　本课内容围绕着如何组织有效的宣讲来展开。Presentation 表示为"宣讲"，是因为其中含有"展示，说明"的意思。而我们通常所说的 Speech 应该叫作"演讲"，更正式化、语言化和艺术化。

　　一般商务环境中涉及的销售、培训、职业学习都需要不断地面向客户、雇员和学习者进行宣讲。然而不是每个人都知道，几乎所有商务人士每年都要作一次大型宣讲和许多次小型宣讲。这些宣讲有的面向客户，有的面向上级或下级，有的是对同事。因此，在宣讲准备阶段，宣讲者必须评估以下三个问题：宣讲属于什么类型？希望在宣讲对象身上达到什么目标？达到这个目标的最佳方法是什么？

　　本课主要要求学习者能够对宣讲内容的组织结构进行规划，突出所讲内容的逻辑性、层次感和主次分明的特点等。

II. EXAMPLES

Presentation 1

　　Here is a presentation given by a Director of NETCOUNT Software Ltd, a supplier of account software to small business users. He outlines the competitive position of the company.

　　What I'd like to do is to outline a SWOT analysis of the company, which we have recently carried out. As I'm sure you all know, SWOT stands for strengths, weaknesses, opportunities and threats.

So let's start with the strengths. It's apparent that our main competitive advantage is our range of products. Our accounts software packages are perceived as the most user-friendly on the market, relatively easy to install, requiring much less training than our competitors' packages and representing better value for money. So, all in all we've got an excellent product. Our other main strength is our people—especially on the after-sales side. Our after-sales team is perceived as faster, more qualified, friendlier and generally more efficient than our competitors. This applies both to the help-desk and the field maintenance people.

Right. Let's turn to the weaknesses. Although we have such a strong product, we haven't achieved the sort of market penetration we should have. Basically this is because our marketing is not so effective as our competitors'. One especially, STERLING, has a much stronger presence in the market both in terms of sales and profile. We've relied too heavily on product quality, not enough on promotion. We've got to put considerably more effort into our advertising and direct mail campaigns.

So, that brings me to the opportunities. We're clearly not taking the opportunity we have to dominate the small business user market. We could be achieving significantly higher sales—I estimate fifty to sixty percent more. We could also be building a much more extensive customer base—this would ensure a more secure future as well.

Our main threat, of course, is STERLING. They've got a much more impressive dealer network and their promotion is a lot more sophisticated than ours. On the other hand, we've got the better range of products. We should be capitalizing on this. One way ...

Presentation 2

Geoff Bridges, Project Manager in charge of the Viscal 2000 videophone is presenting the product and marketing policy to the board of his company.

Geoff: Well, this is the moment we've all been waiting for. At long last I can give you some hard facts about what has become—well—a sort of taboo subject in the company—the Viscal 2000—our first videophone product. My objective today is to inform, not to persuade; hopefully you're all already 100% behind this product. I realize you've got a full agenda so I intend to briefly run through the four P's for the Viscal 2000—the product, the place, the price and the promotion. Please interrupt me if you've got any questions, alright?

To start with, then, the product. I'd like to break this into two parts; firstly, what it consists of and secondly, how it works. If you look at this mock-up drawing, you'll see that it basically consists of four elements; a video screen, a videocamera, an audio receiver and an audio transmitter. Of course, in electronic terms there are some more complex parts but one of the great product benefits of the Viscal 2000 is its simplicity of assembly and therefore also maintenance. Moving on briefly to how it works. It's important to understand how the call is set up. First, the audio signal is established in the same way that any phone call is made; then the video channel will be opened using a separate line, only if the called subscriber also has a videophone set. If he does, then the audio and the video signal will be synchronized and the call with sound and picture can take place. If there is no receiving videophone, then a normal audio call can take place, it that all clear?

Board member: Ah, just one question. Does that mean there is a delay between receiving the audio signal and the video signal?

Geoff: Yes, there is a slight delay of about 2 seconds but by the time they start talking the two channels will be synchronized.

Board member: I see.

Geoff: Anyway, that is a short description of the product and the process. Let me move on now to the place, by which I mean how we are going to distribute the product and where. The launch date for the product is the 1st September 2004 and it will then be in stock in all registered retail outlets throughout the UK. We will also be making the videophone available by mail order with a guaranteed 28 days delivery. However, there's an important aspect of customer acceptance which I'd like to come onto under my third heading of price.

The product will retail at approximately $500 plus VAT but it will only be available to customers who are connected to the integrated digital network—in other words, if they are not connected to this digital network, there will be an additional connection charge—now normally this costs just under $500—but we've agreed a special connection charge of just $300 with the network operator. So, in conclusion, that means a total price of $800 plus VAT for most customers, as the majority are not yet connected to the digital network. I hope that all makes sense. In any case, I'll leave these written specifications with you which you can study at your leisure.

So finally, the last P is promotion. Firstly, I should say that we have allowed a period of two years to achieve a significant penetration in the market—that means more than 25000 terminals installed. The launch advertising campaign will be targeted at the residential user and, to reach them, we've just commissioned a TV ad which will show the benefits of the videophone to users with relatives or close friends who live a long way away. We aim to promote the product throughout the UK but will concentrate initially on the south east. I'll be getting back to you in a couple of months' time with much more detail on the promotion campaign.

Right, I'll stop here. I hope you have now a clearer picture of the product, the distribution, the pricing and some first thoughts on the promotion. I'm also sure that you now share my enthusiasm for the Viscal 2000 which I've no doubt will not only open up a new sector of the market but ensure long-term growth and prosperity for our company.

III. NOTES

A. Purpose and audience analysis

Keeping your purpose uppermost in mind helps you decide what information to include and what to omit, in what order to present this information, and which points to emphasize and which to subordinate.

Most business presentations have one of these four purposes:
- Reporting: Updating the audience on some project or event
- Explaining: Detailing how to carry out a procedure or how to operate a new piece of equipment
- Persuading: Convincing the listeners to purchase something or to accept an idea you're presenting
- Motivating: Inspiring the listeners to take some action

After your presentation is over, the most important question that remains is whether you accomplished your purpose.

In addition to identifying demographic factors such as the size, age, and organizational status of your audience, you need to determine the audience members' level of knowledge about your topic and their psychological needs (values, attitudes and beliefs). These factors provide clues about everything from the overall content, tone, and types of examples you should use to the types of questions to expect and even the way you should dress.

The larger your audience, the more formal your presentation will be. When you speak to a large group, you should speak more loudly and more slowly and use more emphatic gestures and larger visuals. Usually, you should allow questions only at the end of your talk. If you're speaking to a small group, you can be more flexible about questions and your tone and gestures will be more like those used in normal conversation.

B. The elements of an effective presentation are:

1. The effective organization of the information
- Transparency of structure:

Have a clear beginning, middle and end.
- Organization of content:

Identify clearly the main points and the supporting point.

The speaker always follows a number of steps, as the simple chart below:

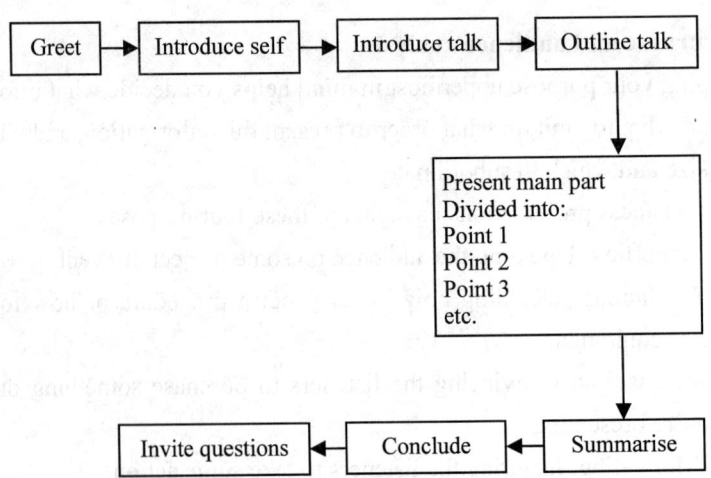

2. The effective delivery of the information

We also take references from the following information to make our presentation effectively.

a. Introduction
b. Statement of objectives:
   My objective today is to inform …
c. Outline of structure:
   Realize you've got a full agenda so I intend to briefly run through the 4P's.
d. Place for questions:
   Please interrupt me if you've got any questions.
e. Starting section 1:
   To start with, then, the product …
f. Dividing section 1:
   I'd like to break this into two parts; firstly … secondly …
g. Referring to visual aids:
   If you look at this mock-up drawing, you'll see that it consists of basically four elements …
h. Closing section 1:
   Is that all clear?
i. Transition and starting section 2:
   Anyway, that's a short description of the product and the process. Let me move on now to the place …
j. Clarifying:
   … by which I mean how we are going to distribute the product …
k. Closing section 2:
   However, there's an important aspect of customer acceptance which I'd like to come onto under my third heading of price.
l. Clarifying:
   … in other words …
   I hope that all makes sense. In any case, I'll leave these written specifications with you which you can study at your leisure.
m. Starting section 4:
   So, finally the last P is promotion.
n. Leaving till later:
   I'll be getting back to you in a couple of months' time with much more detail on the promotion campaign.

o. Finishing:

Right, I'll stop here.

p. Summarizing:

I hope you now have a clearer picture of the product, the distribution, the pricing and some first thoughts on the promotion.

q. Concluding:

I'm also sure that you now share my enthusiasm for the visual 2000 which I've no doubt …

3. The effective use of language.

The effective use of language includes the ability to use connectors to show the relationship between ideas. We put these words or phrases at or near the beginning of a sentence or clause. They connect the following information with the earlier information:

In particular, we've noted our trading strengths as well as our weaknesses. (Highlight)

First of all, let me say it has given me a great personal satisfaction to read in the press that Rossomon is considered one of the hundred best companies to work for in the UK. (Time)

As a result, we can't afford to take on as many employees as our competitors. (Cause)

We can use connectors and sequence markers to signal different types of relationships between ideas. The main ones are:

(1) To signal time relationships

    First   first of all   to start with

    Second   secondly

    Then   after that   next

    Finally   last of all   lastly

(2) To signal logical relationships

a. cause

    therefore   so   as a result   that's why (informal)

b. contrast

    yet   however   but

c. condition
   then   in that case
d. comparison
   similarly   in the same way
e. concession
   anyway   at any rate
f. contradiction
   in fact   actually
g. alternation
   instead   alternatively
(3) To signal textual relationships
a. addition
   also   in addition
b. summary
   to sum up then   in brief   in short
c. conclusion
   in conclusion   finally   lastly   to conclude
d. equivalence
   in other words   that means   namely
e. inclusion
   for example   for instance   such as
f. highlight
   in particular   especially
g. generalization
   usually   normally   as a rule   in general
h. stating the obvious
   obviously   of course   clearly

C. Contrasting with written report

A presentation is a talk given by a speaker to one or more listeners. To be effective, the speaker's message must pass to the listeners, i.e. it must be heard and correctly understood.

When we contrast it with written report, we can find:

a. Spoken language uses a lot more redundant language. However, this is essential in helping the audience to following the presentation and giving them time to absorb the information.

b. Spoken language is more expansive and, because the listener has only one chance to understand, this encourages repetition and clarification.

Contrast:

Written version:

Retailing at approximately £500 per terminal, it will be available through all registered telecom retail outlets to any customer who is connected to the integrated digital network.

Spoken version:

The product will retail at approximately £500 plus VAT but it will only be available to customers who are connected to the integrated digital network—in other words, if they are not connected to this digital network, there will be an additional connection charge …

c. Spoken language is more personal.

Contrast:

Written version:

It is confidently believed that the Viscal 2000 represents a significant market opportunity for the company with its ability to open up a new sector of the residential market.

Spoken version:

I'm also sure that you now share my enthusiasm for the Viscal 2000 which I've no doubt will not only open up a new sector of the market but ensure long-term growth and prosperity for our company.

D. Different techniques to hold attention

1. Emphasis

What I am convinced of is the complete lack of trust that exists amongst most managers in most companies.

What you need to understand is …

2. Repetition

Sure, all these companies have restructured so that there aren't so many layers of management; sure, all these companies have put their junior, may be even middle managers, through teambuilding programmes.

You shouldn't underestimate the strength of feeling. You shouldn't underestimate the power ...

3. Rhetorical question

But I ask you—how many senior managers in your company have gone through this training? Next to none.

Who is responsible for this? I'll tell you who, it's the ...

4. Emotional language

The power-hungry, prima donna, workaholic and totally individualistic senior manager ...

These were the ruthless individuals who carved out empires for the big multinationals.

These people are completely untrustworthy; they'd have the shirt off your back ...

5. Acknowledgement of audience

I'd like to spend just a few minutes of your time exploring ...

Just interrupt me any time you want to.

I realize you've probably had enough of listening to ...

6. Qualification

I don't think it's worth spending a lot of time defining the team but just so we're all roughly on the same pitch.

I would like to try a small sort of experiment—just a short one, of course.

7. Jokes

Yes, this is a golden opportunity for anybody to leave ...

And if you make it to the end of my talk, I'll buy you all a drink.

8. Formal address

Ladies and Gentlemen, Mr. Chairman. It's my pleasure to be here today to represent the Oregon management institute.

Honourable members, Mr Chairman, I am here on behalf of ...

9. Formal structure

I aim to cover the following broad areas: firstly a profile of ...

I will be looking at this problem from two points of view; firstly ...

10. Pomposity

However, they are well-educated, numerate individuals who we plan to mould into the managers of tomorrow …

We should endeavour to recognize the inalienable rights of the individual.

IV. PRACTICE

A. The following 16 sentences (1-16) are taken from a presentation. The purposes of these sentences (a-j) are listed below. Match each sentence with its purpose. The first one has been done for you.

a. greet	f. conclude first main point
b. introduce self	g. introduce second main point
c. introduce talk	h. summarise talk
d. outline talk	i. conclude talk
e. introduce first main point	j. invite questions

1. So, if there are no further comments about the first point, shall we look at the proposed budget? ____g____

2. So, the purpose of today's meeting is to revise the budget. _____

3. Finally, let me say that I look forward to maintaining a good working relationship with all the parties. _____

4. I'd like to welcome you to the team. _____

5. Right, I think that covers the timing. _____

6. Finally, I'd like to say that we shall monitor our performance closely. _____

7. I'd like to explain to you today the plans for the AZ project. _____

8. Good morning, ladies and gentlemen. _____

9. I've divided the talk into three parts: firstly …; secondly …; and thirdly … _____

10. I'd like to start by looking at the old budget. _____

11. That's all I have to say about the old budget. _____

12. So, we've looked at the plans for the AZ project under two main heads—timing and costs. _____

13. And now, if there are any questions, I'll be happy to answer them. _____

14. Okay, let's look first of all at the timing of the project. _____

15. My name is Paul Bailey and I am the operations manager of Rossomon. ___
16. So, let's move on to the next point. _____

B. Complete the following extract from a presentation by putting in the most appropriate connector from those listed on pages 56-57.

That's all I have to say about the environment. So, _____ we come to training. When we started up ten years ago, we offered on average half a day's training per employee per year. _____, by industry standards, that was quite generous at the time. In the last three years, the time has gone up to seven days per employee. _____ this shows our commitment to providing training opportunities. _____, our training falls into three broad categories, _____ understanding the business, improving skills and adding to general education _____, adding languages. _____, developing our trading position is a key concern.

_____ we need to train people so they have a good level of knowledge. _____, those people need to be able to apply that knowledge to the market place, _____ in our sector. _____, to get truly committed staff, you need to help them develop as individuals; _____ you need to give them a chance to grow.

C. Reading by yourself

English Presentation Skills

At some time or other, most of us will have to give a presentation. The idea of speaking in public can be frightening enough if you're a native English speaker, but it's even more so if English is your second language.

In this article on presentation skills, we show you how to take the stress out of giving presentations with eight tips to help you plan a perfect presentation.

1. Know your audience

To give an effective presentation, you need to know something about your audience. How good is their English? How much do they know about the subject of your talk? Why will they be interested in listening to you? It's a good idea to find out who is attending your presentation so that you can make the information relevant and interesting to them. For example, a presentation on your company's financial results to financial analysts will focus on results, reasons and analysis. A presentation on new auditing software will focus on the benefits and features of the software.

Also ask yourself what you want to achieve from your presentation. Sales presentations are different from information-giving presentations, for example. It's always a good idea to work out what you want your audience to think or do at the end of your talk, as this will help you focus on the language and content of your presentation.

2. Use a strong opening statement or question to interest your audience

The first minute of your presentation is crucial. In this time you should interest your audience and give them a reason to listen to you. What you say in the first minute depends on your audience and their interests, but it must mean something important to them. Perhaps it is a problem that you know how to solve, or a fact or statistic that they need to know.

3. Don't forget the physical details

You'll need to make sure the room is big enough for the number of people attending, and that you have all the equipment you need. Find out when you are giving your presentation—your audience may be less attentive if it's right before lunch or at the end of the week and you'll need to make especially sure that the presentation is interesting if it's at a difficult time.

4. Plan the content of your presentation

Planning helps you focus on your presentation goals, and minimises the chances of anything going wrong.

If you know who you are talking to and why you are talking to them, you can put yourself in your audience's position. You can decide what information to include and how to order it.

Aim to speak for no longer than 30 minutes, and leave time for questions and answers at the end. Remember that it's difficult to absorb lots of new information, so don't aim to include too much.

Many presentations are divided into five areas:

a) The introduction (Get someone else to introduce you to the audience. This gives you credibility as a speaker and means that you don't have to waste time telling people who you are and why you are there).

b) The overview.

c) The main body of the presentation.

d) Your summary.

e) A question and answer session.

Make brief notes about all the points you want to make in your presentation and make a plan. Organise your presentation into main points and supporting evidence.

During the presentation, remember that it is a good idea to refer back to your opening statement and remind your audience why they are listening to you.

5. Use index cards

Put your points on individual index cards to help you during the presentation. If you put the key words onto cards (1 card for 1 key word or point) you can refer to them at any time if you forget where you are in the presentation.

Use your index cards for any words that you might find difficult to remember, or words that are difficult to pronounce.

You can also use the index cards to write the links between points, such as:

"This brings me to …"

"Now I'd like to move on to …"

"Right …"

6. Keep visuals simple

Don't put too much information in visuals and only use them to illustrate information that would otherwise take too long to explain.

Simple graphic visuals such as pie charts and bar graphs work better than visuals with lots of labelling or words. Use colour and different fonts to help information stand out.

7. Practice makes perfect!

Practise your presentation as often as you can using your index cards. By practising, you will know how long it will take, and where the difficult areas are in your talk. The more you practise, the more confident you will feel!

8. Prepare questions and answers

You're likely to have questions at the end of your presentation, so try to think of some in advance, as well as possible answers. The more you prepare these, the better you'll feel able to deal with them.

V. WORDS AND EXPRESSIONS

Outline v. 概述，描略图
　　Make an outline before trying to write a composition.
Stand for 代表，拥护
　　What do the letters N.B. stand for?
Package n. 包裹，包装袋
　　Software package 软件包
Perceive v. 察觉，理解
　　I can't perceive any difference between these coins.
Help-desk n. 服务台，前台
　　For Lufthansa booking, please call Helpdesk for name change after obtaining Lufthansa's authorization.
Field adj. 实地的，在实地工作的
　　I also conducted a field study among the boys about their attitude to relationships.
Profile n. 轮廓，简介
　　The newspaper publishes a profile of a leading sportsman every week.
Capitalize on 充分利用某事物
　　Everyone should capitalize on his opportunity.
Taboo n. 禁忌
　　Something was said that happened to be taboo with him.
Behind prep. 支持
　　He had the state's judicial power behind him.
Run through 匆匆查阅，贯穿
　　Please run through these names again from the top of the list.
Mock-up n. 实物模型
　　There's a mock-up of the high street where the Goodwins go shopping.
Transmitter n. 传送者，发射机
　　They tested the range of this transmitter.
Assembly n. 装配，集会
　　cheap self-assembly kitchen units

Maintenance　n. 维持，保养，维修
　　The school pays for heating and the maintenance of the buildings.
Subscriber　n. 用户，订户
　　The subscriber to a government loan has got higher interest than savings.
Synchronize　v. 同时发生，共同行动
　　The sound track did not synchronize with the action.
Distribute　v. 分配，散布
　　Please distribute the examination papers round the class.
Launch　n. v. 发动，开展，投入
　　The company proudly announced the launch of its new range of cars.
In stock　有现货的，备有现货，现存
　　We have many patterns in stock for you to choose from.
Outlets　n. 廉价经销店，奥特莱斯
VAT　value added tax　增值税
Specification　n. 规格，详述
　　This instrument demands stringent specification.
At leisure　有空，闲暇的
　　He put the idea by until he was at leisure to consider it carefully.
Penetration　n. 渗透
　　There have been around 15 attempts from outside France to penetrate the market.
Terminal　n. 终端，终点站
　　Flights for Rome depart from Terminal 3.
Residential　adj. 住宅的，与居住有关的
　　The residential blocks were integrated with the rest of the college.
Prosperity　n. 繁荣，成功
　　I wish you the life of happiness and prosperity.

Unit 7   PRESENTATION SKILLS

Visual aids

宣讲技巧之可视辅助材料

I. INTRODUCTION

现如今，观众已经熟悉于借助多媒体途径来接收大量的信息。他们通常认为正式的宣讲都会伴有某种形式的可视材料的辅助，比如翻转图、字幕片、幻灯片、电影、录音或模型。

可视辅助材料的运用可以比较容易地让观众理解宣讲的内容，特别是其中涉及一些复杂的统计数字、设计参数或新的外形等。宾夕法尼亚大学的一项研究显示，宣讲者如果使用可视辅助材料可以成功地说服67%的观众。在会议期间使用可视辅助材料可以使会议缩短28%，提高效率。类似地，明尼苏达大学的一项研究发现，图表的应用可以使宣讲者的说服效率提高43%。能够使用可视辅助材料的宣讲者也被认为是更专业的、准备更充分的，内容也是更有趣的。

电子设备是可视辅助材料的新型媒介。幻灯片和视频可以从电脑中直接播放，通过投影仪投影到屏幕上。因此，我们不需要制作传统的幻灯片了，而且还可以直接在电子幻灯中轻松地加入多媒体效果。

广泛地说，可视辅助材料不仅可以在商业宣讲中运用，还可以运用到各类会议以及学术展示等方面。

本课比较多地介绍了幻灯片的辅助作用，而可视辅助材料中的图表是在"图表设计"一课中详细介绍的。这两部分可以结合着学习。

II. EXAMPLE

PRESENTATION 1

Below is an extract of one presentation and its visual aids.

"THE GREAT CHINESE INTERNAL MIGRATION: CAUSES AND IMPLICATIONS"

I. PRELIMINARY REMARKS

Good afternoon. Let me begin by expressing my appreciation to President Yang and Economics College for making this conference possible, to Professor Zhao for coordinating the conference, and to President Potter for making it possible for me to be part of today's events. It is truly a pleasure and honor to be here.

II. INTRODUCTION

In the history of human migration, there are a handful of episodes frequently characterized as famous or extraordinary. The most famous Western episode is "The Great Atlantic Migration," the movement of about 55 million people from Europe to the Americas and Australia between 1850 and 1914. The most famous episode of migration within the United States is the "The Great Black Migration" of approximately 6.5 million descendants of African slaves who left the American South and headed to cities in the North. More recent, famous episodes include: (i) the migration of Eastern Europeans to Western Europe following the expansion of the European Union; (ii) the reversal of Ireland from being a net sender of immigrants for many decades to, very recently, a large net receiver; (iii) the migration of several million Iraqi refugees to Syria and other Middle Eastern countries; (iv) the huge movements of persons born and raised in the former East Germany to the Western part of what is now united Germany; and (v) the estimated 10-11 million undocumented immigrants in the U.S., many from Mexico and Central America.

Receiving much less attention in the West is an ongoing migration episode that dwarfs the previously described episodes. It is the massive migration within China taking place since the 1980s, what I call the "Great Chinese Internal Migration."

Slide 1

Period of migration	Persons moving within their home province	Persons moving to another province	Total migration
1985-90	22,569,100	10,660,600	33,229,700
1995-2000	88,932,440	32,282,000	121,214,440
2000-05	128,408,500	66,181,000	194,589,500

The surge in Chinese migration is evident when one compares Chinese census data across three periods—1985-1990, 1995-2000 and 2000-2005. During 1985-1990, approximately 33 million Chinese moved within or across provinces, with roughly one-third of that amount consisting of flows of people across provincial lines. During 1995-2000, the level of migration soared to over 121 million persons, approximately three-fourths being people moving within the same province. During 2000-2005, nearly 195 million persons moved within China, approximately one-third moving between provinces.

Where are the migrants going? Most of the migration, both within and across provinces, is rural to urban, and is focused on the eastern coastal centers. If you examine province-to-province migration, some clear-cut patterns emerge.

Slide 2

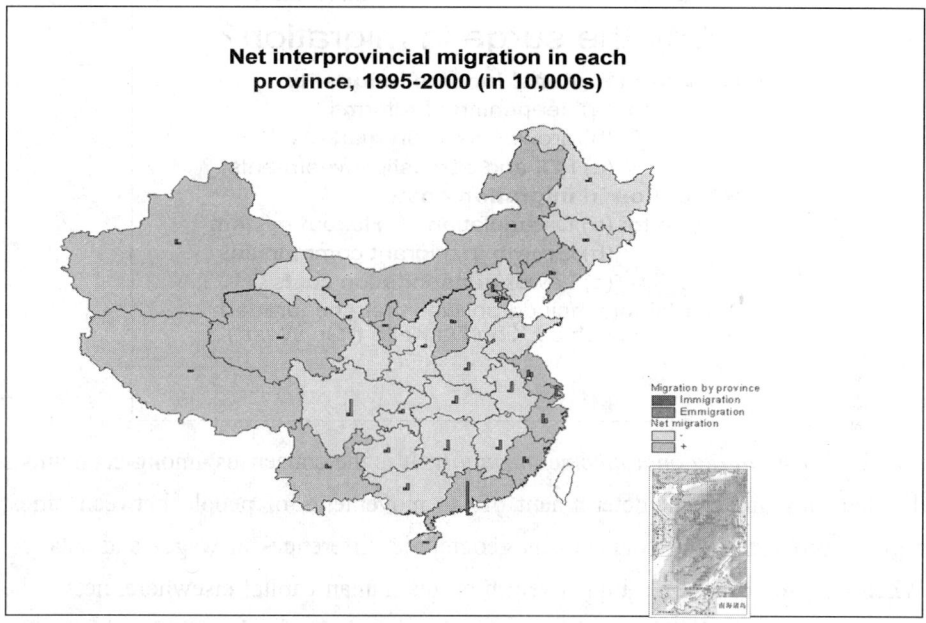

The province minus outflows from the province, for the period 1995-2000. Provinces in gray are those where more people came in than left, while the provinces light gray are those where more people left than came in. Provinces with net gains were the eastern coastal provinces, a few of the northern provinces, and some large western provinces. Provinces that experienced net losses in peoples were the central and some southern provinces. The provinces that have noticeable bars are those which experienced significant levels of migration activity. If the red bar is high, that means the province experienced very large inflows of people, whereas if you have a high right bar it means there were large outflows of people. The biggest net receivers of migrants were the eastern coastal cities, Hong Kong, and Beijing. There was some noticeable net in-migration in a few of the western provinces as well.

This extraordinary surge in internal migration over the last three decades can, I believe, be attributed to two major factors.

Slide 3

> # Why the surge in migration?
> - **Growth in regional income inequality**
>   due to: (a) deepening of reforms
>   　　　　(b) growth in export markets
>   　　　　(c) FDI and domestic investments
> - **Reduction in migration costs**
>   due to: (a) Deregulation of "Hukou" system
>   　　　　(b) Growth in migrant communities
>   　　　　(c) Lower transportation costs
> * Other factors include policies that encouraged migration such as Xibu Da Kaifa ("Go West")

1. *Growth in regional income inequality.* It is the consensus among economists that the most important determinant of the movements of people between cities, regions, provinces, and countries, is geographic differences in wages and salaries. When a person can earn a higher return on his human capital elsewhere, net of the costs of moving, he will move. Thus, China's migration surge has, first and foremost, been driven by rural / urban differences in wages and salaries. These differences grew substantially in response to three broad changes that took place beginning in the late 1970s:

(a) The first was the Comprehensive Economic Reforms, which have been moving China away from central planning to an economic system more closely resembling a decentralized market system. By shifting the responsibility of price determination away from central planners to decentralized competitive markets, the prices of labor services in China became much more closely aligned with labor productivity. This had the effect of widening income differences between towns, cities, regions and provinces.

(b) Global prosperity, driven by advances in technology (especially information technology), deregulation and privatization (particularly in the global financial industry), the collapse of the Soviet Union and its satellites, and expansionary monetary policies around the World, all contributed to tremendous growth in China's export markets. While labor demand grew all over China, the growth was very heavy in the eastern coastal cities, Hong Kong, and Beijing. This had the effect of driving up wages and salaries in export-producing cities and regions, encouraging inflows of migrant labor to these places, and encouraging outflows of labor from other parts of China, especially the central provinces.

(c) Some provinces and cities were recipients of very large infusions of foreign direct investment (FDI) and domestically-financed investment, which stimulated labor demand in those areas.

2. *The costs of moving have fallen dramatically in China over the last thirty years.* There have been three reasons for this:

(a) As Chinese members of the audience well know, China has regulated internal migration through its "Household Registration" or "Hukou" system, since the 1950s. Hukou is effectively an internal passport system. Local and provincial governments have gradually been making it easier for people to change their local registrations. Quotas on local registration permits have been raised and the criteria for obtaining urban Hukou status have been loosened. What is very important to note, though, is that despite China's rigidly structured internal passport system, many people have been moving without obtaining local registration in the destination. These undocumented migrants are the "floating population" in China. The existence of the large floating population, despite relatively strict restrictions on moving, is evidence of the power of wage and salary differences in accounting for China's migration surge.

(b) The rapid growth in migrant communities. A big influence on the migration decision is whether or not you have friends, family and contacts from your home region living in the destination. Having a migrant network to access not only at the time of arrival, but also prior to arrival, can help greatly in reducing the costs of acquiring information about job opportunities in the destination. A thriving migrant network will also reduce the psychological costs of moving, as it is comforting and reassuring to have familiar faces, language, customs, practices, etc., available to you in the destination.

(c) There have been great improvements in China's transportation infrastructure. Air travel within China is much more prevalent than before, thanks to lower air fares, the opening of new airports, the growth of new airlines, etc. The same is true for rail transportation in China. Finally, migration patterns have been influenced by some government policies encouraging migration. The most prominent is "Xibu da Kaifa" (Go West), which helps explain the reason that the western provinces gained population after 1999.

In the next three slides, I would like to highlight the correlation between the migration surge and China's growing prosperity, foreign direct investment and fixed asset investment.

Slide 4

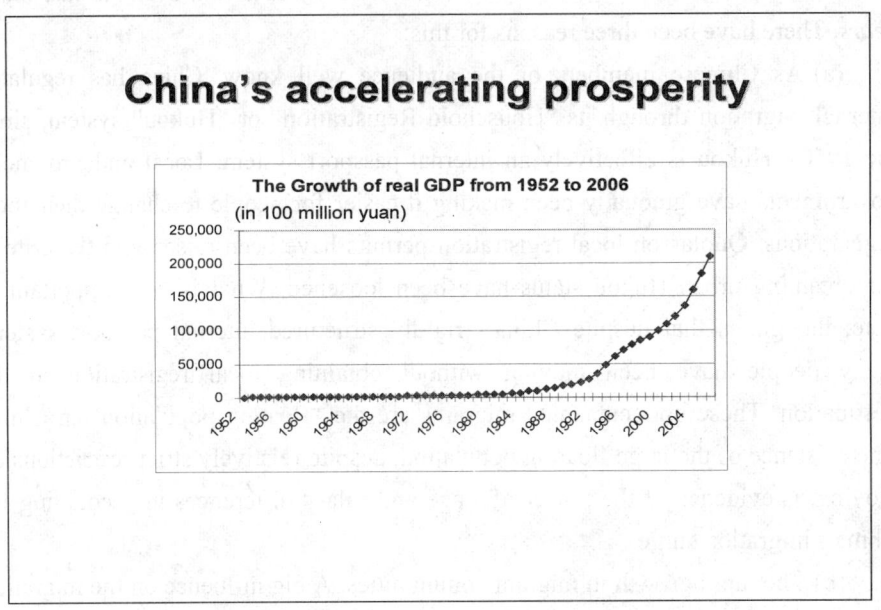

This slide shows the growth of China's real GDP from 1952 to 2006, measured in units of 100 million yuan. GDP began growing in the mid-to-late 1980s, just as migration was beginning to pick up. GDP was accelerating in the beginning in the early-to-mid 1990s, when migration was accelerating ...

PRESENTATION 2

Geoff Roberts is Financial Director of Aoro International. He is taking the Aoro board through the annual results, highlighting some significant figures.

Right, let me take you through some of these figures and try to spell out the implications.

Firstly, as a raw measure of profitability, you need to look at total turnover minus direct costs here on the Income Statement, or Profit & Loss Account, as you guys call it in the United Kingdom. So, as you can see, we shifted $6.5 million worth of goods at a direct cost of $3 million—can you all see that?—so that gave us a gross profit of $3.5 million. That's ok, basically in line with budget but the next figure is more worrying—that's our fixed costs—at $1.85 million—nearly 10% up on last year, they're far too high. It means our operating profit is only $1.65 million, down by nearly $100000 on last year. Ok, I'll come back to that. The only other figure I'd like to draw your attention to on this statement is the tax figure, which fortunately is rather low—just $120000—this is because of a readjustment of liability on overseas profits. Anyway, the important thing is that the net profit figure benefits from this low tax demand—as you can see, after one or two other deductions, it comes out at $1.43 million.

	Income Statement	
	Year ending 31 December	
	2004 $000	2005 $000
Turnover	6500	6300
Direct costs	(3000)	(3000)
Gross profit	3500	3300
Fixed costs	(1850)	(1570)
Operating profit	1650	1730
Tax	(120)	(240)
Profit after tax	1530	1490
Extraordinary items	(100)	(80)
Net profit	1430	1410
Shareholders' dividends	(125)	(115)
Earning retained	1305	1295

Balance sheet
As at 31 December

	2004 $000	2005 $000
Fixed assets		
Intangibles	1500	1400
Tangibles	7500	7200
	9000	8600
Current assets		
Stocks	3100	2700
Debtors	500	1400
Cash	150	250
	3750	4350
Current liabilities		
Bank	1400	1300
creditors	2800	2700
	(4200)	(4000)
Current assets less liabilities	(450)	350
Total assets less current liabilities	8550	8950
Long-term loans	(2550)	(3150)
Deferred taxation	350	
Net assets	5650	5800
Capital and reserves		
Share capital	4000	4000
Share premium account	345	505
Retained profit	1305	1295
Shareholders' funds	5650	5800

Anyway, let's leave that and turn to the Balance Sheet. The key thing I want you to notice here is how our current ratio has deteriorated—this is important because it shows the liquidity of the company. Basically, to measure this we divide the current assets by the current liabilities. Normally we would expect to see a healthy ratio of more current assets than liabilities, but as you can see, at the moment, the company is carrying particularly heavy short-term debts—to the bank and other creditors—and this has coincided with a downturn in sales—which means a drop in the debtor figure under the current assets. We need to do something about this quickly. I suggest we look at rescheduling some of these debts—our fixed assets are, if anything, undervalued, so we could manage to increase our gearing a bit by transferring some short-term debt into long-term loans.

Right, gentlemen. That about covers it. It could be better but, on the other hand, it could be a hell of a lot worse. So, any questions?

III. NOTES

A. Avoid using too many visual aids

Overuse of visual aids keeps the emphasis on the visual aid rather than on the presenter. Instead, use visual aids only when they will help the audience grasp an important point, and remove them when they're no longer needed.

B. Keep it clear and simple

If you do not keep your visual aids clear and simple, your audience can easily become overwhelmed, with their attention drawn to the technology rather than to the content. One of the biggest mistakes is overusing technology.

As general rule, each slide or transparency should contain no more than 40 characters per line, no more than six or seven lines per visual, and no more than three columns of data. The slide needs a simple typeface and plenty of white space. Use bulleted lists to show a group of related items that have no specific order and numbered lists to show related items in a specific order. Establish a color scheme and stick with it for all your visual aids; that is, use the same background color for each slide or transparency. Ensure that your visual aids are readable by testing them beforehand; look at them from the back seat of the room in which you will be presenting.

C. Presentation assessment checklist

Content and structure

1. Did the speaker take account of the following?
   - the audience's needs and interests
   - the objectives
   - the scope
   - the length

- the structure

Techniques

2. Comment on the following:
- the speaker's stance
- the speaker's dress
- the speaker's body language / movements / eyes communication

3. What did you think of the speaker's visual aids?
- clear / unclear
- too much / little information
- words / charts / diagrams
- color / no color
- too many / few visual aids

4. What was the speaker's manner like?
- shy
- reserved
- hesitant
- unassuming
- calm
- confident
- superior
- arrogant

Language

5. What sort of language did the speaker use?
- long / short sentences
- complex / accessible vocabulary
- fast / medium / slow delivery
- varied / monotonous intonation

Other comments

e.g. using examples or analogies

D. Language of integrating the visual into the text

Visual are related to the text. Integrate the visual to the text properly.

Normally, give the table or figure number in the text but not the title. Put the visual as soon after the reference as space and page design permit. If the visual must go on another page, tell the reader where to find it, e.g. as figure 3 shows.

Summarize the main point of a visual before you present the visual itself. This helps the reader get the message the visual intends to convey. How much information to provide depends on the prior knowledge of the readers. The more familiar they are with the visual, the less information is required to summarize. Whatever, give concise summaries. Compare the following two:

Listed in figure 4 below are the results.

As figure 4 shows, sales doubled in the last quarter.

The second summary is better as it provides the essence of the information while the first is doing no more than stating the obvious.

Some practical sentences are followed.
- Take a look at the company's current product lines.
- Let's turn our attention to the company's three current product lines.
- As you can see from this bar graph, the relative level of sales among the three lines has remained consistent.
- The horizontal axis represents the quarterly development. The vertical axis shows millions of units sold.
- As you can see, the blue column in the third quarter representing east was the high point of the year.

E. PowerPoint slides

Slides are powerful visuals. The popular use of Microsoft PowerPoint makes slides easier to prepare and more effective in presenting information.

In making PowerPoint slides, note the following:
- Choose a consistent template, or background design, for the entire presentation. The template should be appropriate for the subject matter.
- Choose a light background if the lights will be off during the presentation and dark background if the lights will be on. Make sure that the words and the background are in high contrast to make them easier to read.
- Use lists of phrases instead of complete sentences. Thus phrases or even words are used in lists. There are two types of lists: numbered lists and bulleted lists. Use bullets when the number and sequence don't matter. Make sure that all of the items on the list are parallel both grammatically (using the same grammatical structure) and conceptually (ideas of equal importance are put at equal hierarchical

levels).

- Make only three to five points on each slide.

IV. PRACTICE

A. Read the following three presentations and evaluate them with rational opinions.

Presentation 1

... what I am convinced of is the complete lack of trust that exists amongst most managers in most companies. Sure, all these companies have restructured so that there aren't so many layers of management; sure, all these companies have put their junior, maybe even middle managers through team-building programs. But I ask you—how many senior managers in your company have gone through this training? Next to none! The power-hungry, prima donna, workaholic and totally individualistic senior manager still prevails in most companies. Of course, these companies needed managers like that in the eighties—these were the ruthless individuals who carved out empires for the big multinationals. But the question is, are they the right managers for us now? You're not going to change these guys even if you can persuade them to attend a team-building course ...

Presentation 2

... I'd like to spend just a few minutes of your time exploring some new approaches to management development. Just interrupt me any time you want to. Right, so management development ... what do we mean by this term? I don't think it's worth spending a lot of time defining the term but just so we're all roughly on the same pitch, I intend to confine myself to middle management and above—I won't be talking about graduate development programs, nor junior management courses ... (someone gets up to leave) yes, this is a golden opportunity for anybody to leave ... so we're going to confine ourselves to middle management and above and I'd like to start by considering a leadership program which we recently ran for an international group based in Brussels ...

Presentation 3

... Ladies and gentlemen, Mr. Chairman. It's my pleasure to be here today to represent the Oregon Management Institute. My presentation is on our long-term management program and I aim to cover the following broad areas: firstly, a profile of a typical freshman, secondly, the curriculum and the main management disciplines and finally, our own internal assessment and graduate placement record. So most freshmen join our program after their ninth grade. They have little or no work experience and they have had no previous education in any aspect of business administration. However, they are well-educated, numerate individuals who we plan to mold into the managers of tomorrow ...

B. Locate two journal articles on some aspect of business news. The two articles should be about the same topic. Integrate information from both articles, and present your findings to the class in a five-minute presentation with some visual aids.

V. WORDS AND EXPRESSIONS

Visual   adj. 视觉的，形象化的
   I have a very good visual memory.
Migration   n. 迁移，移居
   Swallows begin their migration south in autumn.
Implication   n. 含义，言外之意
   He smiled, with the implication that he didn't believe me.
Coordinate   v. 协调，整合
   They appointed a new manager to coordinate the work of the team.
Episode   n. 片段，插曲
   This episode remains sharply engraved on my mind.
Descendant   n. 后代，后裔
   He is a lineal descendant of the company's founder.
European Union   欧盟
Reversal   n. 倒转，颠倒
   That would be a reversal of the order of host and guest.

Refugees   n. 难民，避难者
   They were granted refugee status.
Immigrant   n. 移民，从异地移入的动植物
   Immigrant tales have always been popular themes in fiction.
Dwarf   v. 使显得矮小，使相形见绌
   His figure is dwarfed by the huge red McDonald's sign.
Surge   n. 大浪，汹涌
   The crowds surge out of the sports stadium
Census   n. 人口普查
   A census of population is taken every ten years.
Soar   v. 高飞，剧增
   The eagle can soar without flapping their wings.
Coastal   adj. 临海的，沿海的
   The coastal path is a popular route for walkers.
Clear-cut   adj. 清晰的，轮廓鲜明的
   This was a clear-cut case of the original land owner being in the right
Tan   adj. 黄褐色，棕色
Consensus   n. 一致，合意
   It is difficult to reach a consensus about electoral reform.
Determinant   n. 决定因素
   The windows and the views beyond them are major determinants of a room's character.
Resemble   v. 与……相像，类似于
   China's south does not at all resemble the U.S. south.
Decentralize   v. 权力分散，地方分权
   If you were a manager, would you decentralize authority?
Align   v. 使成一线，排整齐
   Click on this icon to align or justify text.
Deregulation   n. 违反规定，解除管制规定
   In addition, deregulation provided things that voters wanted, such as cheap loans.
Privatization   n. 私有化
   Is the trend towards privatization reversible?

Expansionary adj. 扩张性的，膨胀的
This budget will have a net expansionary effect on the economy.
Infusion n. 注入，灌输
Old families need an infusion of new blood from time to time.
Destination n. 目的地，终点
Life can be likened to a journey with an unknown destination
Thriving adj. 兴旺的，繁荣的
Our country is thriving and prospering day by day.
Infrastructure n. 基础设施
Vast sums are needed to maintain the infrastructure.
Prevalent adj. 流行的，盛行的
The habit of travelling by aeroplane is becoming more prevalent.
Fare n. 费，票价
They quoted 756 dollars for the single New York—London fare.
Correlation n. 相互关系
A high correlation exists in America between education and economic position.
Spell out 读出，拼出，阐述
Will you please spell out your request?
Turnover n. 营业额，成交量
The store greatly reduced the prices to make a quick turnover.
Income statement 损益表
Liability n. 责任，债务
Article 19 A joint venture is a limited liability company.
Balance sheet 资产负债表
Current ratio 流动比率
Deteriorate v. 恶化
There are fears that the situation might deteriorate into full-scale war.
Liquidity n. 资产流动性
The demand for and the supply of credit is closely linked to changes in liquidity.
Creditor n. 债权人，债主
A bank is a creditor when it issues a $30,000 mortgage.
Coincide v. 与……一致，相符

His tastes and habits coincide with those of his wife.
Debtor n. 债务人
He crowded the debtor for payment.
Undervalue v. 估价过低，轻看
Don't undervalue Jim's contribution to the research.
Gear v. 调和，接上
We have to gear our lives to the new changes.
Loan n. 贷款
The loan was denominated in US dollars.
A hell of a （用来加重语气）极恶劣的，使人受不了的

Unit 8 NEGOTIATION
谈判

I. INTRODUCTION

在谈判中，语言是双方进行沟通和交流的重要工具。特别是在国际谈判中，语言是阻碍谈判顺利进行的首要因素。由于语言上的差异，使一方不能准确地、正确地理解另一方所表达的内容及含义，而造成误会、分歧，进而影响谈判的顺利进行的例子有很多。再有，一般谈判人员都来自不同的国家，他们在信仰、生活习惯、价值观念、行为规范、道德标准、乃至谈判心理上都存在极大的差别，所有这些方面都是影响谈判进行的重要因素。

在国际谈判中，不能单凭己方的想法和意愿去推测对方的意图和打算。这种一厢情愿的做法常常是造成沟通失败的主要原因。进行这类谈判时，谈判的准备工作是及其重要的。要尽可能利用一切资料、一切机会去了解对方的行为特点、生活方式、谈判风格，做到心中有数，临阵不乱。同时，在谈判中，要避免用自己所习惯的价值、观念去衡量对方，要充分体谅、理解和尊重对方的行为。彼此间的沟通与交流是十分重要的，这将为达到预期目的奠定坚实的基础。

国际商务谈判中的一个非常重要但又往往容易被忽略的问题就是谈判双方人员的心理障碍。这是由于不同的文化背景导致人们行为差异而形成的心理反射。例如，在谈判中，当一方表达其立场、观点时，往往担心对方不能很好地理解，而对方也可能有同感。在语言运用上，选择词汇十分慎重，唯恐用词不当，有失礼节。对所应采用的策略、方法顾虑重重。许多在国内的谈判场合潇洒自如、从容不迫、临危不乱的谈判人员，在这类谈判中常常表现出拘泥呆板、犹豫不决、瞻前顾后的反常行为。所以，在国际商务谈判中，要重视和加强谈判人员的心理训练，使其具备在各种压力下的心理承受能力。

谈判通常经历几个不同的阶段：

1. 准备阶段

在谈判开始前，双方都要考虑好自身的谈判最高目标（top line）、底线（bottom line）和目标（target objective），并且尽可能准确地评估对方的优劣势。

与此同时，谈判团队需要确定采取哪种谈判策略。例如协调协作策略（collaborating）、妥协让步策略（compromising）、通融策略（accommodating）、主导控制策略（controlling）、避免针锋相对策略（avoiding），等等。

在谈判开始后，首先是双方互相了解、问询并逐渐进入正题的时间段。比如，提出本方的一些疑问，"That's one of the things which worries me."；消除对方的疑虑，"That's true but …"；强调某些要点，"It's critical to meeting deadlines."，等等。

2. 谈判阶段

谈判阶段会由一方作出简单陈述，双方应确定谈判的议程。

正式谈判阶段会充满了问题与回答，而在提问与回答之间则体现了谈判者对于本方利益及诉求的争取和对于全局的控制力。

开场问题，例如 "What sort of delivery periods did you have in mind?" "What do you think you could manage?"

避而不答，例如 "I'd have to get back to you to confirm." "Would you mind waiting while I phone…?"

引导谈判话题，例如 "I suppose we'd be looking at a reduction …" "I'm surprised you're not prepared to offer …" "I was hoping for a more substantial discount." "Would you be willing to consider …?"

捍卫本方立场，例如 "I'm sure you understand …" "I'm afraid that's as far as we could go."

3. 达成结果

如果谈判取得成果，一般是双方签订相关合同以进行今后的项目合作。例如："May I suggest we sign a 6-month contract at a 5 per cent discount on your quoted prices and then we'll meet again to see if we can reduce the prices further?" "You're a tough negotiator. Ok. Let's shake on that and draw up the details of the first contract …"

II. TEXTS

Negotiation 1

Sophmore Electronics are looking for a supplier of components. Price and delivery terms are very important but even more so is a long-term relationship from which both supplier and customer will benefit. Northern Components are relatively new in the market. Sophomore would be their first major customer. Sophmore's purchasing manager, Kate Nelligan, is in the final stages of negotiation with Pete Boardman, Northern Component's sales manager.

Kate: So, you've only recently started up?

Pete: That's right, but Geoff Stanton, the managing director, has been in components supply for a good 20 years.

Kate: Oh, that's interesting. Who was he with before?

Pete: Both he and I were with Standard Telecom, in their electronics division. We were both ready for a change and when he got the capital to start up Northern Electronics, he asked me to join him.

Kate: And how's business?

Pete: Well, it's gradually building up. We've got a number of fairly small-scale contracts for components supply—you know, mainly specialized operations.

Kate: Yes. That's one of the things which worries me. You see, you've no track record of meeting large-scale orders ...

Pete: That's true, but you've seen we've got the capacity and our quality control procedures are very exacting.

Kate: Yes. I'm impressed by the investment you've made in that area. Er, shall we turn now to the actual terms?

Pete: Certainly. Well, we've already discussed price in some detail. I suppose you'd be interested in delivery?

Kate: Yes, we would. It's critical to meeting our deadlines, as you can imagine.

Pete: Sure. What sort of delivery periods did you have in mind?

Kate: Well, you've seen the order quantities, what do you think you could manage?

Pete: Well, on the AX 2000 components, we could certainly …

Kate: No, I didn't mean on the individual order. What about the whole consignment, on a monthly basis?

Pete: Oh, I see. I hadn't realized we'd be talking about that. I'd have to get back to Geoff to confirm times on that.

Kate: Surely you could give me some idea.

Pete: Well, I reckon … we could manage 15 days from confirmed order. But, as I say, I'd have to get back to you to confirm that.

Kate: That's at your quoted prices?

Pete: Um … well, actually we quoted for those batch by batch. We hadn't realized you'd be thinking of ordering the whole lot.

Kate: I see. So I suppose we'd be looking at a reduction for bulk orders?

Pete: Look, I'm sorry. To be perfectly frank, you've caught me on the hop here. Would you mind waiting while I speak to Geoff on the phone?

Kate: No, of course not … did you get through ok?

Pete: Yes, I did. I apologise for keeping you waiting. Anyway, we can now talk more concretely about delivery terms.

Kate: Good.

Pete: We can deliver the whole consignment at 15 days at the prices already quoted. This would mean dispatch from our premises …

Kate: I'm surprised you're not prepared to offer some sort of bulk discount considering the size of the order.

Pete: Well, I'm sure you understand that meeting this sort of order will mean quite a lot of overtime—it would be very difficult to come down on the price.

Kate: But we are offering you a large amount of regular business.

Pete: That's true. Would you be willing to sign an annual contract on the basis we discussed?

Kate: Um, possibly, subject to quality and delivery guarantees.

Pete: Of course. Well, in that case we could offer a 5% discount for a confirmed monthly order for the next 12 months.

Kate: I was hoping for something a bit more substantial.

Pete: I'm afraid that's as far as we could go. We'd already be stretching ourselves to the limit.

Kate: Right, Mr. Boardman. May I suggest we sign a 6 month's contract 5% discount on your quoted prices and then we'll meet again to see if we can reduce the prices further?

Pete: You're a tough negotiator. Ok, let's shake on that and draw up the details of the first contract ...

Negotiation 2

A: Good morning! Nice to meet you again!

B: Today we are going to discuss the tender price. Generally speaking your price is very high compared with the other bidders.

A: The price of this project is worked out on the basis of our experience for power plant construction. We have reduced our profit to a very low level. Considering the benefit of the employer, we believe that the timed completion of the works with good quality at a reasonable price is more significant than the delay of power generating. Nobody would expect a problematic situation just for a little lower price. In fact the construction cost of the civil works compared with the benefit from the earlier power producing is much smaller.

B: Why can't you do a job with a competitive price?

A: There is an old Chinese saying that you cannot let a horse run fast without feeding enough grass.

B: Now let's have a review of the tender price in your submission. A breakdown of your prices will give us explanation whether your price is reasonable or not.

A: We are pleased to do so. The total price consists of 9 items. They are: (1) labor cost; (2) staff cost; (3) construction equipment cost; (4) material cost; (5) technology transfer and training cost; (6) co-ordination cost; (7) tax cost; (8) camp cost and (9) major sub-contractors cost. Let's tackle them one by one. Item 1 is the labor cost. The total labor cost is $ 6.39 million, around 10% of the total price.

B: How many man-hours do you estimate to spend for this project?

A: About 8.9 million man-hours in minimum. So the labour cost is only $ 5 per day, which is rather low. Nearly all labor force will be employed locally. Item 2 is the staff cost. It is around USD 1.9 million in total.

B: From our calculation your staff cost is rather high. The monthly salary is about USD 1500, which is very high compared with average staff salary in your country.

A: This amount is not the actual salary of the staff. In fact only 65% become their incomes, the other 35% is the cost of transportation, telecommunication, tax, insurance, on-cost off site and so on.

B: Can you tell us what percentage you calculate for the depreciation of the equipment?

A: There are several depreciation periods we used for the equipment. For example, for large and durable equipment it is 15 years. Some equipment is 10 years and some consumable machinery is only 3 years. For such a large project with a tight program a lot of highly efficient equipment, such as concrete pumps, high capacity concrete batching plants, concrete mixing trucks and many kinds of cranes would be employed, which are shown in our construction equipment list.

B: We understand that you should mobilize enough equipment for the construction of the project, but in order to control the machinery cost you'd better prepare a schedule of equipment mobilization which is closely matched with construction schedule to avoid any idling of equipment on site.

A: Ok. We will check the equipment cost and see if there are any costs that can be deducted. Item 4 is the material cost which is the largest one and occupies 55% of the total cost. Shall we discuss it now?

B: We have discussed it for a long time. Shall we resume our talk in the afternoon?

A: That's no problem with me.

Negotiation 3

A: Now, let's talk about the payment term for this deal.

B: Very good. Our party, as the buyer, hopes to pay your shipment by D/A so that we can have some time to raise the funds and resell the merchandise.

A: We, as the seller, think that payment by D/A will put us at great risk since the banks involved in it do not guarantee payment or assume any credit risk as they do in L/C transactions. In D/A terms, the collecting bank will release our documents to you against your acceptance of the bill of exchange promising to pay at a later date. After the acceptance, you can immediately take possession of the goods shipped by us. If you refuse to honor payment at maturity, we may then suffer great loses.

B: Please don't be too much worried about our creditworthiness. We are sure to pay the accepted bill of exchange at maturity.

A: What about the payment term of D/P? We may have higher degree of security and protection. In this term, the collecting bank will release our documents to you only upon your full and immediate cash payment.

B: That's reasonable. But we would prefer to accept the D/P types. In this term, after our acceptance of the time draft, we still can not take possession of the shipment until we actually pay it at maturity.

A: However, this term of payment does give you some time to raise funds and make payment. At the same time, our security will also be guaranteed to some extent since the title to our shipment will not be handed over to you until your payment has been made.

B: What you have said is absolutely correct. So we've reached our consensus on the payment term of D/P after sight. Then, what is your expected expiry date of the draft?

A: Do you agree the time draft will fall due on September 20, this year?

B: We have no different idea.

III. NOTES

A. There are four tips about the negotiation skill.
1. Push until they push back

Because the pressure is on, gentler forms of probing may be ineffective, and you may have to push harder than you did earlier. The critical point is to push for concessions and watch their reactions. If they do not communicate any readiness to walk away, they are probably not at their limits yet. You should therefore keep pushing, seeing how far they will go.

In diplomacy this approach is called brinkmanship. One country pushes another closer and closer to the brink of war, watching intently for their reactions. Of course, in most business negotiations you do not want to push that hard or get close to the brink. You should therefore decide how strong their finality signals have to be before you will back off.

2. Encourage them to make concessions

Many people actively discourage concessions by taking positions which essentially punish the other side for yielding. For example, they say, directly or indirectly, "Take it or leave it." However, the visceral and qraceful concessions make you look like a winner.

You should also communicate that they can benefit from negotiating, that compromising will produce better results than stonewalling. Many people do just the opposite; they say, in effect, "Don't negotiate because you will not gain anything by it."

3. Watch for signs that you have gone too far

Because the tension is so high, you must listen and observe very, very carefully. That tension can cause overreactions: people often get angry, storm out, or take extreme positions. You should therefore balance pushing with delicacy and sensitivity. Put on the pressure, but back off quickly—if they seem ready to blow up.

4. If necessary, accept their last offer

If their last offer is within your range, and they seem unwilling to go any further, accept it. A surprising number of people ignore that obvious principle. They get so involved in the competition, so intent on beating the other side, that they forget that the purpose of negotiations is to reach mutually satisfactory deals.

Of course you want to win, but winning—especially if the contest is over a symbol or an unnecessary concession—is much less important than avoiding a defeat. Losing a satisfactory deal is a defeat for both parties.

You set your MSP (Major Strategy and Purpose) before negotiating because you were more rational then. That firm limit was set to help you to resist the natural tendency to go a little further, then further still until you reached a bad deal. But the MSP should also help you to resist the tendency to fight for every penny on the table, and perhaps a few that are not even there. Since it is within your range, their last offer is, by definition, objectively satisfactory. Take it while you can. It might not still be there tomorrow.

B. Businessmen from different cultures also behave differently during negotiations. Here are five different types of negotiators.

1. The calm and collected negotiator

Does a lot of homework and gathers information in advance: "According to the figures I have …"

Doesn't play games: "I'll be frank with you."

Goes very straightforward and direct to the point: "Let's get down to business."

Expects a fair price: "I'm here because I want to get my money's worth."

2. The impatient negotiator

Acts as if he is superior: "My time is valuable."

Doesn't get angry but shows his impatience: "I don't have all day."

Tries to put the blame on the other party: "If we bought at this price, we'd go bankrupt."

3. The persistent negotiator

Doesn't take 'no' for an answer: "Don't give up now. Let's talk some more."

Shows a competitive spirit: "I'm not going to bargain. This is my stand."

Continues to push: "Can you do it or not?"

Encourages further negotiations: "It will work. We just need to work on it."

4. The hotheaded negotiator

Frequent emotional outbursts: "Unacceptable! No way!"

Uses big gestures.

Speaks with a loud voice.

Protests strongly: "Do you think I'm crazy?"

Makes extreme statements: "Oh, come on, you are killing me!"

Belittles the other party: "That's absurd. You make me laugh."

5. The deceptive negotiator

Doesn't tell the whole truth: "This is the only stock left. None of the other supplies will be able to help you."

Withholds vital information: "Oh, didn't I mention those taxes and tariffs? Perhaps you misunderstood me."

Tries to catch people off guard: "There are other people waiting to see me."

C. Typical stages and practical sentences

1. Preparing the ground

Expressing doubts:

That's one of the things which worries me.

Reassuring:

That's true but …

Stressing importance:

It's critical to meeting deadlines.

2. Bargaining

Opening question:

What sort of delivery periods did you have in mind?

What do you think you could manage?

Avoiding the answer:

I'd have to get back to you confirm.

Would you mind waiting while I phone …?

Leading the negotiation:

I suppose we'd be looking at a reduction …

I'm surprised you're not prepared to offer …

I was hoping for a more substantial discount.

Would you be willing to consider …?

Defending a position:

I'm sure you understand …

I'm afraid that's as far as we could go.

3. Closing the deal

May I suggest we sign a 6-month contract at a 5 per cent discount on your quoted prices and then we'll meet again to see if we can reduce the prices further?

You're a tough negotiator. Ok. Let's shake on that and draw up the details of the first contract …

IV. PRACTICE

A. Recognizing the purpose of a particular statement or question in a negotiation is vital. You can then better understand your partner's position.

Match the purpose with the expression:

Expression

1. That's difficult to say. I'd have to check.
2. I assume you'd be willing to offer a discount.
3. I think you have to bear in mind our costs.
4. There's something which concerns me …
5. It's absolutely vital to keep prices down.
6. Could you tell me what sort of figure you're thinking of?
7. That's no doubt true but you should know …
8. You strike a hard bargain. But let's shake on that.

Purposes

a. opening question
b. defending a position
c. stressing importance
d. avoiding the answer
e. leading the negotiation
f. closing the deal
g. expressing doubts
h. reassuring

B. At the Harvard Negotiation Project we have been developing a new method of negotiation explicitly designed to produce good results efficiently and amicably. This method, called principled negotiation or negotiation on the merits, can be boiled down to four basic points.

(1) The first point recognizes that human beings are not computers. People have strong emotions, often see things very differently, and do not always communicate clearly. In negotiation it often happens that emotions get mixed up with the objective rights and wrongs of the situation. Taking up a fixed position makes this worse because people's personalities become identified with their positions. So before the actual negotiation begins we need to distinguish between personal differences and differences over solutions to the problem.

(2) The second point distinguishes between what people say they want, their stated positions, and what they really want, their underlying interests. Negotiating positions often hide what you really want. A compromise between two positions is

not likely to produce an agreement which satisfies the needs underlying each position.

(3) The third point acknowledges the problem of having to find a perfect solution while you're under pressure. Making up your mind in the presence of your opponent restricts your ideas. Deciding on something very important or trying to find the perfect answer limits creative thought. You can get around these limitations by arranging a set amount of time to think up a wide range of possible solutions which help both sides and creatively bring them together.

(4) When both sides find that their interests are directly opposed, one negotiator may try to win simply by being stubborn. However, you can respond to such tactics by insisting that his opinion alone is not enough and that some fair independent standard is needed. This does not mean that you yourself select the independent standard, rather that both of you decide on one, such as market value, expert opinion, or law. By discussing such criteria neither side need give in to the other.

Question 1-4

Choose the correct title for each paragraph from the box

1. Paragraph (1) _____
2. Paragraph (2) _____
3. Paragraph (3) _____
4. Paragraph (4) _____

A	Opening negotiation	E	Invent options
B	Firmness and success	F	Compromise and flexibility
C	Objective reference points	G	Interests not positions
D	Separate people and problem		

Question 5-8

Complete each sentence with a phrase from the list below

5. You need to agree on a fixed period to _____
6. An example of the use of objective reference points is to _____
7. It can be difficult to see the problem clearly if you _____
8. A negotiating position often makes it hard to _____

A	analyse problems systematically	E	show strength and firmness
B	take an emotional approach	F	identify real needs
C	make up lots of options	G	insist on your opinion
D	consult a specialist		

C. Make up dialogues according to the following situation

A businessman from the U.K. wants to import your red beans, 2013 crop, grade A. You offer him USD 680 per metric ton FOB Xingang. But the British businessman counter offers you USD 612, a 10% cut in your original offer. Have a negotiation with him about the price of the red beans. When negotiating the price, consider also the quality of the product, the size of the order and the market trend.

How about the businessman is coming from America or Japan? The following information is for your reference.

The American negotiation style
- Getting down to business quickly
- Handling any negotiation situation independently and having full authority to finalize the agreement without checking the home office unless something unexpected and beyond his authority come up
- Placing high value on informality and equality in human relations, emphasizing individual equality rather than social status
- Viewing honest information and direct answer as the token of mutual cooperation
- Attacking a complex negotiation task piecemeal, that is, separating the issues and settling them one at a time.
- Relying on the law, not friendship
- Being constant and predictable, treating everyone and every situation with an action-oriented and forthright style

The Japanese negotiation style
- Emphasizing hierarchical personal and business relationships
- Emphasizing the importance of long-term relations
- Placing high value on interpersonal harmony over frankness, so difficult to get a "yes" or "no" from the Japanese
- Making decision by consensus
- Communicating nonverbally through tone of voice, eye contact, silence, body movements, etc.

V. WORDS AND EXPRESSIONS

Supplier   n. 供应商
　　By changing its supplier, the company saved thousands of pounds in import duty.

Managing director   总经理
　　He rose from office boy to managing director in ten years.

Division   n. 分开，分隔，分支
　　the bank's Latin American division

Exacting   adj. 严格的，费劲的
　　Privately they seem to have the same exacting standards.

Consignment   n. 托运，装运的货物
　　We have to ask you to dispatch the consignment immediately.

Batch   n. 一批
　　Each summer a new batch of students tries to find work.

Bulk   n. 大块，大量
　　The bulk of the population lives in cities.

Catch on the hop   出其不意，措手不及
　　I'm afraid your order has caught us on the hop—the goods aren't available yet.

Premises   n. 复数用作房屋
　　There is a kitchen on the premises ...

Stretch   v. 伸展
　　The procession stretched for several miles

Shake on   （非正式）握手成交
　　Then, let us shake on 70 US dollars.

Draw up   草拟，折叠
　　We'll notify her to draw up a contract

Bidder   n. 出价者，投标人
　　The house went to the highest bidder, ie the person who offered the most money.

Power plant   发电厂

Construction   n. 建造

Work has begun on the construction of the new airport.

Generate　v. 形成，造成，引起

We need someone to generate new ideas.

Problematic　adj. 成问题的，不确定的

Such an operation is problematic to implement and explain.

Civil work　土建工程

Our civil work includes construction of roads, buildings, foundations and reinforced concrete structure.

Submission　n. 递交，呈递

I demand the submission of the signature to an expert.

Technology transfer　技术转让

Sub-contractor　n. 分包商，转包商

The company was considered as a possible sub-contractor to build the aeroplane.

Tackle　v. 着手处理

The government is determined to tackle inflation.

On-cost　原材料及人工费用以外的间接成本

Depreciation　n. 折旧，贬值

They wrote off 500 for depreciation of machinery.

Durable　adj. 耐用的，长期的

These shoes are durable.

Consumable　adj. 可消费的，会用尽的

Consumer economy behavior is affecting consumable market with indirect ground directly.

Pump　n. 泵，打气筒

She washed her face at the pump in front of the inn.

Crane　n. 塔吊，起重机

We used a crane to lift the piano into the theatre.

Mobilize　v. 调动，动员

He is trying to mobilize all the supporters.

Idle　v. 虚度，空转，闲着

Mike doesn't study at all. Instead, he sits idle all day.

Shipment　n. 装运，载货

The shipment is destined for America.

D/A documents against acceptance 承兑交单（出口人的交单以进口人在汇票上承兑为条件，即出口人在装运货物后开具远期汇票，连同商业单据，通过银行向进口人提示，进口人承兑汇票后，代收银行即将商业单据交给进口人，在汇票到期时，方履行付款义务）

Raise v. 筹措，筹集

They held a harambee meeting to raise funds for a new classroom.

Merchandise n. 商品，货物

L/C letter of credit 信用证（是指开证银行应申请人的要求并按其指示向第三方开立的载有一定金额的，在一定的期限内凭符合规定的单据付款的书面保证文件）

Collecting bank 代收行

Bill of exchange 汇票

Possession n. 拥有，占有物，所有权

They were imprisoned for possession of drugs.

Maturity n. 票据的到期

Customers are told what their policies will be worth on maturity.

Creditworthiness n. 商业信誉，信贷价值

But also follows a fundamental reassessment of the creditworthiness and prospects of emerging, versus developed, economies.

D/P documents against payment 付款交单（出口人将汇票连同货运单据交给银行托收时，指示银行只有在进口人付清货款时，才能交出货运单据）

Hand over 交出，让与

Yuan Shikai forced the emperor to abdicate and hand over power to him.

Expiry n. 期满，届期，终止

You have to apply for a renewal within six months before expiry.

Unit 9　E-MAIL

电子邮件

I. INTRODUCTION

　　商务英语电子邮件以其方便快捷，在现代商务活动中起着重要作用。商务往来中的电子邮件代表着公司的形象，显示着公司的水平和实力，直接影响到客户对公司的评估。所以，商务电子邮件的写作在业务往来中占据着举足轻重的地位。据调查，约有88%的互联网用户使用电子邮件，而在商务领域中约有90%的员工通过电子邮件的形式来联系公务。需要注意的是，商务电子邮件有别于私人邮件，称呼要得体；如果正文含表格或数字比较多，最好使用附件功能。

　　电子邮件的抬头模板和备忘录很像，信件主体的格式可根据实际情况灵活调整，一般采取书信的简化形式即可。电子邮件的内容也可以看作是简化的书信内容，能够完整、礼貌、清楚、准确地表达意思即可。

II. EXAMPLES

E-MAIL 1

To: albert@hb.com
Subject: Product information

Dear Mr. Gleason

　　Our account representatives are very busy people—often spending as much as half of their time traveling to consult with various clients around the world. Obviously, they make heavy use of their laptop computers when travelling, often tapping into our company database to prepare a proposal for a client. Some of our representatives have requested that we provide them with a portable printer so that they can prepare hard copies immediately for their clients. Therefore, I would like some information on your portable printers, specifically the HB-340. First, I'd like to know if this is a laser printer. Our reps would also need a battery-operated model because they print out legal-size forms while travelling.

If I can provide any further information about our printing needs, do not hesitate to let me know.

Sincerely,
Carolyn J. Ryerson

E-MAIL 2

To: ＊＊＊@＊＊＊
Subject: Request for Replacement (Re: Photoshop)

Dear Sir

On June 23 I received Electric Razor and Photoshop, which I ordered via your on-line shopping website.

Electric Razor is running smoothly and I'm very pleased with it. However, I'm experiencing a lot of trouble with Photoshop. It hangs up very often while in operation for no apparent reason. I can no longer afford the interruptions and irritation caused by constant hang-ups.

There obviously is something wrong with this software. I believe that I'm entitled to a replacement, but please let me know what you would propose to do about this matter.

Your prompt reply will be most appreciated. Thank you.

Greatwall@sina.com.cn

III. NOTES

A. Heading of an e-mail
To: (name of the recipient)
From: (name of the sender)
CC(carbon copy): (name of another recipient who is also expected to receive the e-mail)
BCC(blind carbon copy): (name of another recipient who is also expected to receive the e-mail, but without being known by other recipients listed in "TO" or "CC"
Date: (date of sending the e-mail)
Subject: (subject of the e-mail)
Attached/attachment: (any files to be sent together with the e-mail)

B. Useful sentences
I have the honor to inform you that ...
I would like to remind you that our office is in want of ...
I have several proposals for ...
In response to your request for ... I have to inform you that we can not approve it.
This is further to your memo dated June 6, in which you proposed that ...
The board of directors approved your proposal at the meeting last week.
Please let me know your response to ...
Please feel free to contact me if you need further information.
I highly appreciate your considerations to these proposals.
I enclose the evaluation report for your reference.
I add some comments to the document for your reference.
Please let me know if you have any questions on this.
For other known issues related to individual features, please see attached release notes.

IV. PRACTICE

A. The following e-mail has many errors either in grammar, wording or style. Read carefully and then correct them.

To: all the staff

Subject: safety precautions at work

Attachment:

Last Thursday, when "B" shift were clocking off, one of the men hit his head against a safety lader which someone had carelessly left down. He had to have stitches in his head because of this.

I am fed up with telling you about this kind of things. One of these days, we'll have a serious accident, and then it will be too late. Unless I see a great improvement in your attitude towards keeping the place tidy and safe. I'm afraid I'll have to punish the offenders.

B. Suppose you are a secretary of a general manager, and the manager will go to Paris to visit Mr./Ms about the opening of a sample room. Now write a letter to inform him/her.

V. WORDS AND EXPRESSIONS

Repersentative n. 代表

The President nominated me as his representative at the meeting.

Laptop n. 便携式电脑

Do you know which one is better, a laptop or a desktop?

Tap into 利用，开发

They made success by tapping into recent developments in technology.

Proposal n. 提议，建议，投标

His proposal was outvoted by 10 votes to 8.

Portable adj. 手提的，轻便的

There is a pretty portable pair of steps in one corner of the room.

Laser n. 激光

Laser discs can store prodigious amounts of information.

Replacement　n. 更换

　　As Jack is ill, we have to get a replacement for him.

Razor　n. 剃刀

Hang up　停下，使等候

　　Looking back, she feels she should never have hung up her backpack.

Irritation　n. 恼火

　　For the first time Leonard felt irritation at her methods ...

Unit 10　MEMOS
备忘录

I. INTRODUCTION

　　备忘录是企业员工之间相互联系、交流信息的信函，一般不像公司与顾客之间的通信那样正式。它是一种录以备忘的公文，但在公文函件中，它的等级是比较低的，主要用来提醒、督促对方，或就某个问题提出自己的意见或看法。在业务上，它一般用来补充正式文件的不足。

　　企业内部上下级之间、部门主管与下属之间、公司总部与分部之间普遍使用这种形式沟通情况、下达指示或报告近况。备忘录在业务上的作用通常包括提供资料、传达信息、解释问题、提出建议、作出指示、描述产品等。因此，备忘录的抬头一般都很明确地给出备忘录的发出人和接收人以及主题。备忘录的内容也很直入主题，较少客套话，每段都表达了一个非常明确的议题。而备忘录的落款也被简化掉了。

　　备忘录的基本要素包括：
1. 书端
TO：收阅者的姓名和职务
FROM：作者的姓名和职务
DATE：当前的准确日期
SUBJECT：备忘录所陈述和强调的内容
2. 开头
　　这部分可以简要陈述如下信息：背景和研究的问题、特定的任务或工作及备忘录的目的等。

3. 正文

这部分可以给收阅者提供所需要了解的信息或细节，也可以就某个事项提出指示建议，或就某些问题进行解释说明等。

4. 结尾

这部分通常用一个客气的祈使句来陈述希望收阅者采取的行动，以及其在行动后可以获得的益处。

有的备忘录，根据情况还可以在后面提供誊写备忘录的人、附件的数目、抄送给谁等信息。

由于备忘录的写作目的之一是快捷方便地传达信息，文字应该简练、易读易记，因此备忘录的写作原则包括：

1. 明确交流目的，直截了当、准确完整地表达信息。
2. 段落短小，以每段不超过五六个句子为宜，以方便收阅者阅读。
3. 可使用醒目的编号排列内容要点。
4. 避免重复，删去一切不必要的词句。
5. 首句要交代清楚写备忘录的目的。在回复对方的备忘录时要标明对方写备忘录的时间。
6. 在备忘录中交代的事情要简明扼要，每一件事情要另起一段来写明。
7. 在备忘录中通知一些事项时要力求准确、不引起歧义。
8. 在备忘录的最后，一般用一句概括性的话强调希望备忘录的收阅者对备忘录的内容尽快作出反应。

II. TEXTS

Memo 1

Memo to: Elliott Lamborn, Vice president
From: Janson J. Peterson, Marketing supervisor
Date: April 3, 2010
Subject: Proposal to reassign employee parking lots

As one way of showing our support for the Ford Motor Company, which accounts for nearly half of our annual sales, I propose that the close-in employee parking lots around our headquarters be restricted to use by owners of Ford vehicles.

During their frequent visits to our headquarters, Ford personnel must pass the employee parking lot. When they do, they will see that approximately 70 percent of our employees drive vehicles manufactured by competitors of Ford. In fact, a Ford purchasing agent asked me last week, "How can you expect us to support you if you don't support us?"

The purpose of this memo, then, is to seek approval to have our close-in employee parking lot restricted to use by Ford vehicles. The maintenance department estimates that it will need four weeks and about $500 to make the needed signs.

Our labor contract requires union approval of any changes in working conditions. However, Sally Marsh, our shop steward, has told me that she would be willing to consider this matter—especially if similar restrictions are imposed on the executive parking lot.

Since our next managers' meeting is on May 8-10, I look forward to being able to announce the new plan to them. By approving this change, Newton will be sending a powerful positive message to our visitors: Our employees believe in the products we sell.

Memo 2

To: All heads of departments
From: Walter Jobs, Training Manager
Date: December 3, 2011
Subject: Secretarial Training Scheme

The company has arranged a number of secretarial training courses in the spring of next year.

The courses include:
- Book-keeping
- Typewriting
- English for business
- Information systems

Please note that enrollment will be free of charge to all administrative staff on the first-come-first-served basis.

Please put up the poster.
Thank you.
Walter Jobs

III. NOTES

A. Components of a memo
1. Heading
   Memo to: (reader's names and job titles)
   From: (your name and job title)
   Date: (complete and current date)
   Subject: (what the memo is about, highlighted in some way)
2. Content
   a. Information giving
   b. Action taking
      Problems
      Solutions
      Closing remarks

B. Functional expressions

This memo responds to your request that the weekly meeting be moved from 9 am to 10 am.

This memo presents my impressions of the meeting last week.

If possible, I would like to receive your report before the next Board Meeting.

Please feel free to contact me if you need further information.

We would appreciate hearing from you in regard to this matter.

If there's any problem about this arrangement, please let me know.

IV. PRACTICES

A. Do exercises and find the definition of business memo.

setting	deadline	persuade	policy	little
short	inform	change	attend	increase

A business memo is a _____ piece of writing to _____ or _____ people. It is often used in an office _____. You can write a memo to:

1. Inform _____ change;
2. Inform price _____;
3. Persuade people to _____ meeting;
4. Persuade people to use _____ paper;
5. Meet a _____;
6. _____ a current production procedure, etc.

B. Translation

我想让你交给我你所有有关……的资料。

我想确切地知道采取了什么样的行动。

如你们3月2日的备忘录中所要求的，我调查了……

本周晚些时候咱们能集合一下讨论……吗？

C. The sentences of the following memo got mixed. Number the correct order you think they should be. One is done for you as an example.

MEMO

To: Students in my class
From: Jenifer Tanner, 7 grade student
Date: June 5, 2011
Subject: results of phone inquiry to Craig Air

Fellow students,

  _3_   At ＄180.00 per 207 it will cost the class ＄720.00 to go to Hawaii.

  ___   Please talk to me if you have any questions.

  ___   Yesterday I called Craig Sir and talked to Joe Smith about the class field trip to Hawaii.

  ___   The two planes would be able to fly us Hawaii on December 23 at 9:00 am and return to Seattle the same day at 7:00 pm.

  ___   Mr. Smith said that it would take two 207s to fly the class to Hawaii, and two 270s to fly the class back.

Jenifer Tanner

D. The following extract is from a telephone call. Suppose you wanted to send a memo instead of making the telephone call. Please write the body of the memo.

Hello, Mr. Williams? This is Dennis Tang here. Yes, Senior Accounts Supervisor. Look, Mr. Williams, I'm afraid I made a slight mistake in the figures I sent you recently. Yes, well, well, not really my fault. The computer was down. You know how these things are … Would you like me to send over the revised figures? You would. Ok.

E. Suppose you (Robert Brown) are a supervisor of a big company. The chief of operations (David Green) wants to adopt the "pitch-in" system to increase productivity. Write a memo which covers the following issues.

1. You agree with David in terms of increasing productivity in the company.

2. You express doubts that "pitch-in" system can tighten control over employees and increase productivity.

3. You would like to meet David to discuss other means of incentives.

V. WORDS AND EXPRESSIONS

Reassign　v. 再分配，再指定

　　Only a system administrator can reassign ownership of a job.

Headquarter　n. 总部

Chose-in　adj. 接近中心的

　　The campsite is close to all local amenities.

Steward　n. 理事，管家，干事

　　The steward at the march stood his ground while the rest of the marchers decided to run.

Secretarial　adj. 秘书的，书记的

　　My secretarial duties includes taking shorthand, typing and filing.

Book-keeping　n. 记账，簿记

Enrollment　n. 登记，注册

　　Another federal program was still promoting student enrollment in teaching programs.

Poster　n. 海报

Unit 11　MINUTES
会议记录

I. INTRODUCTION

常规的会议一般要求有一份备忘录或电子邮件作为会议决议的记录。而正式的会议或者是那些存在一些争议观点的会议则会需要一份更正式一些的汇总记录。

会议记录（Minutes）是一种对于会议过程进行正式记录的文件，是如实记载会议参加者、主要议题、讨论过程、开会结果的写作文体。会议秘书通常负责写会议记录，并在会议结束后打印，由会议主持人过目，看是否需要改动，然后分发给所有出席会议的人员并存档。会议记录要求按照与会议议程一致的顺序来写。

会议记录通常由会议标题、会议基本情况、会议记录正文和会议记录的结尾四个部分组成。

- 会议标题通常包括会议名称、开会日期和时间、开会地点及会议主题。
- 会议基本情况包括会议出席人、缺席人、议事日程及会议记录人。
- 会议记录正文是主体，包括各位领导的报告、决议、下次会议的召开日期和议程、动议人姓名、附议人姓名、表决结果及休会时间等。
- 会议记录的结尾部分通常有结尾礼辞、记录人的手写和打字签名。

会议记录汇总了会议上所有的讨论议题和决策。但是要注意它的记录重点是会议上都发生了什么，有那些决策发生，而不是哪个参会者分别说了什么。因此，会议记录可能只是提供了对于某一事项都出现了哪些观点，结论是什么，而没有表明发表观点者的姓名。尽量注意避免会议记录太短而不能反映问题，太长又太过乏味。

在会议记录的语言应用层面，应注意以下几个方面：

- 开会时使用的口头语常常不太规范，因此会后整理会议记录时一般要改成较正式的书面语。
- 会议发言人通常使用的是主动语态，写会议记录时常常要改为被动语态。
- 记录每位发言人的言论时，一般要使用间接引语。
- 会议记录的内容是已发生过的事情，因此要对时态、代词、时间用语进行相应的变化，保持会议记录全文在诸方面的一致性。
- 会议记录的撰写要以客观、详细、明确为原则，不带有个人感情色彩。

第二课中所涉及的会议主持技巧和本课都与会议有关，但是前者偏重口语沟通，后者偏重书面沟通。学习者可以将两课结合起来，相互补充，再结合比如讨论与陈述观点的技巧，从而最终有能力形成一个比较完整的会议过程。

II. EXAMPLES

Minutes 1

COMPUTER USE COMMITTEE
Minutes of the Regular Meeting
May 18, 2011

Member present: S. Llindsey (Chair), L. Anderson-White, F. Griffin, T. King (Secretary), Z. Petrppoulou, G. Ullom, J. West, K. Wolff

Shannon Llindsey called the meeting to order at 8:35 a.m. The minutes of the April 14 meeting were approved with the correction that Frank Griffin be recorded as present.

REPORT OF THE BUDGET SUBCOMMITTEE

Zoe Petrppoulou reported that the Corporate Executive Council had approved an additional $ 58000 for subcommittee allocation for hardware purchases through September 30, 2011. The subcommittee plans to send out RFPs by the end of the month and to make allocation recommendations to CUC at the June meeting. He also distributed a handout (appendix A) showing the current-year hardware and software allocations through May 1.

OLD BUSINESS

None.

NEW BUSINESS

Standardization of Webpage-Development Software. Jenny West moved that "beginning September 1, 2011, CUC approve expenditures for webpage-development software only for Microsoft FrontPage 2003." She summarized the coordination, training, and site-maintenance problems that are now being encountered as a result of individual webmasters using different programs and answered questions from the floor. Gina Ullom moved to amend the motion by inserting the words "or later version" after "FrontPage 2003." The amendment passed, and the amended motion was adopted after debate.

Speech-Recognition Software. Shannon Lindsey reported that she had received numerous requests for information or recommendations for purchasing speech-recognition software and asked for committee input. Extensive discussion followed concerning the cost, the amount of training required, accuracy, resulting noise level for carrel workers, and the overall implications of such software for touch-typing skills. The motion by Lisa Anderson-White that "the chair appoints a task force to study the issue and report back at the next meeting" passed. The chair appointed Lisa Anderson-White and Frank Griffin to the task force.

ANNOUNCEMENTS

Shannon Lindsey made the following announcements:

She has received three positive comments and no negative feedback from her March 15 memo to department heads announcing the new repair and maintenance policy.

She has been asked to represent CUC at the June 18 long-range planning meeting of the Corporate Executive Council to answer questions about planned hardware and software expenditures for the next three years.

Anthem Computer Services has asked permission to make a 30-minutes presentation to CUC. In accordance with committee policy, she rejected the request.

ADJOURNMENT

The meeting was adjourned at 10:40 am. The next regular meeting is scheduled for 8:30 am on June 20.

Respectfully submitted,

Terry King, secretary

Minutes 2

Minutes of a Board Meeting
International Tractors, Inc.
Directors' Meeting
Minutes of April 6, 2012 Regular Meeting, No. 4

A regular meeting of the Board of Directors of International Tractors, Inc. was held on Thursday, April 6, 2012. The meeting was called to order by John Wolfe, Chairman, at 10 am in the founder's Conference Room of the Corporate Office on Gilpin Road in Leechberg, Pennsylvania.

Present Eleven members of the Board were present: Paulin Alt, Charles Fillip, Glenn France, Robert Hazer, Joseph Latina, Richard Linamen, Lorraine Perejda, Ismail Perez, Ethel Rasmusson, Irene Stanick and Elizabeth Walden. There members constituted a quorum.

Absent One member was absent: Louis Jones

Minutes The minutes of the March 5, 2012, special approved directors' meeting were read and approved.

Report The chairman reported on the period of growth, in sales during the last quarter, especially in international business with a 12 percent increase as compared with a year ago. However, mention was made of the increasing difficulties in biding for critical material supplies against strong and affluent foreign competitors.

A plan for organizing for growth was submitted to the board to study.

First, decentralize from our corporate headquarters into each operating company responsibility for its sales, marketing, and accounting operations.

Next, reinstitute the dual management posts of chairman and chief executive officer and of president and chief operating officer. This will assure that undivided attention will be given to current operations and future growth.

Adjournment A motion for adjournment was made by Mr. France and seconded by Ms. Stanick. The meeting was adjourned at 11:45 am.

John Wolfe Chairman
Charlotte Charpnak Secretary

Minutes 3

Resolution minutes of meeting

Date: April 23, 2011, 8:30-11:00
Venue: Room 204, East-Saxon Savings Bank
Participants: All the middle-level managers from Saxony Economic Development Corporation and East-Saxon Savings Bank
Minutes recorder: Ms. Koch, secretary from Saxony Economic Development Corporation

The following resolutions on proceeding further were taken in the subsequent discussion.

Setup of a discussion group "Developers of Economy"
The establishment of a regular Discussion Group that will take place, following a rotation principle, at least twice a year has been agreed upon as a suitable instrument for the exchange of information and for coordination. The Breslau Region has offered an invitation for the next meeting. Visiting interesting projects in the area has been adopted as an idea of inspiration.

There has been agreement that the attractiveness and the profile of the region need to be made visible. Main focus for this purpose should be formed by the economy with concentration on certain branches.

Profile sheet and contact partners
Filling in a profile sheet for participating partners is regarded as helpful for the provision of basic information, contact partners and, probably, core competence.

All partners are requested to return this profile sheet (Attachment) to Saxony Economic Development Corporation by 14 June, 2011. They will subsequently be made accessible to all partners.

The meeting was adjourned at 11:30 am.
Catherine Koch

III. NOTES

The first paragraph of minutes should identify the type of the meeting (regular or special); the date, time, and place of the meeting; the presiding officer; the names of those present (or absent) if customary; and the fact that the minutes of the previous meeting were read and approved.

The body of the minutes should contain a separate paragraph for each topic. According to parliamentary procedure, the name of the maker of a motion, but not the seconder, should be entered in the minutes. The precise wording of motions, exactly as voted on, should also appear in minutes. It is often helpful to use the same subheadings as in the agenda.

The last paragraph of the minutes should state the time of adjournment and, if appropriate, the time set for the next meeting. The minutes should be signed by the person preparing them. If someone other than the chairperson prepares the minutes, the minutes should be read and approved by the chairperson before being distributed.

A. Abbreviations, symbols and meaning

Abbreviations and Symbols	Meaning
i.e.	that is
e.g.	for example
approx.	approximately
b/w	between
i/e	import-export
o/d	overdue
sig.	significant
imp.	important
Q1, Q2, Q3	first, second, third quarter of the year
b4	before
bt	but
=	equals, is
≠	is not equal to

Continuing

Abbreviations and Symbols	Meaning
≈	approximately, about
→	leads to, results in
←	the result of, due to
∴	therefore
∵	because of
↘	drops, reduces
↗	rises, increases

B. Practical sentence patterns

1. + that + sentence

Mr. Tang agreed that he would oversee the move to new premises.

Mrs. Sue declared that the company had spent rather too much on training in the previous year.

2. + to + infinitive

The managing director refused to allow personal issues to come into his consideration.

The senior engineering officer offered to visit the plant in the coming month.

3. + verb-ing

Mr. Bush suggested taking on a number of new members of staff to cover the shortfall.

Mr. Black raised the issue of introducing a new system of stock control.

4. + the fact (or idea) that + sentence

Mr. White argued against the idea that his department could take sole responsibility for the recent downturn in the company's profits.

Mrs. Fan referred to the fact that the company had previously had trading contacts with Hong Kong.

5. + noun

Ms. King explained the background to the acquisition of stock in the new company.

Mr. Jackson recognized the importance of maintaining close links with raw material suppliers.

IV. PRACTICE

A. Here is the extract from a meeting called to arrange a European sales conference. Please complete the secretary's minutes below.

Sheila: Right, I've called this meeting to fix the details for the annual European sales conference. Basically we've got three issues to decide: firstly the date, secondly the location and finally the conference facilities. Let's start with the date. What's your view, Ron?

Ron: I think we're going to have to settle for September—probably the last weekend. I've had a look at the schedule. There's a big trade fair coming up in July—most of the sales people will be there. August is out—most of the sales team are taking their holidays then. The first couple of weeks in September ...

Tracy: Excuse me for interrupting, Ron. Sheila, I've just been looking at your diary. That last week in September you're flying out to Japan ...

Sheila: When do I get back?

Tracy: Well, you are booked on a flight back to Miami on Friday evening. Hardly time to get over to London for the weekend.

Sheila: You're right. Ron, why can't we make it the second weekend in September? That's the ...

Tracy: 15th and 16th.

Ron: It'll be very difficult. As I was saying, the first two weekends in September are pretty busy. Most of the team will be involved in the launch of the new Xion product.

Sheila: Of course, I was forgetting. What about that third weekend? Tracy, when do I leave for Tokyo?

Tracy: Well, at the moment, you're flying out on the Monday morning from JFK.

Sheila: Is there any reason why I shouldn't take a flight from London instead?

Tracy: I don't see any problem.

Sheila: Right. Ron, what about the third weekend—that's the 22nd and 23rd?

Ron: That looks ok. Of course, I'll have to confirm it with Peter.

Sheila: Sure. Get back to us as soon as possible. Now, what about the location?

Ron, any ideas?

Ron: Yes, I think I've found the ideal spot—just outside London, not far from Heathrow. It's called the Swallow Hotel.

Sheila: That sounds great. How much is it going to cost us?

Ron: Well, we're working to a budget of $250 per delegate for the weekend and I reckon we can get this place for less.

Sheila: Good. Does that include everything?

Ron: Yes, all inclusive.

Sheila: Great. Look, I have to go now. My flight leaves in a couple of hours. Can I leave you with Tracy to sort out the details?

B. The following words on the left are extracted from the verbatim notes of a meeting between two companies. Write a minutes accordingly.

HF: On the 23 of this month at 6:30 in the morning, a security guard discovered that a fire had broken out on the roof of the Shafesbury Building. The fire had burnt the outside surfaces of Cooling Tower 14. In particular, the wooden topping and part of the cooling tower's upper casting were completely burnt.	
JC: Well, it certainly looks like the fire started outside. Lighting? **HF**: No, I don't think so. The building is completely sheltered under the lighting protection system, which is routinely checked and serviced, so I don't think lightning is to blame. **JC**: Vandalism? **HF**: I personally think so.	
JC: Tougher security might stop such incidents happening again. Maybe some extra patrol points around the building perimeter and dead corners? **PK**: I see no reason why we can't do that remedial work within the next week.	

PK: I really think the timber of the cooling towers should be protected with flame-retardant paint. We'd be happy to help if we can.	
JC: Let me just recap. First, it looks like the most likely cause of the fire was vandalism, and that increased security may be needed to combat this in the future. Second, Kuen Wah has agreed to carry out the necessary remedial work on Wednesday May 1, and have also offered to undertake repainting with flame retardant paint.	

V. WORDS AND EXPRESSIONS

Council　n. 委员会，政务会

　　The party is expecting to gain control of the council in the next election.

Subcommitee　n. 小组委员会，下属委员会

　　He has resigned from the chairmanship of the subcommittee.

Handout　n. 讲义，印刷品

　　I read the handout carefully.

Appendix　n. 附录，附加物

　　This prospect was the subject of an appendix to the development plan.

Move　v. 提议

　　Labour quickly moved a closure motion to end the debate.

Floor　n. 底部，议员席

　　The issues were debated on the floor of the House.

Amend　v. 修改，修订

　　The teacher advised him to amend his way of living.

Carrel　n. 小单间

　　He then returned to his carrel for his own research.

Adjournment　n. 休会，延期

　　The court met again after an adjournment of two weeks.

Quorum　n. 法定人数

One-half of the members of the Executive Committee shall constitute a quorum.

Bid　v. 出价，投标

Singapore Airlines is rumoured to be bidding for a management contract to run both airports ...

Affluent　adj. 富裕的

He hails from an affluent background.

Decentralize　v. 权利分散，地方分权

If we decentralize, the provinces will have more autonomy.

Dual　adj. 双重的

The airplane had dual controls.

Rotation　n. 轮流，旋转

The workers in this workshop do day and night shifts in weekly rotation.

Instrument　n. 仪器，工具

You can see distant objects with this special instrument.

Inspriration　n. 灵感

The bank has branches all over the country.

Branch　n. 分支，部门

Dreams can be a rich source of inspiration for an artist.

Provision　n. 预备，规定

The government is responsible for the provision of health care.

Attachment　n. 附件，附属物

The girl has a doll with a range of different attachments.

Unit 12   RESUME AND JOB-APPLICATION LETTERS
简历与求职信

I. INTRODUCTION

简历是对某人的经历与素质的简要记录，通常是为申请工作机会而制作。简历的重点应该放在未来的可能性和发展上，而不是曾经的过去。因此，你必须在简历中反映出以你的教育背景和工作经验，是可以胜任今后的工作的。

递交简历的目标就是争取到面试的机会，而面试的目标是拿到工作机会。因此，需要牢记，简历以及随附的求职信是你在芸芸众生中脱颖而出，进而进入小范围选拔面试的关键。

简历的基本要素有标题、工作经历、教育背景、主要成就、证明人和其他项目（特殊技能、个人强项、曾经接受过的相关培训和兴趣爱好等）。

再来看求职信。求职信是你与有望成为你的老板的人之间的一次沟通。沟通的内容就是你有兴趣和能力在他的机构任职。求职信也被称为cover letter，是指信中大致概括了你的简历中的要点，cover在这里是"覆盖、包括"的意思。大多数求职者申请不同的工作都使用同一份简历，但却随附更有针对性的求职信。在这时，求职信的作用就是针对不同的工作岗位而个性化你的技能和素质。

求职信的基本要素有，求职信的信息来源及具体目标、申请工作的原因及胜任工作的理由、恳请对方给予面谈机会和告知对方联系方式及附件。

II. EXAMPLES

RESUME

JAMES J. ARNOLD

OBJECTIVE

Labor relations position in a large multinational firm that requires well-developed labor relations, management, and communication skills.

SKILLS

LABOR RELATIONS
- Majored in labor relations; minored in psychology
- Belong to local 463 of International Office Workers Union
- Was crew chief for the second-shift work team at Wainwright Bank

MANAGEMENT
- Learned time-management skills by working 30 hours per week while attending school full-time
- Was promoted twice in three years at Wainwright Bank
- Practiced discretion while dealing with the financial affairs of others; treated all transactions confidentially

COMMUNICATION
- Developed a webpage for Alpha Kappa Psi business fraternity
- Ran for senior class vice president, making frequent campaign speeches and impromptu remarks
- Took elective classes in report writing and business research
- Be competent in Microsoft Office 2003 and Internet research

EDUCATION

B. S. degree from Boston University to be awarded June 2006

Major: labor relations; minor: psychology

EXPERIENCE

Bank teller, Wainwright Bank, Boston, Massachusetts: 2003-present

Salesperson, JC Penney, Norfolk, Nebraska: summer 2001

REFERENCES

Available from the career information center
Boston University, Boston, MA 02215; phone: 617-555-2001

JOB-APPLICATION LETTER

March 13, 2011

Mr. David Norman, partner
Ross, Russell & Weston
452 Fifth Avenue
New York, NY 10018
Subject: EDP specialist position

Dear Mr. Norman:

My varied work experience in accounting and payroll services, coupled with my accounting degree, has prepared me for the position of EDP specialist that you advertised in the March 9 *New York Times*.

In addition to taking required courses in accounting and management information systems as part of my accounting major at New York University, I also took an elective course in EDP auditing and control. The training I received in this course in applications, software, systems, and service-center records would enable me to immediately become a productive member of your EDP consulting staff.

My college training has been supplemented by internship in a large accounting firm. In addition, my two and one-half years of experience as a payroll specialist for the city of New York have given me firsthand knowledge of the operation and needs of nonprofit agencies. This experience should help me to contribute to your large consulting practice with governmental agencies.

After you have reviewed my enclosed résumé, I would appreciate having the opportunity to discuss with you why I believe I have the right qualifications and personality to serve you and your clients. I can be reached by phone after 3 p.m. daily.

Sincerely,
James White

Aurelia Gomez
225 West 70 Street
New York, NY 10023
Phone: 212-555-3821
Email: agomez@nyu.edu

III. NOTES

A. Résumé Length

Recruiters typically spend no more than 35 seconds looking at each résumé during their initial screening to pare down the perhaps hundreds of applications for a position into a manageable number to study in more detail. Most managers prefer a one-page résumé for the entry-level positions typically sought by recent college graduates, with a two-page résumé being reserved for unusual circumstances or for higher-level positions.

Note, however, that a recent survey of personnel recruiters from big five accounting firms found that recruiters ranked candidates with two-page résumés more favorably than candidates with one-page resumes.

A one-page résumé is not the same as a two-page résumé crammed onto one page by means of small type and narrow margins. Your résumé must be attractive and easy to read. Shorten it by making judicious decisions about what to include and then by using concise language to communicate what is important. But do not make your résumé too short, either. A résumé that does not fill one page may tell the prospective employer that you have little to offer.

B. Résumé Format

Choose a simple, easy-to-read typeface, and avoid the temptation to use a lot of "special effects" just because they're available on your computer. One or two typefaces in one or two different sizes should be enough. Use a simple format, with lots of white space, short paragraphs, and a logical organization. Through the use of type size and style, indentation, bullets, and the like, make clear which parts are subordinate to main features.

C. Résumé Content

One survey of 152 fortune 500 company personnel indicated that 90 percent or

more wanted the following information on a résumé.
- name, address, and telephone number
- job objective
- college major, degree, name of college, and date of graduation
- jobs held, employing company or companies (but not complete mailing address or the names of your supervisors), date of employment, and job duties
- special aptitudes and skills

D. Grammar and Words

Complete sentences are not necessary. Instead, start your descriptions with action verbs, using present tense for current duties and past tense for previous job duties or accomplishments.

Avoid weak verbs such as attempted, endeavored, hoped, and tried, and avoid sexist language such as manpower (use labor instead) and chairman (use chair or chairperson instead).

E. Practical Sentences in Job Application Letter

I have learnt that you are looking for a few qualified teachers of English from an ad in the *People's Daily*.

Your advertisement in this morning's journal for an adjustment manager prompted me to apply for this position.

I am able to speak English fluently and I am fond of teaching career. Besides, I am good at computer operation.

I have been handling most of the bookkeeping for the past 3 years and I trust I am qualified to fulfill your position.

Four years' experience on China Daily gives me the confidence to apply for this desirable job.

I would be very glad of an opportunity to discuss whether I could fit into your organization.

The enclosed resume describes my qualifications for the position advertised. I would welcome the opportunity to personally discuss your requirements with you.

Thank you for your attention to my application. I look forward to meeting you at your convenience.

IV. PRACTICE

A. Put the following sentences into the right order and make it a complete letter of application.

1. Besides, I have studied secretarial skills at Westside Business Institute, and I have completed 85 credits towards my BA degree.

2. I have been a secretary for the past six years. Most recently, I have been working as an assistant to the vice-president of ESCO, Inc.

3. I am writing in response to your ad in Sunday's newspaper. I would like to apply for the position of executive secretary.

4. In addition to general secretarial duties, my responsibilities in this capacity have included the management of the office in the absence of my employer.

5. Yours truly

6. A list of references will be provided on request.

7. I am enclosing my resume for your consideration. My complete job history is included.

8. Dear Sir/Madam,

B. The following job application needs revising. Read and discuss it in groups and try to rewrite it (inside addresses omitted).

Dear Sir or Madam

According to this morning's *Times,* you want an experienced, efficient secretary.

During the past 12 years I have served in that capacity to three prominent executives, all three of whom will vouch for my efficiency and dependability. They are:

Mr. Matthew Borden, Hollins-Borden company, Trenton, N.J. (Hospital Supplies)

Mr. Curris Thompson, Worden associates, New York (Manufacturers of Surgical Instruments)

Mr. John Peterson, Billings, Holt & Company, New York (Advertising Agency)

Following the recent reorganization of Billings, Holt & Company, Mr. Peterson was transferred to Chicago—which is the reason why I am now looking for another connection.

I am 29 years of age, a graduate from People's University, unmarried, living at home with my family. I am in excellent health, and am told that I make an especially good appearance for a secretary.

My former associates will tell you I am neat, accurate and painstaking in my work and I am tactful and courteous, resourceful, loyal to the job, and of pleasing personality. I am well-trained and experienced in all the duties and responsibilities of a good secretary; and I should like the opportunity of coming in and talking with you personally. May I?

The résumé and my self-addressed card is for your convenience. Just write on the card when you would like me to come for an interview.

Sincerely yours
Susan Williams

C. You are finally in your last term of college before graduating and are searching for the perfect full-time post college job. Compose your résumé and application letter.

D. You are going to write a letter of application for the job advertised below to the executive vice president of Faraday Plastics Manufacturing Company and your resume should be enclosed.

VACANCY

Director of Public Relations

Applicants for this position should have college degree, proficiency in English and knowledge of public relations.

Salary and benefits will be very attractive. Please enclose a recent photograph and C.V. to:

Faraday Plastics Manufacturing Company
Executive Vice President, Mr. Robert Johnson
P.O. Box 457, Mombassa
No later than one week after this ad.

V. WORDS AND EXPRESSIONS

Multinational　adj. 多国的
　　The firm was taken over by a multinational consulting firm.

Major　adj. 主要的，主修的
　　We don't anticipate any major problems.

Minor　adj. 较小的，少数的
　　The birth of her son was a minor interruption to her career.

Crew　n. 全体船员，全体，一群
　　None of the passengers and crew were injured.

Discretion　n. 判断力，慎重
　　Visits are at the discretion of the owners.

Impromptu　adj. 即席的，临时的，无准备的
　　The announcement was made in an impromptu press conference at the airport.

Fraternity　n. 大学生联谊会
　　One of writer's favourite themes is the fraternity of mankind.

Payroll　adj. 工资名单，工资总支出
　　They had 87,000 employees on the payroll.

Audit　v. 审计
　　Each year they audit our accounts and certify them as being true and fair.

Internship　n. 实习
　　This is paid internship for the summer.

Nonprofit　adj. 非营利的
　　The council is a nonprofit group that supports liberal arts education.

Unit 13　BUSINESS CORRESPONDENCE
商务书信

I. INTRODUCTION

　　从内容上看，商务书信和前面所介绍的备忘录和电子邮件是基本一致的，因此很多教材也把这三者放在一起讲解。其中的区别就是，书信在格式上与备忘录有所不同，并且商务书信更加正式一些。读者可以复习前面的内容，会发现之前强调过备忘录比较多地用于个体之间或组织内部的信息交流，电子邮件比较突出它的时效性。本课所涉及的商业书信多往来于组织和组织之间，因此在语言构成方面需要更加严谨一些。

　　商务书信与口头沟通不同，因为它提供的是一份永久性的书面文档。因此，商务书信中的语言应用方面多与口语不同。比如口语中的多次重复现象、话题之间的来回转换、漏字或句子不完整等都是在商务书信中不应出现的。

　　商务书信从内容方面划分，通常包括正面/中性消息类型、负面消息类型、投诉信件和推销/劝导型等。例如确认合同、订单、装运安排、通知产品规格或技术指标等都属于正面/中性消息类型；拒绝合作、提高价格等都属于负面消息类型。很多时候，我们也可以把对于产品或服务的投诉信函划归为负面消息类型。而推销产品或服务，推广某项目或计划，争取时间期限的延后，邀请专家出席会议可以被视作劝导型信函。

II. EXAMPLES

Letter 1

Maria da Silva
Boticario Brasil
32, Park Avenue
Sao Paulo SP

Mary Higgins
Customer Service
Wzd Transport
9, Wind Road
Sao Paulo SP

May 17, 2003

Dear Mrs. Higgins,

  Boticario Brasil has had a contract with your company for the last four years, since we decided to outsource our delivery service. The main reason for us to do so was that at the time we felt that a reliable business partner could perfect better our distribution and reduce the costs.

  Your deliveries were satisfactory until last Christmas; however, since January we have been finding the standard of your service absolutely below expectations. Last April, when we were in the midst of launching our new product line, your company failed to deliver our loads to 3 of our major retailers, 2 of them being very important high street sites. Needless to say this had a terribly negative effect on our sales. We had just invested in a high-impact advertising campaign, and when our consumers went to the shops, the products simply were not there on the shelf.

  In April we were faced with yet another problem due to your poor service, when a delivery to Rio de Janeiro was 20 days late.

  I do hope you address this matter as a top priority and re-establish the good service you used to provide, or else, Boticario will have to look for another business partner.

  I look forward to hearing from you.

Yours sincerely …

LETTER 2

Rainbow training institute
53 Bradburn Close
Muswell Hill
London n10

Phone 0818832555
Fax 0818849345

J. Fisher
The personnel manager
DJ Banking Corp.
54 Smithson Ave
London e17 6ty

20 September 1999
Re: International sales workshop 5 November

Dear Ms. Fisher

    I'm writing to inform you that, unfortunately we have had to cancel our November workshop. However, we can include your staff in the October 8 workshop instead if this is convenient.
    I regret that we were unable to inform you of this change earlier, and I hope you will be able to attend at this earlier date.
    I would appreciate it if you could let me know as soon as possible the names of your staff who will be attending on October 8.
    I'm sure that your staff will find the workshop both useful and informative.

Yours sincerely
J. Reading
Training manager

LETTER 3

Gentlemen

With reference to your order No. 672 dated June 3, 2008 and your telephone conversation this morning, I am pleased to inform you that the containers have now been loaded on board, and that the departure time from Southampton docks is confirmed as 08:00 on September 15, 2008.

As we discussed, the shipping documents (Commercial Invoice, Bills of Lading, Insurance Policy and Consular Certificate of Origin) have now been presented to our bankers, together with a sight draft for collection through the Bank of China. The bank has been instructed to release the documents once payment of the draft has been received. A copy of the Commercial Invoice is enclosed.

I trust that the containers arrive safely and that the order has been carried out to your satisfaction. I would be grateful if you could inform me once the containers have arrived in Shanghai.

We would, of course, be glad to receive any further orders, and look forward to hearing from you again in the future.

Sincerely yours
Tom Livingston
Exports Manager
Enc: Copy of Commercial Invoice for Order No 672 dated June 3, 2008

III. NOTES

Business letters typically contain the following features (although they may not all appear in the same letter):

1. Opening and closing greetings

   If you don't have a contact name:

   Dear sir or madam

   Yours faithfully

   If you know the name of the person:

   Dr. Mr. Jones

UNIT 13 BUSINESS CORRESPONDENCE • 133 •

    Mrs.
    Miss
    Ms.
    Yours sincerely

  If you know the person as a friend or close business colleague:

    Dear James
    Best wishes/regards

2. Stating the reference at the beginning of the letter

    You can start with either:
    Subject: _____
    Reference: _____
    Re: _____

  Or an expression like:

    With reference to … (your letter of /email/enquiry of)
    I thank you for your letter of July 1.
    Further to our telephone conversation, …

3. Requesting

    I would be grateful if you could …
    I would appreciate it if you could …
    Could you please …? (informal)
    Would it be possible to …?

4. Explaining the reason for writing

    I am writing to inform you that/apply for/request, etc ….

5. Thanking

    Thank you for …
    We were very pleased to …

6. Enclosing documents

  Where other documents are included with the letter, you can say:

    Please find enclosed / attached …
    I enclosed the …
    I have attached a …
    Here is the …

7. Apologizing

   I regret that …
   I am afraid that …
   I am sorry that …
   I apologise for …

8. Expressing urgency

   … at your earliest convenience
   … without delay
   … as soon as possible

9. Confirming

   I am pleased to confirm that …
   I confirm that …
   This is to confirm that …

10. Ending the letter

    I look forward to … (hearing from you / seeing you)
    I am sure that …
    I hope …
    See you soon. (informal)

IV. PRACTICE

A. Write a reply to the following letter.

Technology in Engineering Conference
45 Broughton Street, Brighton

J. Higgins
Purchasing manager
Zacron engineering
Unit 5
Hempstead industrial estate
Hemel Hempstead HP2 7FX   25 May 1999

Dear Mr. Higgins

We have pleasure in inviting you to our annual conference. This year it will be taking place at the Metropole Hotel, Brington from 24 to 28 July.

We enclose details of the conference, accommodation arrangements and a provisional programme.

Last year you gave a very interesting presentation on the subject of "Purchasing High Technology". We would be very grateful if you would consider giving us an update on this.

We would appreciate it if you could confirm your participation at your earliest convenience.

Yours sincerely
P. Matthews
Conference organizer

Your reply should include the following:
Reference to the above letter
Confirmation of your participation
Request for more information about the programme
Apology for not being able to give another presentation (pressure of work—no time for preparation)
A polite phrase to end the letter
Some parts of the letter have already been done for you.

Zacron engineering
Unit 5
Hempstead industrial estate
Hemel Hempstead

Mr. P. Matthews
Technology in engineering conference
45 Broughton Street
Brighton bn25 1xl
1 June 1999

Dear Mr. Matthews

　　With reference to your letter of 25 may, I am pleased to_____
_____.
　　I would be grateful _____.
Unfortunately, _____.
　　I am afraid _____
_____.

Yours sincerely
J. Higgins
Purchasing manager

B. Clozing

How to write a business letter

　　The business letter is the principal means used by business firm to keep __1__ touch with it's customers; often enough it is the only one and the customers form their impression of the firm from the __2__ and quality of the letter it sends out. Good quality paper and an attractive __3__ play their part in this, but they are less important than the message they carry. Business does not call __4__ the elegant language of the post, but it does require us to express ourselves __5__ in plain language that is clear and really understood.

　　Writing plainly does not mean that the letter must be __6__ to a mere recital of facts. In a style that is dull and unattractive, when we write a letter we enter into __7__ relationship with our reader. Like us he has feelings and we can't __8__ to disregard them. This is a necessary reminder because many people who are warm and friendly by __9__ become reasons of quite another sort when they sit down to write or dictate a business letter.

　　The whole __10__ of good business letter-writing is to write simply, in an easy and natural way—like one friendly human being talking to another. Make your letter then __11__ as much as possible like good conversation. You wouldn't say on the phone "It's regretted that the goods can't be delivered today." You would say

UNIT 13 BUSINESS CORRESPONDENCE

"I am sorry we can't deliver the goods today". So why not say it when you write a letter?

※	A	B	C	D
1	in	on	into	out
2	voice	tone	sound	expression
3	letter-head	letter	words	writing
4	out	on	for	in
5	quickly	slowly	carefully	accurately
6	asked	confined	requested	demanded
7	personal	private	personnel	good
8	decide	determine	afford	obey
9	chance	nature	the way	means
10	secret	principal	rule	method
11	listen	seem	sound	hear

C. The following is a writing assignment finished by a student. It is then discussed and polished in class. The purpose of the letter is to persuade Mr. Thompson to invest in the new project, but the letter fails to arouse the reader's interest in taking out money and to show the benefits he may receive. Please revise it after a discussion in class.

Dear Mr. Thompson

    I am writing to tell you about a very exciting project. My company, Hansu Ltd. is currently planning to build a new swimming pool complex in the city of Joti. The project has already received permission from all the necessary authorities, and we are now at the stage of inviting tenders for various parts of the project.

    We hope having shops and night clubs and bars as well as swimming pools and saunas.

    One of the areas which we need to work on is finance. We would like to offer you the chance to help finance the project. We have heard that you may be interested in such a role. Of course the profits will be considerable, although we cannot say at this stage.

    I suggest we meet up and have a meeting. Could you please come to us next week with some details of your company and also your ability to help us? Thank you.

D. Look at the following extracts from different letter. Match each extract with a description from the box.

> Apology, letter of enquiry, congratulations, cover letter for an invoice, chase-up letter threatening legal action if ignored

Extract 1

Dear Sir

I picked up a copy of your latest catalogue at the recent Print Trade Fair in Rome, and I am writing to enquire about the possibility of having calendars printed at very short notice (we would need delivery by the end of November at the latest). The calendars we would like are the A3 color format (see page 4 of your catalogue), with a different photo for each month.

Extract 2

Despite repeated reminders, including three phone calls and two emails, we have not yet received a satisfactory answer to our questions regarding the faulty KL24 mechanism. Should we not receive an answer by June 30, we would have no other choice but to place the matter in the hands of our lawyers. We are sorry for having to threaten such a drastic action, but unfortunately you leave us with no alternative.

Extract 3

Please find an invoice enclosed for the parts dispatched to your factory on 21 June. We trust you will find everything in order. As always, we may remind you that payment within a month will allow you to claim a 1% discount on your next order.

Extract 4

I was very sorry to hear that the frames you ordered arrived in less than satisfactory condition. It appears that mistake was made by the packaging department, for which I apologize. I have made arrangements for a new consignment to be sent to you without delay, and I have credited your account with the invoiced value of the frames as small compensation for the inconvenience caused.

Extract 5

I have just heard about your appointment as CEO of Knaysas incorporated. May I be among the first to congratulate you and wish you all the very best for the future.

V. WORDS AND EXPRESSIONS

Outsourcing　v. 外购，外部采购
  Already, the outsourcing of human resources is becoming an increasingly common trend.
Reliable　adj. 可靠的，可信赖的
  There was a dearth of reliable information on the subject.
Midst　n. 中部，当中
  Such beauty was unexpected in the midst of the city.
High street site　主干道
Workshop　n. 工作坊，专题讨论会，实验室
  Please take this study material with you to the workshop.
Informative　adj. 提供信息的，有益的，增进知识的
  The book is too long but, nonetheless, informative and entertaining.
Container　n. 容器，集装箱
  Use the formula to calculate the volume of the container.
Dock　n. 码头
  We took the children to the dock to see the ships.
Shipping document　装运单据
Bill of lading　提单（用以证明货物运输合同和货物已经由承运人接收或装船，以及承运为保证据以交付货物的单证）
Insurance pocily　保险单　written contract or certificate of insurance;
Consular certificate of origin　原产地证书
Release　v. 放开，发布，发行
  The fight for his release gathers momentum each day.

Unit 14 CHARTS
图表应用

I. INTRODUCTION

　　本课内容介绍的其实是商业报告和宣讲中的必要工具——图形和表格。在商业报告和宣讲的视觉资料中，都必不可少地需要图与表的配合。通常，我们统称之为"图表"，其实应该将两者区分开来。

　　"表"分为空白表和信息表两种。空白表在英语中我们应该称之为"form"，是需要填写入相应内容的，在公共部门办公领域是非常常见的。在商业领域多用于客户咨询、票据单据、机构管理等方面。这一部分不是本书所要介绍的重点。信息表在英语中对应的用词是"table"，英文解释为 a written set of facts and figures arranged in columns and rows。也就是说，信息表中包含的可以是文字也可以是数字，一般以行和列的形式给出，尤其是包含数字的信息表是我们制图的基础。

　　"图"在英语中主要有 picture, chart 和 diagram。picture 主要是指图画，而我们在这里主要要讨论的是 chart 和 diagram。

　　最常用的三类 chart，是线状图、柱状图和饼形图。这也是本课第二部分举例的重点。

　　线状图（graph, line chart）显示的是随时间变化的趋势或两个变量的关系。在线状图中，纵轴表示的是数量，横轴表示的是时间或其他与数量相对的指标。它的优点是可以很清楚地表现出变量的变化过程和趋势；缺点是理论上，线状图也可以显示两个以上变量的关系，但效果比较凌乱。常用的专业用语有"点线"(dotted line)、"虚线"(broken line)、"实线"(solid line)。

　　柱状图（bar chart, pillar chart）利用其长条的高度和长度来表示数量。它在一次比较多个变量的大小、显示随着时间推移几个变量的组成变化等方面尤其有价值。在这些方面，柱状图弥补了线状图的缺点，因此在很多时候线状图和柱状图是联合出现的。常用的专业用语有"列"（row）、"柱形"（column）、"轴"（axis）和"图例说明"（legend）。

饼形图（pie chart）拥有众人皆知的优势，大多数情况下我们都用饼形图来展示整体与部分的关系，每一扇形区块代表整体中的一小部分。它是一种显示占比或者比较各部分份额的有效方式，例如最常见的就是用于分析市场份额。在制作饼形图时，要注意限制图中的分格数量，对不太重要或很小的部分要进行合并。常用的专业用语有"部分"（segment）。

其他的图形还有流程图 flow-chart，循环图 cycle diagram，射线图 radial diagram，组织结构图 organization chart，示意图 diagram，矢线图 PERT-chart，地图 map 等。在第三部分的注释与补充中可以找到一些例子。

II. EXAMPLES

1. Graph

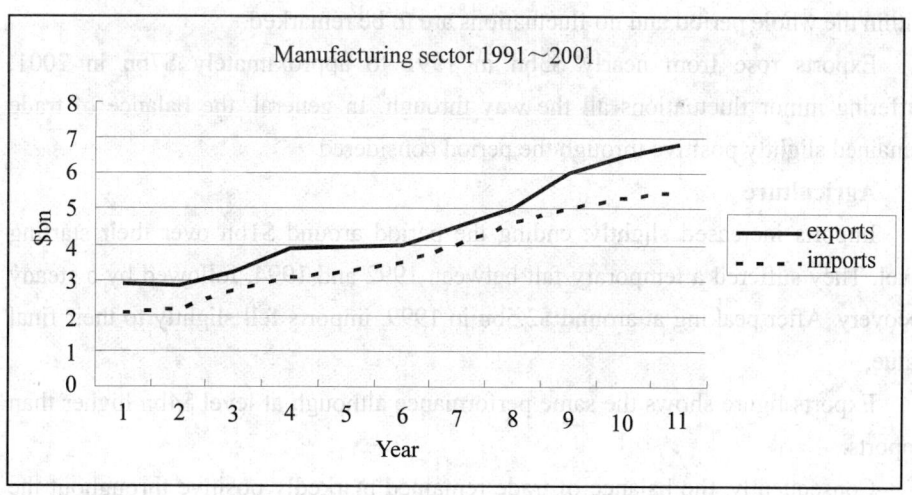

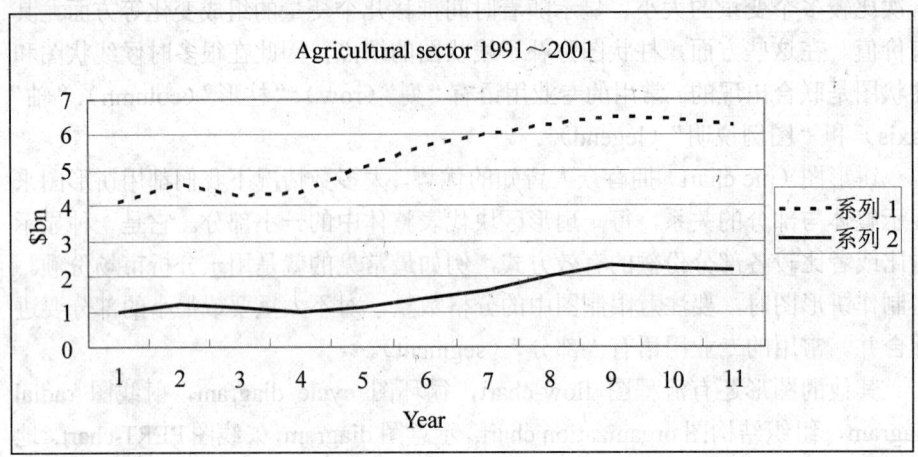

This report describes the movements of the balance of trade between 1991 and 2001, for a particular country, concerning manufacturing and agriculture.

Manufacturing

Imports increased constantly during this period. The figure shows a rise of $4bn within the whole period and no fluctuations are to be remarked.

Exports rose from nearly $3bn in 1991 to approximately $7bn in 2001, suffering minor fluctuations all the way through. In general, the balance of trade remained slightly positive through the period considered.

Agriculture

Imports increased slightly, ending the period around $1bn over their starting level. They suffered a temporary fall between 1992 and 1994, followed by a steady recovery. After peaking at around $2.5bn in 1999, imports fell slightly to their final value.

Exports figure shows the same performance although at level $4bn higher than imports.

Consequently, the balance of trade remained markedly positive throughout the period.

2. Bar chart

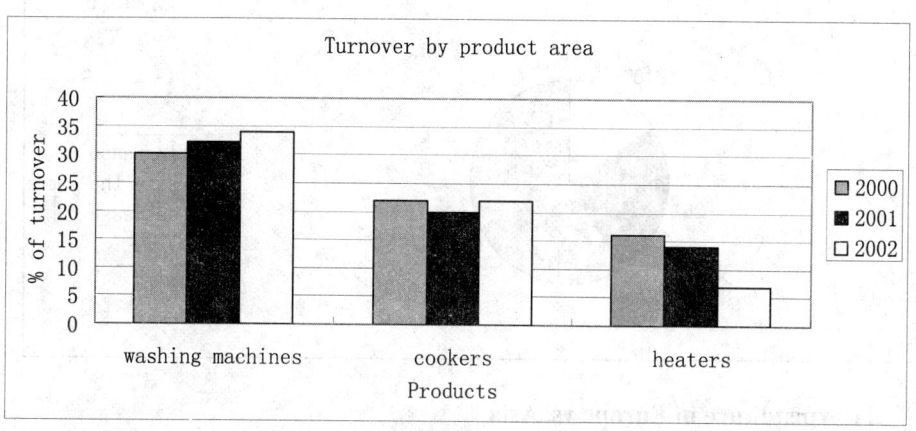

The chart shows how much of the turnover of a certain company was contributed by each of its three main product areas in the year 2000, 2001 and 2002.

Generally speaking, washing machines are the strongest and heaters the weakest of the three products. This basic difference between the two became even more pronounced in this three-year-period with the contribution of washing machines to the company's turnover rising from thirty percent in 2000 to thirty-four percent in 2002, while the share which the heaters contributed dropped from sixteen percent in 2000 to seven percent in 2002. The contribution of the third product—cookers—remained relatively steady during this period; it dropped slightly from twenty-two to twenty percent in 2001, but recovered again in 2002.

3. Pie chart

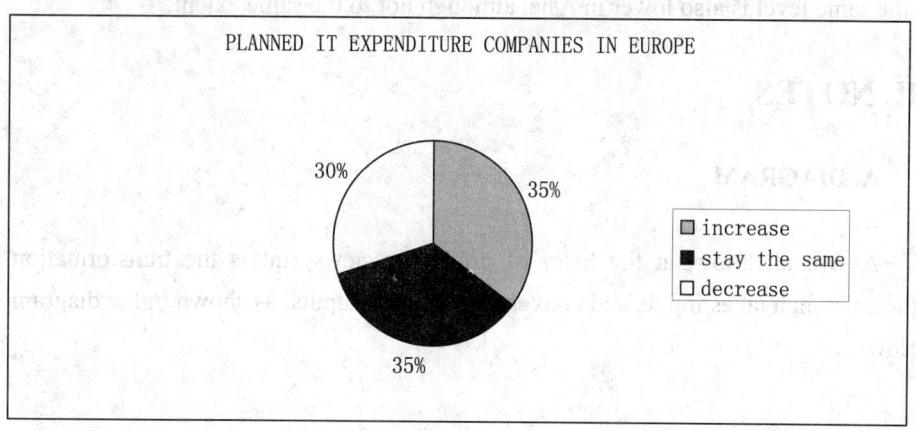

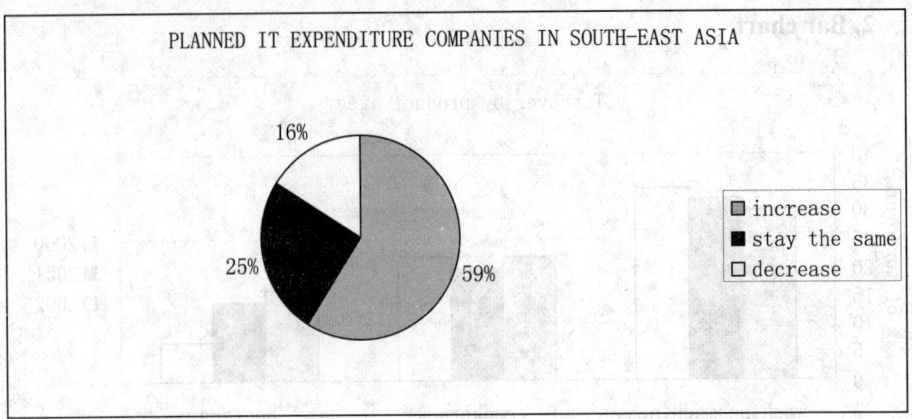

IT expenditure in Europe vs. Asia

The overall result of this international survey on planned IT expenditure for next year shows significant differences between Europe and Asia.

According to the survey results, European companies are almost equally divided between increasing their IT spending, keeping it at this year's level or decreasing it.

The situation in Asia is quite different. Almost 60% of the surveyed Asian companies plan to increase IT expenditure next year, compared to just over a third in Europe.

Moreover, Asian companies seem less keen on cutting IT spending, as only 16% are planning to decrease it, compared to 30% in Europe.

Finally, the percentage of companies who are planning to keep IT expenditure at the same level is also lower in Asia, although not to the same extent.

III. NOTES

A. DIAGRAM

...

As we all know, at the heart of producing newsprint is the transformation process, which takes inputs and converts them into outputs, as shown in the diagram below ...

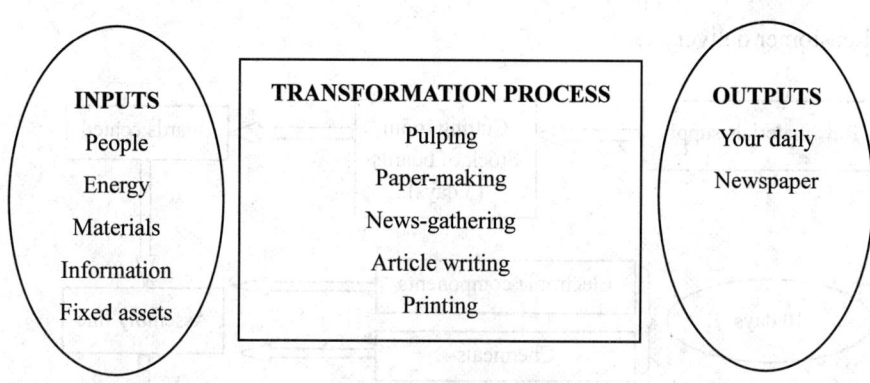

B. Organization chart

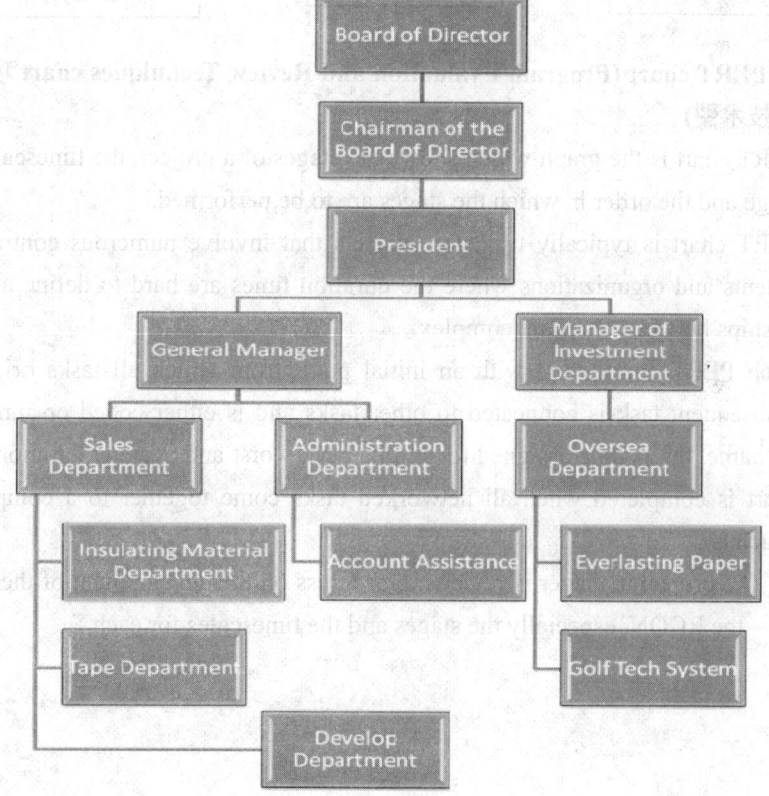

C. Flow-chart

... one of the key areas of our operations is logistics—namely the management of materials movement—all the way through from raw materials supply to end-customer delivery ...

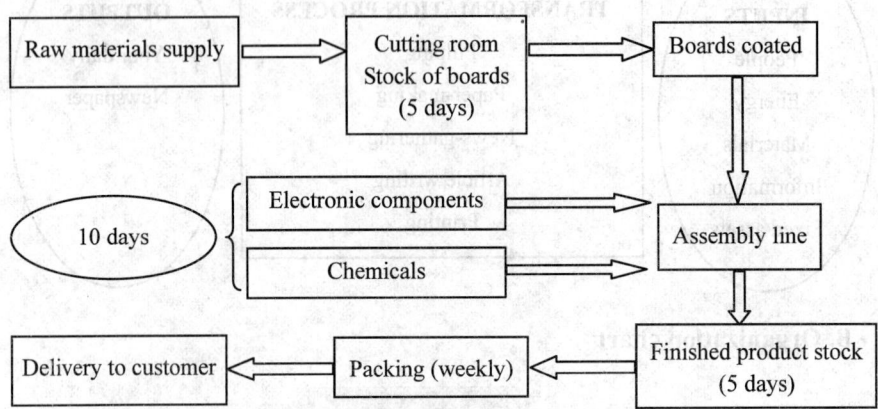

D. PERT-chart (Program Evaluation and Review Techniques chart 项目计划评审技术图)

PERT chart is the graph which shows the stages of a project, the timescales for each stage and the order in which the stages are to be performed.

PERT chart is typically used for projects that involve numerous contractors, departments and organizations where the duration times are hard to define and the relationships between tasks are complex.

Each PERT chart starts with an initial point from which all tasks originate. Each subsequent task is connected to other tasks and is either coded or annotated with its name, the people assigned to, and its best, worst and average duration time. The chart is completed when all networked tasks come together to a completion point, such as:

... The project manager is reviewing progress on the development of their new product – the RCDN, especially the stages and the timescales for each ...

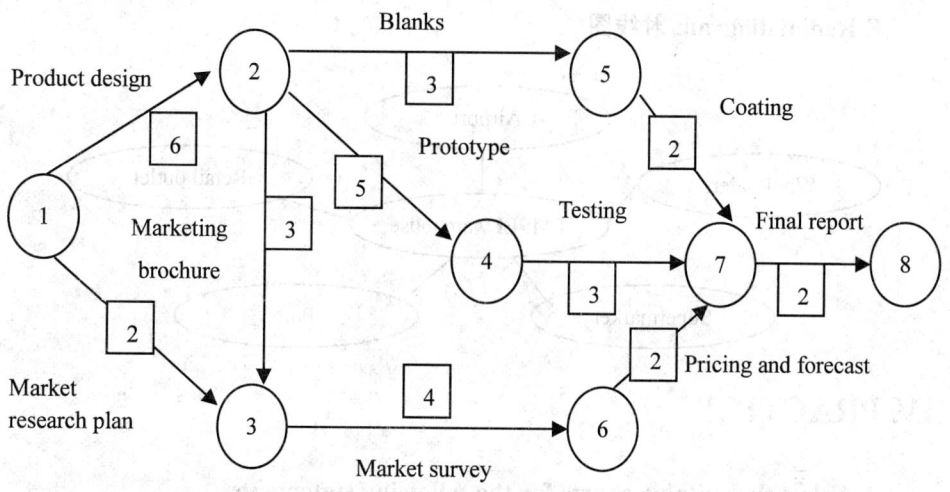

E. Cycle diagram 循环图

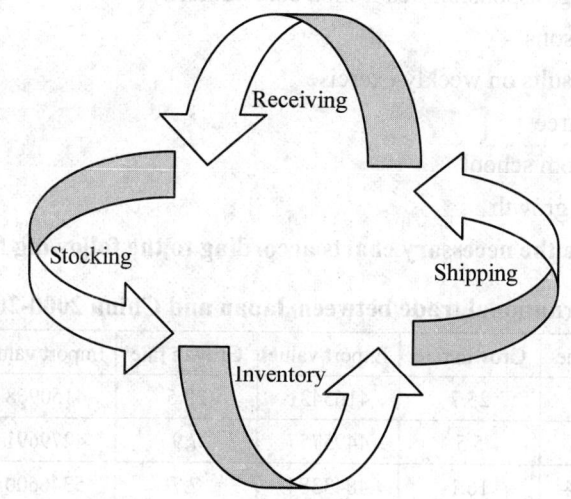

F. Radial diagram 射线图

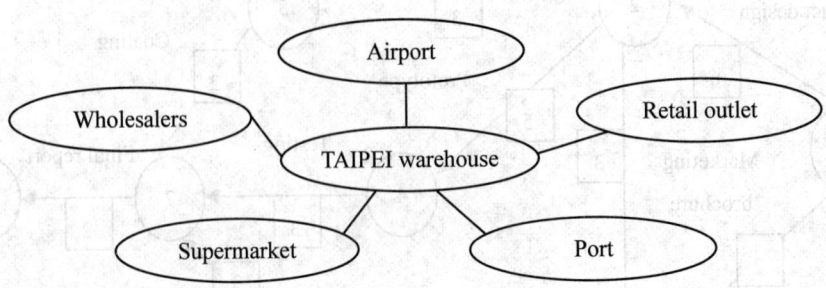

IV. PRACTICE

A. Select the suitable charts for the following statements.

1. Production efficiency
2. Subway routes
3. Delegating responsibilities from a core authority
4. The 4 seasons
5. Survey results on weekly exercise
6. A family tree
7. Grades from school
8. Financial growth

B. Compose the necessary charts according to the following figures.

International trade between Japan and China 2000-2008

Year	Trade value	Growth rate	Export value	Growth rate	Import value	Growth rate
2000	8316399	25.7	4165431	28.5	4150968	22.9
2001	8775448	5.5	4495757	7.9	4279691	3.1
2002	10189984	16.1	4843384	7.7	5346600	24.9
2003	13355683	31.0	5940870	22.7	7414813	38.7
2004	16783577	25.7	7350904	23.7	9432673	27.2
2005	18439396	9.9	8398628	14.2	10040768	6.4
2006	20735592	12.5	9163920	9.1	11571672	15.2
2007	23602193	13.8	10207129	11.4	13395064	15.8
2008	26678510	13.0	11613414	13.8	15065095	12.5

C. Look at the following PERT chart for the development of a brand new toothpaste. Then complete the extract from a report. You should use sequence markers, subordinating conjunctions of time and process verbs.

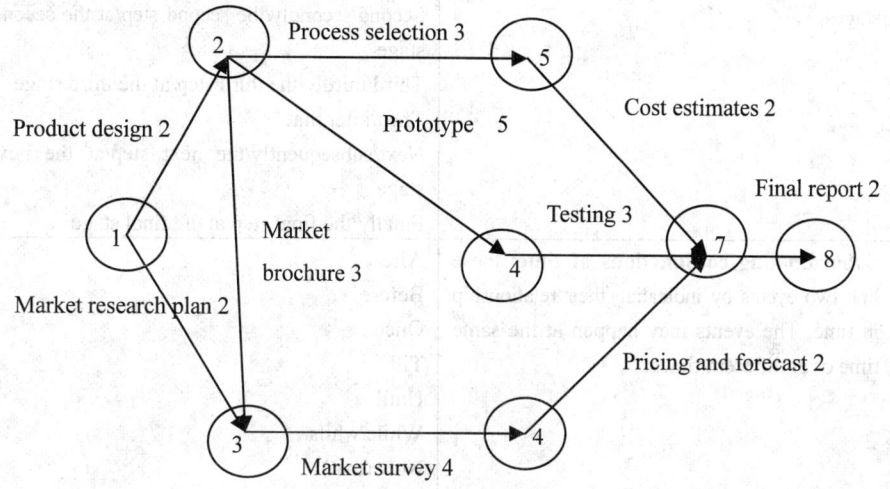

Zing toothpaste project

_____ _____ _____ _____ R&D will start working on the product design at the beginning of March and _____ it in 2 weeks. _____ R&D are designing the product, the Marketing Department will be working on the market research plan. The plan, _____ completed, will provide a report detailing the various steps that will be followed.

_____ _____ drawing up the plan, the _____ _____ will be the market survey itself and _____ pricing and forecasts.

_____ the market research plan has been drawn up, the advertising department can _____ working on the advertising material. The production team can't start process selection _____ the product design stage _____ _____ _____. However, _____ this stage is under way, our chemists will finalize the prototype and then send it to the labs for testing. _____ _____ _____ _____ _____ testing is going on, two teams will be working on figures: the production team on production cost estimates and the sales team on price estimates and sales forecast. _____ _____ _____ all the figures have been collected, they will be put into a report for submission to senior management. _____, a decision about the product will be made in the early autumn.

Sequence markers: these signal the time or sequence relationship between two or more stages	First/first of all/ initially/to start with/the first step/at the first stage Second/secondly/the second step/at the second stage Third/thirdly/the third step/at the third stage Then/after that Next/subsequently/the next step/at the next stage Finally/the final step/at the final stage
Subordinating conjunctions of time: these link two events by indicating their relationship in time. The events may happen at the same time or at different times.	After Before Once Till Until While/whilst Now (that) As soon as At the same time as
Process verbs to show the beginning, middle or end of a stage: these verbs are all followed by a verb stem +ing.	Start Begin Continue Go/Carry/Keep On Finish Stop Cease Leave Off Quit Complete
Duration verbs which indicate a change of state during the process: as a process normally has a duration, these verbs can be used in the continuous form.	Develop Extend Shorten Lengthen Improve Speed up Slow down Reduce Warm up Widen

V. WORDS AND EXPRESSIONS

Manufacture   n. v.制造，生产
　　The date of manufacture of the jewellery has not been authenticated.
Fluctuation   n. 波动，起伏
　　Wild fluctuations in interest rates are the typical sign of finance crises.
Recovery   n. 复原，重获
　　The government is forecasting an economic recovery.
Peak   山峰，最高点
　　She's at the peak of her career.
Heater   加热器
Pronounce   v. 宣称，宣布
　　He is best qualified to pronounce upon such a matter.
Cooker   n. 灶具，炉灶
　　Mum has just won a microwave cooker.

Unit 15　DISCRIPTION OF TRENDS
（图表）趋势描述

I. INTRODUCTION

（图表）趋势描述其实不是独立的一项内容，这一点学习者看过后面的课文可以有所体会。（图表）趋势描述一方面和图表应用密不可分，一方面又大量地体现在宣讲、书信、报告或谈判中。（图表）趋势描述的基础是词汇的掌握，包括动词、动词词组、介词、副词几个方面。在词汇的基础之上，应做到用正确的句子如实反映（图表）趋势的变动，并且要能突出重点，掌握大趋势。更高一级的要求是，读者能够结合自身的专业知识，例如金融、财务、营销、经济分析等，来对于（图表）趋势进行解释和预测。

II. EXAMPLE

Text 1

Here is a presentation given by the director of the milk marketing board about trends in the milk drinks market.

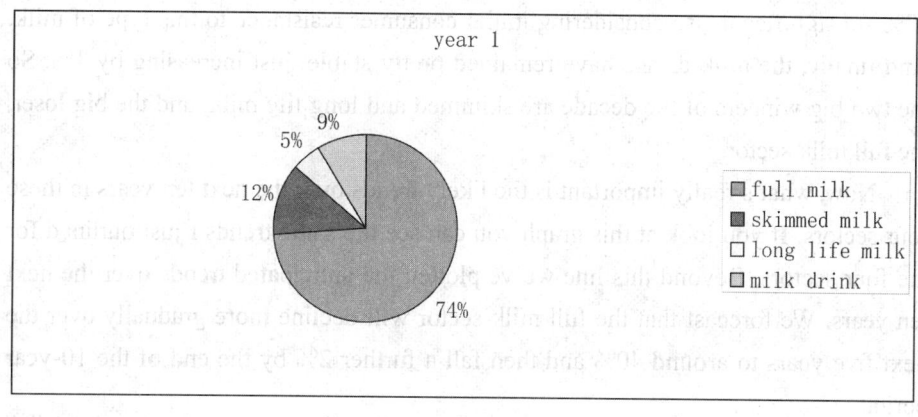

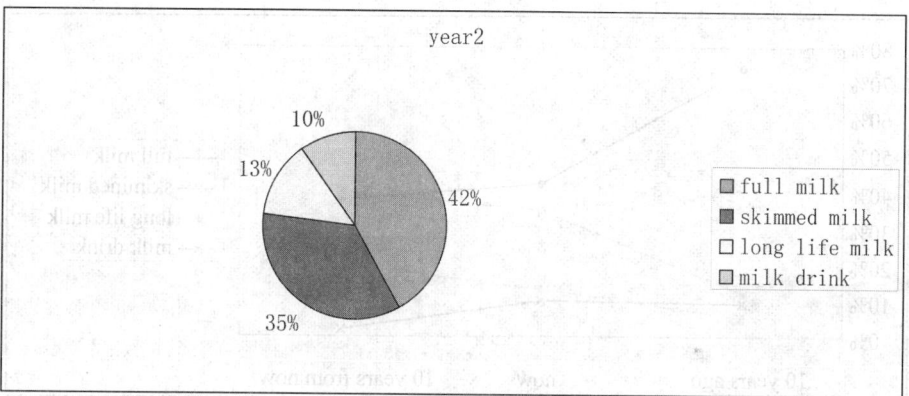

Presenter: We all know that there have been some major changes in our market over the last ten years, and we can expect further changes over the next ten years. I'd like to present the trends over the last ten years and also anticipate the trends we predict over the next ten years.

Let's start by looking at trends over the last ten years. On this first transparency you'll see two pie charts—the first represents the milk product market ten years ago, the second, how it looks now. There are two outstanding features: firstly, the total market has grown substantially from 280 million litres to 440 million litres; secondly, the actual sector share of the four main milk products has changed radically. The full milk sector has fallen dramatically from 74% to just 42%—here on the pie chart; the skimmed milk sector has rocketed from only 12% to 35%, reflecting the weight of publicity directed towards low fat diets. The other two sectors are long life milk and milk drinks. It's interesting to see that the long life sector has risen from 5% to

13%—a significant rise considering initial consumer resistance to this type of milk. And finally, the milk drinks have remained pretty stable, just increasing by 1%. So the two big winners of the decade are skimmed and long life milk, and the big loser, the full milk sector.

Now, what's really important is the likely trends over the next ten years in these four sectors. If you look at this graph you can see the same trends I just outlined for the four sectors. Beyond this line we've plotted the anticipated trends over the next ten years. We forecast that the full milk sector will decline more gradually over the next five years to around 40% and then fall a further 2% by the end of the 10-year period.

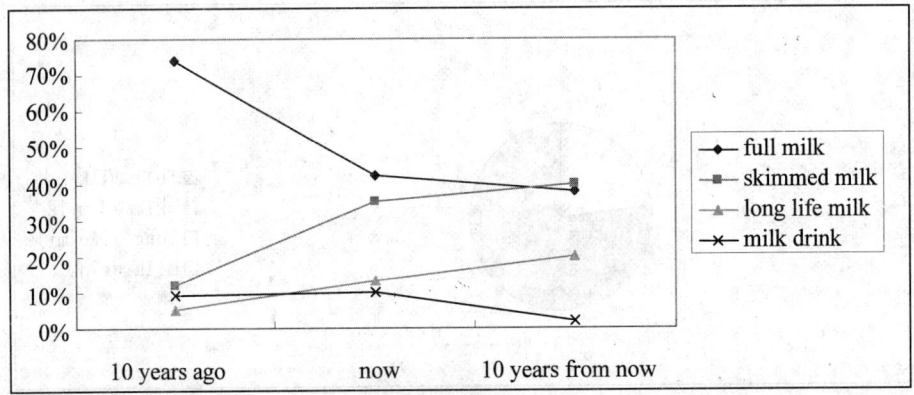

The skimmed milk sector should continue to rise steadily to 40% over the next five years and then level off around this figure for the next five years. We expect long life milk to continue rising moderately so that at the end of this period this sector will represent a significant 20%. Finally we project a fairly marked decline in the milk drink sector as consumer awareness of the sugar content of these drinks increases. We forecast an eventual fall to just 2% by the end of the period.

Text 2

It's now 6 o'clock and the dealers have all gathered in the meeting room to wait for Augustus Faraday.

The reason you're here is that yesterday was quite a day on the stock markets. So, it is important that we stay ahead of them. But, let me first bring you up to date over the last 24 hours or so. Before I go into the specific performance of some key

UNIT 15   DISCRIPTION OF TRENDS   • 155 •

stocks, I'd just like us to look at how the three markets have shaped up during their last trading session.

Ok, let's take the Nikkei first. Now, you'll have seen some of these figures during Monday afternoon's trading here. It was looking pretty good at the start of trading at 23920. During the first second hour it rose again, reaching another peak, before falling back gradually in midmorning trading. Now during that period it was mirroring the upward surge of our market. After that the Nikkei remained fairly level for a couple of hours until after our markets had wound down for the evening. Then, by early afternoon their time, it was beginning to wobble and by late afternoon it was back down to its morning starting point. In the late afternoon, the release of some healthy trading results pushed it back up temporarily, but there was not enough good news to sustain the rise and the downward slide continued. So, apart from a brief rally in the middle of the evening, the day was pretty dismal and the Nikkei ended at 22980, a fall of 940 points on the day.

Now the FT-SE opened up in buoyant shape on Monday morning. By mid-morning it had reached 3267, the highest point since Black Thursday. However, then came a couple of interim results from the construction industry. And the index fell like a stone by 40 points, back to where it started the day. Then came a late-morning rally, and as we opened, London had overtaken its morning opening position. Apart from a little dip, it continued to rise in the early afternoon to 3412, reflecting a little peak we had here around 11 o'clock. Then the rot set in and rumours of a couple bankruptcies in the depressed electronic sector sent prices down for the rest of the trading day. By the time the market closed, London had all but lost its early gains.

Ok, just to compare that with our own performance. The market started yesterday in a fairly jittery shape. The increase in the value of the dollar at the end of last week was continuing to drive the market down. The good news was that the drop didn't go on for long. By mid-morning we had the first signs of some market confidence, and, although it initially fell back again, by the early afternoon the signals were all very positive. When buying picked up, the market responded and we saw a good rise for a couple of hours. I, for one, felt that it couldn't be sustained.

However, despite a small but dramatic drop, the market continued its upward surge throughout the evening, ending the day on 3742.85. So, that was the performance of the three key markets. Now, I'd like to take a closer look at some of the key stocks that we'll be trading today. As I said, our objective is to vigorously defend our position; consolidate the gains we made yesterday.

Text 3

FDI in China falls for sixth month

Foreign direct investment (FDI) into China fell for a sixth straight month in April amid global economic woes.

FDI edged down 0.74 percent year-on-year to $8.4 billion in April, following a 6.1 percent drop in March, 0.9 percent decline in February and 0.3 percent fall in January.

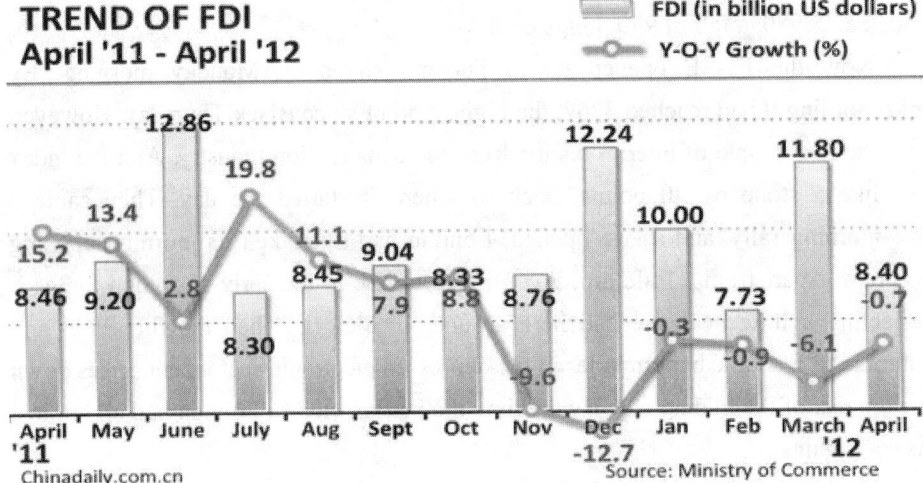

The country received $37.88 billion of FDI in the first four months, down 2.38 percent from a year earlier.

Investment from the debt-ridden European Union plunged 27.9 percent in the January-April period from a year ago. However, that from the United States and Japan climbed 1.9 percent and 16 percent, respectively.

The nation approved the establishment of 7016 foreign-invested companies in the first four months, down 13.94 percent from a year ago.

However, as investment into China drops, the country's outbound investment has surged. The country's non-financial overseas direct investment totaled $23.16 billion in the first four months, up 72.8 percent from a year earlier.

III. NOTES

A. Describing trends impressionistically

A simple statement, e.g. the sector share increased, can be modified to give a stronger impression:

The sector share increased dramatically.

Modifying words can be classified in the following ways:

Size	Speed	Impact
Substantially	Rapidly	Remarkably
Considerably	Fast	Dramatically
Moderately	Gradually	Significantly
Slightly	Steadily	Noticeably
Modestly	Slowly	Markedly

Notice it is also possible to use strong verbs:
   To rocket
   To climb
   To sink
   To plummet

It is possible to use modifiers which generalize:
   Pretty (stable)
   Fairly (constant)
   Quite (stagnant)

B. Describing trends specifically

Sometimes the audience wants to know the precise extent of change. In this case the prepositions are important:

From ... to expresses the start and end figures.	... has fallen from 74% to just 42%
By expresses the difference between the start and end figures when you make use of phrasal verbs.	... has fallen by 32%

Of expresses the difference between the start and end figures when you make use of phrasal nouns.	From 1995 to 1996, there was an increase in expenditure *of* 10000 dollars.
During or *between* are used for the timescale when you make use of *from* ... *to* ... to express figures.	*During/between* March and April there was a cut in number of accounts from 45 to 37. March and April the number of accounts was cut from 45 to 37.
To expresses the result point of a changing procedure.	The market has increased *to* the level of ...
At expresses the level of the situation.	The market opened *at* 4539.59.

C. Words about describing the trends

1. Upward

Verbs/phrases	Nouns
Increase	
Raise	Increase
Put/push/step/drive up	Rise
Extend	Growth
Expand	Extensive
Shoot up	Expansion
Increase	Boom(dramatic rise)
Rise	Improvement
Go/be/pick up	Pickup
Grow	Takeoff
Boom	Climb
Improve	
Get higher	
Edge up	
Go up	
Take off	
Climb	

2. Downward

Verbs /phrases	Nouns
Decrease	Decrease
Drop	Fall
Put/push/drive down	Drop
Cut	Slide
Reduce	Decline
Fall	Cut
Go/be down	Reduction
Slide	Dip
Decline	Collapse (dramatic fall)
Dip	Slump (dramatic fall)
Collapse	Downturn
Slump	Dive
Lower	Plunge
Lessen	
Shrink	
Plunge	

3. Static

Verbs/ phrases	Nouns
Keep/hold … stable/constant	
Maintain … (at the same level)	Stability
Sustain a trend	
Remain stable/level	
Stay constant	
Level out	
Even out	
Calm down	
Chill out	
Stabilize	

4. Fluctuation

Peak	Max out Top out Hit the roof Reach the high point
Plunge	Fall Decline Slide Decrease Drop
Low point	All-time low Bottom out Rock bottom Nadir
Recovery	Rebound Turnaround Upturn Revitalization Recuperate Resurgence Return to normal Bounce back

IV. PRACTICE

A. Fill in the blanks with the correct words (An indication of which type of modifier is given in brackets).

1. The full milk sector has declined _____ (size) over the last ten years.
2. In the same period, skimmed milk sales have risen _____ (speed).
3. The milk drink sector share has remained _____ stable.
4. The long life sector share has risen _____ 8%.
5. Over the next ten years, we expect the full milk sector to continue to decline _____ (speed).
6. The skimmed milk sector will rise _____ (impact) _____ 35% _____ 40% over the next five years.
7. The long life sector will reach a _____ (impact) sector share of 20% by

the end of the period.

8. Milk drink sales are likely to decline _____ (size).

9. During the last ten years skimmed milk sales _____ while full fat milk sales _____.

10. Over the next ten years, the changes will be more _____ (size), except for the virtual disappearance of milk drinks from the market.

B. Complete the following passage about the performance of the Dow Jones on the following day.

It has been a disappointing day for the Dow Jones. The market opened at 3742.85, having _____ _____ that level from 3682 the previous day. In the morning, the market, although slow, registered a _____ increase, before _____ _____ before lunch. Then there was a further _____ _____, caused by the announcement of a _____ _____ in unemployment figures, which were better than expected. This helped to _____ _____ the index _____ a further 30 points.

During the middle of the afternoon, the index _____ _____, consolidating the earlier gains. In the early evening, as the Nikkei opened, we saw a _____, as dealers lost confidence. The market closed the day at 3744.52, a rise _____ less than 2 points on the day. The market is very cautious at the moment, but we hope to _____ it _____ _____ 3750 tomorrow.

C. Write a brief report on the topic of *Retail Sales of Consumer Goods* according to the following chart.

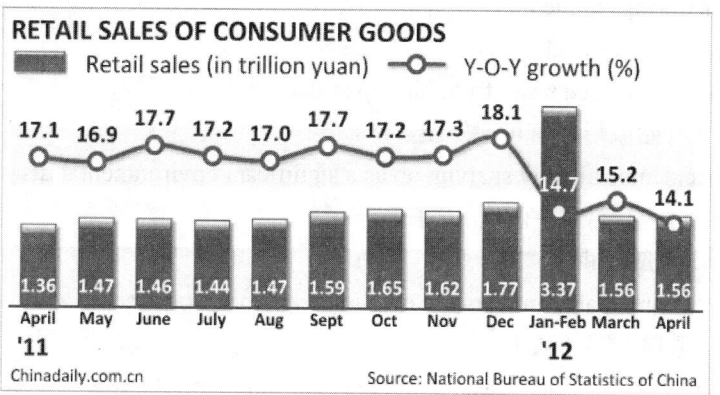

V. WORDS AND EXPRESSIONS

Transparency　n.（用于投影的）透明正片，幻灯片
　　A transparency is a small piece of photographic film with a frame around it which can be projected onto a screen so that you can see the picture.
Litre　n.（容量单位）升
　　Litre is a unit of capacity in the metric system.
Full milk　全脂奶，全乳
Skimmed milk　脱脂奶
Rocket　v. 急速上升，飞快地移动
　　Fresh food is so scarce that prices have rocketed.
Weight　n. 权重，重要性
　　The scientists involved put different weight on the conclusions of different models.
Long life milk　保存期较长的牛奶
Outline　v. 梗概，概述
　　The outline of the mountain in the distance is dim.
Plot　v. 计划，制定
　　Yesterday's meeting was intended to plot a survival strategy for the party.
Level off　（数字或数量）趋向平缓，趋于稳定
　　Inflation is finally levelling out at around 11% a month.
Moderately　adv. 适度地，适量地
　　He only drinks moderately.
Up to date　至今，到目前为止
　　I have not received news from him up to date.
Shape up　开始成形，有可能发生
　　The accident is already shaping up as a significant environmental disaster.
Midmorning　早晨，上午十点左右
Mirror　v. 反应，再现
　　The book inevitably mirrors my own interests and experiences
Surge　n. 激增，突飞猛进
　　Specialists see various reasons for the recent surge in inflation.

Wind down 逐渐减小（工作规模），放松

Foreign aid workers have already begun winding down their operation.

Wobble v. 晃动，颤动

Don't wobble the desk when I'm writing.

Rally v. 振作，复苏

Markets began to rally worldwide.

Dismal adj. 惨淡的，忧郁的

He felt dismal after reading a piece of bad news in the newspaper.

Buoyant adj.（经济）繁荣的

We have a buoyant economy and unemployment is considerably lower than the regional average.

Interim adj. 在间歇期，其中的

But, in the interim, we obviously have a duty to maintain law and order.

Fall like a stone 直线下降

Overtake v. 追上，压倒

I had to walk very fast to overtake you.

Dip n. 蘸，浸

Quickly dip the base in and out of cold water.

Rot n. 胡说八道

What a load of pompous, pseudo-intellectual rot.

Jittery adj. 紧张不安的

Being a gun, the old man's action became jittery.

Vigorously adv. 猛力地，精神旺盛地

The orator gestured vigorously while speaking.

Consolidate v. 巩固，加强

We will consolidate and develop the broadest possible patriotic united front.

Amid prep. 在……中间

His resignation passed almost unnoticed amid the furor of the election.

Woe n. 灾难，麻烦

He did not tell his relatives and friends about his woes.

Edge down 慢慢向下移动

Inflation may edge down only slowly.

Debt-ridden n. v. 负债累累

Plunge　v. 突降，俯冲
　　Don't plunge head first into another person's room.
Outbound　adj. 开往外地的，开往外国的
　　The outbound tourists carrying cultural relics must pass through that checkpoint.

Unit 16　BUSINESS REPORT
商务报告

I. INTRODUCTION

　　为什么说商务报告很重要呢？原因是，虽然可能前期已经经历了长期且复杂的工作过程，但是最终的这份书面报告却是你对于项目所付出努力的唯一证明。辛苦工作的成功与否有赖于这份报告的呈现。精心准备的书面报告可以展示数据的重要意义并且帮助报告阅读者作出决策或解决问题。

　　商务报告可以根据内容分为市场研究报告（marketing report）、进展报告（progress report）、调查报告（investigation report）、建议书（proposal）、可行性报告（feasibility report）、日常报告（routine report）、意见调查报告（survey reports）等。对于不同大类的报告，撰写的时候应注意时态的选择。

　　商务报告使用的语言多为正式语言。此外，报告的内容和篇幅也决定了其写作预期比一般商务信函要正式得多。在商务报告中，可以适当多使用一些能提高语言正式度的英语语法结构，比如使用被动语态、复杂词汇、长句子、名词短语、分词短语、动词不定式、介词短语等。

　　报告的主体内容应包括介绍、提出问题以及总结、给出结论和建议。结论可以在开头给出，也可以在结尾给出。英文报告使用开头给出结论的比较多，而中文报告一般将结论放在后面。如果是较长的报告，要分章节。较短的报告可以用副标题的方式区分不同的部分。

　　商务报告的结构必须要足够清晰，便于读者阅读。因此在商务报告中应增加一些信息或符号用来降低阅读难度，加快阅读者的阅读速度。具体的方法有在正文中提供小标题、段容量缩小、段内内容紧凑、使用星号或下划线强调重点内容等。

II. EXAMPLES

A. INVESTIGATION REPORT

Sales Performance of the Shanghai Branch

Following your instruction, we examined the cause of the decline in sales of Shanghai Branch. We visited the offices and most of their major customers there. This is our findings.

Findings

1. Some of the major customers in Shanghai have closed down, and some have moved to other areas.

2. Other customers are planning to move to new Suzhou or Wuxi as business there is booming and then they can enjoy favorable policy from the local government there.

3. The Shanghai office has not kept an up-to-date mailing list for sending circulars to existing customers who have moved, or potential customers moving in.

4. The customers I visited were interested in more advanced air-conditioning system instead of the traditional model we supply them with at present.

Conclusions

1. A more favorable after-sales mix is needed to keep our customers there.

2. An up-to-date circular list should be made.

3. The supply needs adjustment as to replace the present model with new ones.

Recommendations

1. A traveling sales representative is positioned in Shanghai as the personnel will keep contact with customers who have moved out of Shanghai but may still purchase our goods.

2. Shanghai Branch needs technical support in dealing with information or data sorting.

3. Replacement should be made in supply with latest models.

B. PROPOSAL

A Proposal for Determining the Feasibility
of
Marketing Dead Western White Pine

Introduction

Over the past four decades huge losses of western white pine have occurred in the Northern Rockies, primarily attributable to white pine blister rust and attack of the mountain pine beetle. Estimated annual mortality is 318 million board feet. Because of the low natural resistance of white pine to blister rust, the high mortality rate is expected to continue indefinitely.

Statement of Problem

White pine mortality results in a reduction in value of white pine stumpage, since the commercial lumber market will not accept it. There are two major implications of this problem. First, in the face of rising demand for wood, vast amounts of timber are not being used; second, dead trees are left to accumulate in the woods, where they are rapidly becoming a major fire hazard.

Proposed Solution

One possible solution to the problem of white pine mortality and waste is to search for markets other than the conventional lumber market. The last few years have been a bust of popularity and a growing demand for weathered barn board and wormy pine for interior paneling. Some firms around the country are marketing defective wood as specialty products. There is a good possibility that distressed white pine might find a pace in such a market.

Methods

My primary data sources will include consultations with Dr. James Hill, Professor of Wood Utilization, and Dr. Steven Bergman, Forest Economist—both members of the College of Forestry, Wildlife and Range. I will also inspect decks of dead white pine at several locations and visit a processing mill to evaluate it as a possible base of operations. I will round out my primary research with a letter and telephone survey of processors and wholesales of distressed material. Secondary sources will include selected publications on the uses of dead timber, and a review of and ongoing study by Dr. Hill concerning the uses of dead white pine.

My Qualification

I have been following Dr. Hill's study on dead white pine for two years. In June of this year, I will receive my B.S. in forest management. I am familiar with wood milling processes and have firsthand experience at logging. My association with Dr. Hill and Dr. Bergman creates the opportunity for an indepth feasibility study.

Conclusion

Clearly, something should be done to reduce the vast accumulations of dead white pine in our forests. The land on which they stand is among the most productive forestland in northern Idaho. By addressing the six areas of inquiry mentioned earlier, I can determine the feasibility of directing capital and labor to the production of distressed white pine products. With your approval I will begin my research at once.

C. ROUTINE REPORT

Report on the first year of activity of our polish subsidiary

It has been a year now since our new subsidiary called "Alpha" opened its doors in Varsaw. Before pointing out its successes, the problems faced and the plans for the coming year, let me remind you the reasons for its opening.

Reasons for opening

In fact, there was only one main reason for choosing to settle down in Poland: reducing labor cost rates. Indeed, our activity as cosmetics producers requires a lot of staff, and labor costs are much cheaper in Poland than in Switzerland!

Successes

Knowing this aim, we decided to go on. We managed to build new factory on time, and the line works! That was our greater success: being able to respect the opening date and to produce efficiently.

Problems experienced

But, we met difficulties in two areas:

- Transportation: the roads' network in Poland is not so good and time spent on transportation is higher than predicted.
- Staff: we still have to learn a lot about staff's culture and expectations.

Plans for the coming year

Our plan for the coming year is mainly to improve the above mentioned points (as production is running quite well). Therefore, we will study the opportunity of buying a few lorries (not to depend on others for delivery). We will also organize seminars for both local staff and overseas managers, to understand each other better.

Finally, I would like to take the opportunity of this report to invite the top management for a visit of Alpha, whenever they want.

General Manager
In charge of the polish subsidiary

III. NOTES

A. Introduction

The introduction sets the stage for understanding the findings that follow. In this section, present information such as the following:
- Background of the problem
- Need for the study
- Authorization for the report
- Hypotheses or problem statement and subproblems
- Purpose and scope (including definition of terms, if needed)
- Procedures used to gather and analyze the data

The actual topics and amount of detail presented in the introductory section depends on the complexity of the report and the needs of the reader. For example, if the procedures are extensive, you may want to place them in a separate section, with their own first-level heading.
- Practical sentences

The purpose of this report is to ... investigate/evaluate/study ...
The objective of this report is to ... recommend/analyze/give ...
The aim of this report is to ... feedback/estimate/assess ...

B. Findings

The findings of the study represent the major contribution of the report and make up the largest section of the report. Discuss and interpret any relevant primary and secondary data you have gathered. Organize this section using one of the plans, such as by time/location/importance/criteria. Use objective language to present the information clearly, concisely, and accurately.

- Inquiries

The data ananlyzed is completely, accurately and appropriately.

The data is interpreted (its importance and implications discussed) rather than just presented.

All calculations are correct.

Visual aids are correct, necessary, clear, appropriately sized and positioned and correctly labeled. They should appear immediately below the first paragraph of text in which the reference to it occurs. Avoid splitting a table or figure between two pages.

- Practical sentences

Several staff members expressed the view that …

The findings of the investigation indicate that …

It was proposed/found/felt/discovered that …

As it can be seen from the table/chart/figure …

The table/chart/graph/diagram/figure/statistics shows/describes/illustrates that …

Sales witnessed a great rise/increase/drop/fall between … and …

C. Summary, conclusions, and recommendations

Summary is brief reviewing the problem and the procedures used to solve the problem, and providing an overview of the major findings. Repeating the main points or arguments immediately before presenting the conlusions and recommendations reinforces the reasonableness of those conclusions and recommendations. To avoid monotony when summarizing, use wording that differs from the original presentation.

If your report includes both conclusions and recommendations, ensure that the conclusions stem directly from your findings and that the recommendations stem directly from the conclusions. The conclusions can answer the questions or issues raised in the introduction. Provide ample evidence to support all your conclusions and recommendations.

D. Writing style and format

Regardless of the structure of your report, the writing style used is typically more objective and less conversational than the style of an informal note. Avoid colloquial expressions, attempts at humor, subjectivity, bias, and exaggeration.

The overall report takes into account the needs and desires of the reader.

The material is organized appropriately.

Emphasis and subordination are used effectively.

Proper verb tense has been used throughout.

An appropriate level of formality has been used.

The length of the report is appropriate.

The report is free from spelling, grammar and punctuation errors.

E. Reference report outline

STAFF EMPLOYEES' EVALUATION OF THE BENEFIT PROGRAM
AT MAYO MEMORIAL HOSPITAL

Loretta J. Santorini

I. INTRODUCTION
   a. Purpose and scope
   b. Procedures

II. FINDINGS
   a. Knowledge of benefits
      1. Familiarity and benefits
      2. Present methods of communication
         Formal channels
         Informal channels
      3. Preferred methods of communication
   b. Opinions of present benefits
      1. Importance of benefits
      2. Satisfaction with benefits
   c. Desirability of additional benefits

III. SUMMARY, CONCLUSIONS, AND RECOMMENDATIONS
   a. Summary of the problems and procedures
   b. Summary of the findings
   c. Conclusions and recommendations

IV. PRACTICE

A. Pierre is a French area salesman. Please compose a business report for him according to the telephone conversation between the European sales manager Alison and him.

Alison: Hello, Pierre. This is Alison. How are things?

Pierre: It's not easy. The market's very slow.

Alison: Oh, really? We're getting some very good results in the rest of Europe.

Pierre: I know. But the French situation is not the same.

Alison: Sure. Right. Um … let's go through your quarterly results by product. How has the new Zellon range been sold?

Pierre: Well, last quarter we cleared 450000 worth—that's French francs of course.

Alison: Oh, didn't we fix a target of 600000?

Pierre: That's right. I had hoped to pick up a big order from one of the supermarket chains.

Alison: Yes, I remember you telling me about it. What happened?

Pierre: They've cut their stock levels on perfumes and we only got an order for 150000.

Alison: Oh, that's disappointing. What about the other lines?

Pierre: Artemis is sold very well—we hit 880000—well above the target.

Alison: Oh, good. It hasn't done so well elsewhere—obviously it appeals to the French more!

Pierre: Could be. I'm afraid we weren't so successful with our two main brands—Hedon aftershave and Minos face-cream. The market in these sectors has become very competitive.

Alison: Hmmm. So what were the quarterly figures?

Pierre: For the aftershave, just 800000—and for Minos we reached 550000.

Alison: Oh, I've got the forecasts here. We reckoned we'd reach 1.5 million on the aftershave and 750000 for Minos. So they are both far below the target.

Pierre: I know. I was obviously over-optimistic. I thought we were going to pull out of the recession quicker than we are. Consumer spending on luxury items is well down on last year.

Alison: I can appreciate that, but the economic situation is bad everywhere. We must have missed some other factors in your market.

Pierre: Well, I don't think so. The recession has definitely bottomed out but the predicted consumer boom just hasn't materialized.

PRODUCT	FORECAST	ACTUAL (LAST QUARTER)
ZELLON RANGE	600000	450000
ARTEMIS	650000	880000
HEDON AFTERSHAVE	1500000	800000
MINOS FACE-CREAM	750000	550000

B. You are the assistant sales manager of Hopewell Incorporated. Recently you were asked by the sales manager to go to Richmond to investigate the heavy turnover of sales representatives there and to submit a report after your investigation. Write the report, describing how you investigated the matter and what your findings are. Suggest ways of improving the situation.

V. WORDS AND EXPRESSIONS

Boom   n. 繁荣，激增

Record profits in the retail market indicate a boom in the economy.

Up-to-date   adj. 现代的，新式的

He bought an up-to-date textbook.

Circular   n. 广告传单

The proposal has been widely publicised in BBC-TV press information circulars sent to 1,800 newspapers.

Air-condition   n. 空调

Keep contact with   保持联系

Attributable   adj. 可归因于……的

Their illnesses are attributable to a poor diet.

Blister   n. 水疱

Mortality   n. 死亡数，死亡率

Poor hygiene led to high mortality among children.

Indefinitely adv. 无限期地，遥遥无期地
　　The government can't expect the taxpayer to bail this company out indefinitely.
Stumpage n. 立木，直木材，未砍伐的树
Lumber n. 木材
　　The truck was sent to carry lumber.
Timber n. 木材，林场
　　These trees need more time to grow into useful timber.
Hazard n. 危险，冒险的事
　　He climbed into the car at the hazard of his life.
Bust n. 突然事件，狂欢
　　The handful of them often went on a bust together.
Weathered adj. 风化的
　　The softer rock has been weathered away into soil.
Barn n. 谷仓，车库，大而空荡的房屋
　　Don't worry—he'll be all safe and snug in the barn.
Wormy adj. 虫蛀的
　　When I bit into the apple, finding it wormy, I flung it away.
Paneling n. 嵌板，镶板
　　The guide drew our attention to the magnificent carved paneling.
Defective adj. 有瑕疵的，有错误的
　　The firm had received bad publicity over a defective product.
Distress n. 悲痛，不幸
　　The newspaper article caused the actor considerable distress.
Milling n. 磨
　　Put the rice in steep for some time before milling.
Round out 丰满起来
　　Her figure is beginning to round out.
Publication n. 出版物
　　Publication dates are given in brackets after each title.
Logging n. 伐木搬运业
　　They cleared large tracts of forest for farming, logging and ranching.
Polish adj. 波兰的
Poland n. 波兰

Poles   n. 波兰人

Subsidiary   n. 附属机构，子公司

　　The company is a wholly-owned subsidiary of a large multinational.

Settle down   定居，平息

　　Tom, when are you going to stop tearing around and settle down?

Cosmetics   n. 美容品，化妆品

　　Cosmetics do not always cover up the deficiencies of nature.

Lorry   n. 运货卡车

Seminar   n. 研讨班

　　The seminar was to discuss diversification of agriculture.

Unit 17　INTERCULTURAL BUSINESS COMMUNICAITON
跨文化商务沟通

I. INTRODUCTION

　　文化与沟通的关系紧密相连、密不可分，犹如鱼水关系，缺一不可，因为沟通的载体——语言与文化相互制约从而影响人们的思维和表达，而沟通内容所体现的价值观念也受文化的影响而具有鲜明的文化特征。不同的国家具有不同的文化，也就决定了各国不同的人文环境，包括服饰及饮食习惯，决定了人们不同的欣赏角度和审美观念，决定了人们不同的道德标准和行为规范。我们往往会理所当然地认为，我们的标准是正确的，我们的行为是得体的，我们的语言表达是礼貌的，与之相反的就是不正确的、不得体的、不礼貌的。虽然这是很自然的倾向，但是当我们与其他文化背景的人共事、交流时，跨文化的困惑、误解或冲突就由此产生了。

　　中国人学英语往往学习其词汇的字面意思，而忽视这些词的用法或文化含义，更忽略使用语言时的语境。产生跨文化沟通失误的原因是多方面的，其中最常见的失误是语用失误，即将母语的表达方式或话语迁移至目的语之中，而不考虑这些话语是否遵守交际规则，因而造成交际失误。

　　随着国际交流与合作的不断扩大，跨国企业管理、跨国项目团队组织、进出口交易和国际谈判等方面都会频繁出现跨文化沟通的问题，并且特别突出地体现在商务操作层面。跨文化冲突的出现是不可避免的，但可以通过相互学习与了解并正确运用国际通行的语言规范来尽可能地改善。

II. TEXTS

TEXT 1

TRANSLATION PROBLEM

Even when cultures speak the same language—as the United States and Great Britain—there can be vocabulary differences. When cultures speak diverse languages, translation is critical—but always imperfect. Estimates of number of languages spoken worldwide vary from nearly 5000, including variants and dialects, to approximately 200 main language groups. We have identified five translation problems that can become barriers to intercultural communications:

Vocabulary equivalence

First is the lack of vocabulary equivalence. The arctic peoples have many different words to refer to snow. Were you to translate on a word-for-word basis, you would translate all those different words into the one English word "snow". Much of the meaning of their more specific and more descriptive words – for example, qualities of slushiness or hardness or newness – would be lost. As another example, imagine having to translate all shades of pink, burgundy, orange-red, and so on into the one word "red". As you might imagine, such a limitation would be frustrating to you if you were accustomed to using more descriptive words.

One frequently quoted example of the lack of vocabulary equivalence is from World War II. The allies had issued the Potsdam ultimatum demanding the surrender of the Japanese military to end the war. At a press conference, Prime Minister Suzuki was asked for his opinion. He responded, "The government does not see much value in it. All we have to do is *mokusatsu* it." The Japanese cabinet had carefully chosen that word to convey their intended meaning. Later, Japanese cabinet officials said they intended to convey a bland "no comment" at that time, as there was interest in negotiating a surrender and more time was required for discussions. Unfortunately, the word *mokusatsu* can mean anything from "to ignore" to "to treat with silent contempt". Western translators used the latter meaning and the Potsdam ultimatum was then considered to have been rejected. After-the-fact reasoning argues that that translation led to the continuation of the war and the first use of atomic weapons.

Idiomatic equivalence

The second barrier to successful translation is the problem of idiomatic equivalence. The English language is particularly replete with idioms. Take the simple example of "the old man kicked the bucket". Native speakers know that this idiom means the old man died. If the sentence is translated word for word, the meaning conveyed would be exactly that the old man kicked the bucket – quite different from the intended meaning. You can no doubt think of many other examples. Just think of how the idioms "out to lunch" and "toss your cookies" could cause communication problems!

Not understanding idioms can be fatal. In 1993, an exchange student from Japan looking for a Halloween party went to the wrong address and was shot for apparently not understanding the word "freeze". It's easy to think of many idioms in common use in spoken American English that can be misunderstood: "back off", "cut that out", "get lost", "duck", and "hands in the air". This is one reason why English is a difficult language to learn as a second language. However, learning the ideas of a culture can be an effective way of learning the culture.

Grammatical-syntactical equivalence

Third is the problem of grammatical-syntactical equivalence. This simply means that languages do not necessarily have the same grammar. Often, you need to understand a language's grammar to understand the meaning of words.

For example, words in English can be nouns or verbs or adjectives depending on their position in a sentence. In English you can say "plan a table" and "table a plan" or "book a place" and "place a book" or "lift a thumb" and "thumb a lift".

Experiential equivalence

Fourth is the problem of experiential equivalence. If an object or experience does not exist in your culture, it is difficult to translate words referring to that object or experience into that language when no words may exist for them. Think of objects or experiences that exist in your culture and not in another. "Department store" and "shopping mall" may be as difficult to translate into some languages as "wind surfing" into others.

Conceptual equivalence

Finally, the problem of conceptual equivalence refers to abstract ideas that may not exist in the same fashion in diverse languages. For example, in the United States we have a unique meaning for the word "freedom". That meaning is not universally shared. Speakers of other languages may say they are free and be correct in their culture, but that freedom they refer to is not equivalent to what you experience as freedom.

In a 1994 interview, former president Jimmie Carter identified conceptual equivalence problems with the term "human rights". According to Carter, each country defines the term by what it has. In the United States, human rights refer to the Bill of Rights. Other countries define the term by adequate housing or universal health care.

TEXT 2

THE CHALLENGES OF INTERCULTURAL COMMUNICAITON

Cultural diversity affects how business messages are conceived, planned, sent, received, and interpreted in the workplace. Today's increasingly diverse workforce encompasses a wide range of skills, traditions, backgrounds, experiences, outlooks, and attitudes toward work—all of which can affect employee behavior on the job. Supervisors face the challenge of communicating with these diverse employees, motivating them, and fostering cooperation and harmony among them. Teams face the challenge of working together closely, and companies are challenged to coexist peacefully with business partners and with the community as a whole.

The interaction of culture and communication is so pervasive that separating the two is virtually impossible. The way you communicate—from the language you speak and the nonverbal signals you send to the way you perceive other people—is influenced by the culture in which you were raised. The meaning of words, the significance of gestures, the importance of time and space, the rules of human relationships—these and many other aspects of communication are defined by culture. To a large degree, your culture influences the way you think, which naturally affects the way you communicate as both a sender and a receiver. So you can see how intercultural communication is much more complicated than simply matching language between sender and receiver. It goes beyond mere words to beliefs, values, and emotions.

TEXT 3

ENSURING SUCCESS BY EMBRACING DIVERSITY

The "I" in IBM stands for "international", but it could just as easily stand for "intercultural" as a testament to the computer giant's longstanding commitment to embracing diversity. Ted Childs, IBM's vice president of global workforce diversity, knows from years of experience that communicating successfully across cultures is no simple task, however – particularly in a company that employs more than 325000 people and sells to customers in roughly 175 countries around the world.

Language alone presents a formidable barrier to communication, when you consider that IBM's workforce speaks more than 165 languages, but language is just one of many elements that play a role in communication between cultures. Differences in age, ethnic background, gender, sexual orientation, physical ability, and economic status can all affect the communication process. Childs recognizes that these differences represent both a challenge and an opportunity, and a key part of his job is helping IBM executives and employees work together in a way that transforms their cultural differences into critical business strength. As he puts it, workforce diversity has "moved from being a moral imperative to being a strategic imperative".

IBM's diversity efforts help the company in virtually every aspect of its operations, starting with attracting the most talented people it can find and then helping those employees communicate effectively, regardless of cultural background. Employees are supported through more than 100 networking groups that unite IBM staffers with a variety of backgrounds and personal and professional interests. Diversity efforts extend outside the corporation, too, reaching out to both suppliers and customers. In fact, one of the key advantages that Childs sees in IBM's diverse workforce is the ability to communicate more effectively with an increasingly diverse marketplace.

While workforce diversity has become a hot topic in recent years, respect for the individual has long been a core value in the IBM corporate culture. For instance, the company decreed in 1935 that women would receive equal opportunities and the same pay for the same work—28 years before pay equity was written into U.S. law. IBM was also the first corporation in the United States to establish a policy ensuring equal employment opportunities for people of all races and religions—more than a decade before the Civil Rights Act made such principles the law of the land.

Throughout its long history of employing and working with people from different cultures, IBM has learned some powerful lessons. Perhaps the most significant is the recognition that successfully managing a diverse workforce and competing in a diverse marketplace starts with embracing those differences, not trying to ignore them or pretend they don't affect interpersonal communication. And it's a lesson that every aspiring business professional can take to heart. As Ted Childs puts it, "No matter who you are, you're going to have to work with people who are different from you ... and manage people who are different from you."

III. NOTES

Seven suggestions for people from individualistic cultures to enable them to deal with conflict effectively in a collectivistic culture are as follows:

1. Understand the opponent's face-maintenance assumptions in order to keep a balance between humility and pride, besides, between shame and honor in interactions.

2. Save the opponent's face by carefully using go-between or informal consultation to deal with low-grade conflicts before they fall irrevocably into face-losing situations.

3. Give face to opponents by not pushing them into a corner with no leeway for recovering face.

4. Avoid using too much verbal expression, and learn how to manage conflicts by effectively reading implicit and nonverbal messages.

5. Be empathic by listening attentively and respecting the opponent's needs.

6. Put aside the effective communication skills practiced in the west and learn to use the indirect communication style.

7. Tolerate the opponent's tendency to avoid facing the conflict by being patient, thereby maintaining a harmonious atmosphere and mutual dignity.

IV. PRACTICE

A. Please find out the definition from column B for the terms in column A

A	B
1. communication	a. the communication between African Americans and European Americans
2. international communication	b. the process whereby one person transits a message through a channel to another, with some effect
3. interpersonal communication	c. the communication between culturally similar individuals
4. interracial communication	d. the communication between two people
5. intercultural communication	e. the communication of cultural phenomena in different cultures
6. cross-cultural communication	f. interactions among people from different nations
7. intracultural communication	g. face-to-face interactions among people of diverse cultures
8. intrapersonal communication	h. communication we have with ourselves

B. Please choose the suitable words to fill in the blanks

| empower | foster | productive | well-balanced | random | commitment |
| cohesive | multinational | dimensions | incremental | evolves | individuals |

1. Managers should remember that some people perform better in one type of role; some are inclined toward social concerns and others toward task concerns. A _____ team members and permit the accomplishment of team tasks.

2. Research findings suggest that team development is not _____ but evolves over definitive stages.

3. The greater the amount of contact among team members and the more time spent together, the more _____ the team.

4. When a team succeeds in its task and others in the organization recognize the success, members feel good, and their _____ to the team will be high.

5. Leadership plays an important role in determining whether a team successfully _____ to the performing stage.

6. Team leaders must encourage the specific _____ contribution of each

member, because overlooking one person would sacrifice potential benefits form his or her unique perspective.

7. An effective team enjoys a sense of freedom of expression that allows _____ to speak freely, challenge others on core issues, question flawed logic, and suggest candid proposals without fear of threat.

8. Because groups can break down or even _____ hostility when poorly managed, conflict or unproductive compromise always threatens potential performance.

9. A transnational team is a work group composed of _____ members whose activities span multiple countries.

10. Team leader ship works to establish a democratic decision-making climate that _____ employees as active participants in team decision and activities.

11. Team development, nevertheless, has followed a slow process of _____ change for many Western companies.

12. Teamwork itself takes on different _____ in various societies, and managers must be able to adapt to different cultural expectations.

V. WORDS AND EXPRESSIONS

Vocabulary　n. 词汇
　　The basic vocabulary of a language is those words that must be learnt.
Diverse　adj. 不同的，多种多样的
　　Spain is a composite of diverse traditions and people.
Variant　n. 词的变体，字音的转化
　　There are so many variant spellings of his name.
Dialect　n. 方言，土语
　　Cockney is the colourful dialect spoken in the East End of London.
Intercultural　adj. 不同文化间的
　　Actually, the use of foreign teacher's resources means intercultural permeation.
Arctic　adj. 北极的，寒带的
　　This ship was designed expressly for exploring the Arctic waters.
Descriptive　adj. 描写的
　　He wrote a book descriptive of the frontier provinces.

Slushiness n. 泥泞的情况（slushy adj. 泥泞的）
Burgundy n.（法国的）勃艮第葡萄酒 col. 紫红色
Frustrate v. 挫败，阻挠
　　But this didn't frustrate Einstein. He was content to go as far as he could.
Accustom v. 使习惯
　　It took him a while to accustom himself to the idea.
Ally n. 同盟国，协约国
　　In that war England was not an ally; she was neutral.
Ultimatum n. 最后通牒，最后条件
　　The ultimatum expires at noon tomorrow.
Surrender n. 投降，解约
　　He preferred to die rather than surrender to the enemy.
Press conference 新闻发布会
Cabinet n. 内阁
　　The Prime Minister eventually decided against reshuffling the Cabinet.
Convey v. 传达，输送
　　Don't forget to convey my regards when you see him.
Bland adj. 温和的，平和的
　　He eats bland food because of his stomach trouble.
Continuation n. 继续
　　They are anxious to ensure the continuation of the economic reform programme.
Atomic adj. 原子的，
　　You may conceive a new world in the atomic age.
Idiomatic adj. 符合语言习惯的，含有习语的
　　She speaks fluent and idiomatic English.
Replete adj. 充满的，比比皆是
　　History is replete with examples of populations out of control.
Bucket n. 水桶
Fatal adj. 致命的，攸关的
　　Fatal road accidents have decreased in frequency over recent years.
Syntactical adj. 依照句法的
　　A compiler structured on the syntactical relationships of the character string.

Universally adv. 普遍地，一般地
They believed these principles to be universally true.

Diversity n. 多样化
The exhibition is designed to reflect the diversity of the nation and its regions.

Encompass v. 围绕，包含
The course will encompass physics, chemistry and biology.

Supervisor n. 监督者，管理者
He said I was too flighty to be a good supervisor.

Motivate v. 激发，促动
You have first got to motivate the children and then to teach them.

Foster v. 培养
The club's aim is to foster better relations within the community.

Coexist v. 同时存在，和平共处
In some cases the public estates coexist with private markets and influence their price through competition.

Pervasive adj. 普遍的，弥漫的
Such dominance and dependence relationships are indeed pervasive.

Virtually adv. 实际上，实质上
This new material is virtually unbreakable.

Gesture n. 手势，举止，动作
She opened her arms wide in an expansive gesture of welcome.

Embrace v. 拥抱，欣然接受
The new rules have been embraced by government watchdog organizations.

Testament n. 确实的证明
The new model is a testament to the skill and dedication of the workforce.

Formidable adj. 强大的，可畏的，难以对付的
In debate he was a formidable opponent.

Ethic n. 道德，伦理
They also boldly championed the Christian ethic and Western Culture tradition.

Gender n. 性别；某些语言的性的区分
French differs from English in having gender for all nouns.

Imperative adj. 必要的，命令的
Job creation has become an imperative for the government.

Reach out　伸出

Decree　v. 颁布，规定

　　The UN Security Council has decreed that the election must be held by May.

Principle　n. 原则，准则

　　Respect for life is a cardinal principle of English law.

Take to heart　在意，对……想不开，在乎

　　He won't take such trifles to heart.

Comprehensive Modules
综合模块

GROUP WORK 1：Business Meeting

内容涉及会议主持人，讨论与陈述观点，会议记录。

Every group of students can decide on a meeting subject by themselves and through the following process:

1. Decide on a subject (brainstorm ideas—professional / personal).
2. Decide on the objectives and type of meeting (informational / brainstorming / decision-making).
3. Draw up an agenda (also set time limits)
4. Decide on roles during the meeting (chairperson, speakers, minute-taker).
5. Decide on style of meeting (formal / informal, structured or not).
6. Prepare your contribution to the meeting (content).
7. Prepare the language you need for the meeting (go through the language above).
8. Hold the meeting (audio or video-record it).
9. Use the recording for feedback and correction.

GROUP WORK 2 ：Finding a Job

内容涉及简历，推荐信，面试。

Divide the students into several groups. Some of them need to prepare their resumes and application letters according to the following recruitment information. Some of them can act as the interviewees whose responsibilities are selecting suitable applicants and organizing an efficient interview.

Company Introduction:

The Brose Group, founded in 1908 in Berlin, Germany, is one of the fastest growing international automotive suppliers. Worldwide, more than 14000 employees work at almost 51 international locations in 21 countries. As a partner of the international automotive industry, we are supplying products for more than 40 vehicle brands and leading seat products. In average, every third car in the world is equipped with Brose products.

With the first plant set up in China 10 years ago, Brose has now 7 production and development facilities across over China. Brose Shanghai Automotive Systems Co., Ltd. is the newly setup Asian headquarter of the Brose group, located in Jing An Ting, Shanghai. The purpose is to coordinate all business within Asian countries from this new headquarter in Shanghai.

For further information about the Brose Group, please visit our website: www.brose.com

Positions:

1. Intern—Test Department

Job responsibility:

—Support on motor testing machine

—Support test reports

—Support test fixture design

—Support motor sampling

—Support special motor tests

Job requirement:

1) University student

2) Major in mechanical eng. or electrical eng

3) Fluent English, both spoken and written (German preferred)

4) Strong sense of responsibility

5) Clear thinker & fast learner

6) Three days available one week

2. Intern—IT Job Description:

—Work as an intern to assist IT department

Requirement:

—Bachelor degree student; the third grade

—Fluent English

—Major in IT

—Available at least 4 days a week

—Self-motivated, patient, good team player.

3. Intern—Business Division Seat Adjuster Job Description:

—Responsible contact (internal and external) for all sales related issues.

—Support to the seat business division team regarding the customer relationship.

—Support to the engineering for issues at customer side.

—Responsible regular project meeting and follow up.

—Responsible arrangement all business trip.

—Other administration activities.

Requirement:

—University students, major in German language

—Good at communication.

—Excellent business sense.

—Fluent English, both writing and speaking, fluent German preferred.

—Practical experience with MS Office software, especially Word, Excel, Outlook and Powerpoint.

—Self-motivated, patient, good team player.

Starting date: as soon as possible

Intern period: at least half a year

Please send both English and Chinese CVs to "jobs.shanghai@brose.com"

GROUP WORK 3: Report of a Project

内容涉及图表分析，书面报告，口头宣讲，可视辅助材料。

The following graphs show the economic climate of china. The students in one group should prepare some market analysis according to that and work on a written business proposal about their company's product, either production or sale. Then give a presentation to the board in order to let them adopt your suggestions.

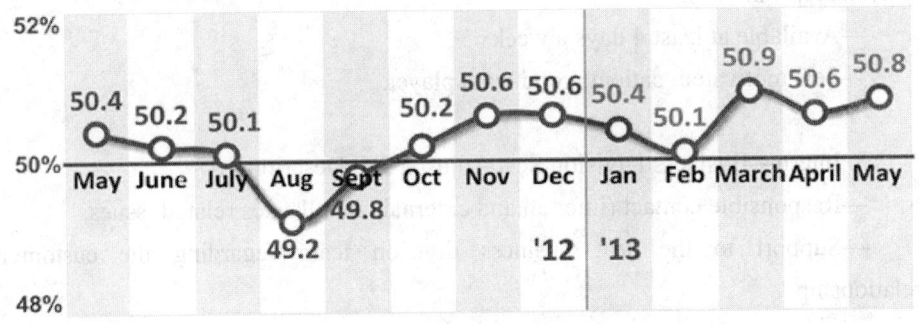

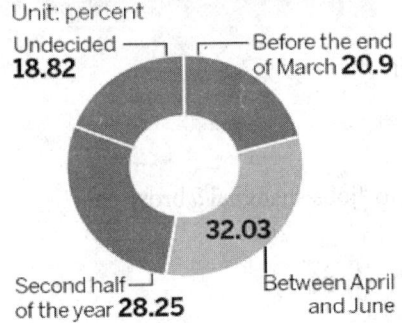

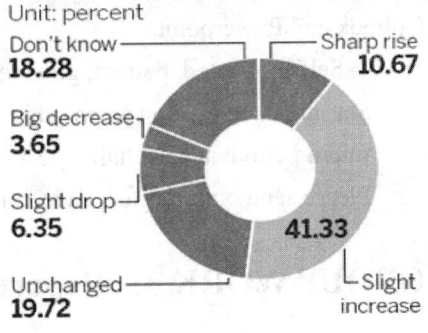

GROUP WORK 4: Negotiation between Two Company Coming from Different Countries

内容涉及跨文化商务沟通与谈判。

Six months have passed. Sophomore Electronics and Northern Components meet again to renew the terms of the contract. Divide into two groups.

Group 1: Northern Components (coming from country A)

You have met all the monthly delivery dates. However, you have found that high overtime payments have meant that your margin on the contract is very small. You want to negotiate a slight increase in the price. Use the following arguments:

1. Delivery dates all met.
2. No problems with quality.
3. Overtime payments higher than expected.

Your best outcome should be a 5 per cent increase in price. The bottom line should be that prices are fixed at the same level for another 6 months.

Group 2: Sophomore Electronics (coming from country B)

Northern Components have met all the delivery dates and you are very happy with the quality standards. However, there is a lot of pressure on your prices and you would like to reduce the price further.

Your arguments are as follows:

1. Market is very competitive: in order to stay in business, you need a further reduction in price.
2. If Sophomore can reduce their price, they will increase market share and therefore will need to order more components next year.
3. If Sophomore cannot reduce price, they risk losing market share and therefore Northern Components' order would be reduced.

Your best outcome should be 5% reduction in price. The bottom line should be the promise of reducing the price only if the orders increase by move than 10%.

课文译文

第一课　电话沟通

电话一

A：这里是 Krondike 电子（公司）。有什么需要帮助的吗？
B：是的，请帮我找爱德华先生。
A：请问你是哪位？
B：我是约翰·伯德。
A：请稍等，伯德先生。我来帮您接通。
C：我是泰勒小姐。
B：我是约翰·伯德，我可以和爱德华先生通话吗？
C：很抱歉他现在不在。我可以帮您留个口信吗？
B：好的，可以麻烦您告诉他尽快给我回电话吗？
C：当然可以，您的电话号码是多少？
B：他有我的电话号码，不过以防万一嘛，我的电话是 071-253 4686。
C：071-253 4686。谢谢，伯德先生。我保证把口信捎给他。
B：谢谢，再见。
C：再见。

电话二

S1：这里是系统支持（公司）。
贝奈特：早上好。可以帮我接通采购部吗？

S1：请问要通话的主要内容是？

贝奈特：软件开发。

S1：那您想要找谁通话？

贝奈特：部门经理。顺便问一下，您能告诉我他的名字吗？

S1：格兰汉姆·乌兰汉姆是本公司的软件开发经理。

贝奈特：可以请您拼写一下吗？

S1：好的，W-A-R-E-H-A-M。

贝奈特：好的，我可以和他通话吗？

S1：请稍等。

S2：这里是软件开发的詹妮特·帕克。

贝奈特：早上好。我可以和格兰汉姆·乌兰汉姆通话吗？

S2：当然。

乌兰汉姆：这里是乌兰汉姆。

贝奈特：早上好，乌兰汉姆先生。我是 Access 电脑公司的，我的名字是艾力斯塔尔·贝奈特。

乌兰汉姆：早上好，贝奈特先生。

贝奈特：乌兰汉姆先生，我从我们的文件中得知，去年您有意委托我公司制作一些软件。我想知道这个项目后来的进展。

乌兰汉姆：嗯，最终我们将这个系统控制软件项目交给了您的一位竞争者。

贝奈特：我知道了。那么，我今天打电话的原因是由于我 9 月 21 日将要到达伦敦，想知道是否有必要和您会面商谈一下其他的项目。

乌兰汉姆：没有什么不可以的，虽然目前没有什么要进行的项目。但是我们当然可以大体上讨论一下。

贝奈特：好的。可以定在 21 日的两点钟吗？

乌兰汉姆：好的，21 日的两点钟很合适。

贝奈特：我期待着与您见面。

乌兰汉姆：再见。

贝奈特：再见。

电话三

在这一对话中，A（洛奇）是一家小型生产休闲快艇的公司的经营者。他正和处在另一国家的海滨度假村的经营者 B（杰克斯）通话。

A：早上好，杰克斯。很高兴再次和你通话。你那里的天气怎么样？

B：好的不能再好了，洛奇。晴朗，29度，微风……

A：别说了，我听不下去了。那么，杰克斯，我能为你做点什么呢？

B：我需要两艘你们的SY2000快艇，打算出租给客人。你能报个价吗？

A：让我看一下……嗯，报价单上是6500美元。你是老主顾了，所以可以给你百分之十的优惠。

B：这个价格很合理了。你现在有存货吗？

A：当然有。去年我们安装了新的库存监管系统，因此我们再不会有过多的积压库存了。

B：那很好。旅游旺季就要到了，所以我急着要。你最早能什么时间装运？

A：装运准备要两到三周。

B：很好。洛奇，成本加保险运费的价格是多少？

A：稍等……运到你通常的港口价格将达到15230美元。可以成交吗？

B：成交！把所有信息传真给我，我马上发给你我的订单。像往常一样，我用不可撤销信用证付款。条件与以往相同，可以吗？

A：当然可以。

B：太好了！洛奇，很高兴和你又做了一笔生意。再见，代我向你的家人问好。

A：我会的，也代我向你的家人问好。再见，杰克斯。

第二课　主持会议

会议一

这里是三位经理在讨论一些决策。

道格：听着，让我们进入正题吧。基本上，今天下午我们要完成两项内容：第一，有关任命新的英国营销经理的短期决策；第二，所谓在集团内发展国际型经理人的长期战略。那么，有关任命的问题，大家持什么立场？哈格？

哈格：如果选择比较突出的一个，即玛丽·沃特斯，我们的决策将是稳妥的。假如选择另外一个更有竞争力的候选人，即乔治·麦斯威尔，我们将会冒更多风险，也会有更多机遇。

道格：我明白你的意思。你怎么看，维恩？

维恩：我是从公司的角度看的。如果我们从内部选人，即沃特斯，以后我们再说到"集团内的机会"就没有人相信了。我理解哈格对于乔治·麦斯威尔的看法，他是个特立独行的人，而有时候公司需要这样的人。但是，假如我们任命他为营销经理，我将不得不辞职，而你，道格，也是一样的。

道格：我觉得你言重了，但是我明白你的意思。那么，就选择玛丽·沃特斯吧。咱们还是把这部分话题搁置一会儿，先来讨论关于发展国际型经理人的相关问题。维恩，我知道你有很坚定的观点。

维恩：确实是这样。对于集团来说，我们能团结起来是很关键的。这里有两种选择：要么通过内部长期发展途径，即培训；要么我们到公司外寻找国际型经理人。如果选择第一种，我们会花费五年时间打造具有真正国际经验的一组经理人。假如选择第二种，明年我们就能做到这一点，但是我不确定对于现有员工士气的打击有多大。

哈格：确实是。国际型经理人是什么？没有，我认为我们没有其他的选择。我们必须培养我们自己的人。假如我们启动一个在各个国家的销售和生产部门之间交换人员的系统，我们不用等上五年。这样还能识别出这些经理们的能动性和潜能。

道格：好的。我感觉你们两个都倾向于内部培养的选项。维恩，你可以将这些整理成书面材料以便我们上交董事会吗？

维恩：当然可以，道格。

道格：好的，让我们再回到玛丽·沃特斯的问题。

会议二

蒙特森是全球最大的娱乐集团之一。他们在全世界拥有并经营着一些主题公园。他们的欧洲区总部设在阿姆斯特丹。欧洲区业务协调员，简纽拜，召集了一次会议来讨论是否关闭位于巴黎郊外的麦格德姆主题公园的问题。参加会议的有弗朗西斯·皮卡德（麦格德姆主题公园经理），哈姆特·瑞特（欧洲区财务总监）和帕姆·科汉（欧洲区营销总监）。

简：好了，你们都知道我为什么召集这次会议。麦格德姆主题公园在过去的6个月里收入严重下降。弗朗西斯已经发给大家一份报告，明确说明了这一情况，即他觉得这只是一次暂时性的挫折，并且他预计公园能在明年上半年恢复盈利。现在，我们面临三种选择：第一个是完全关闭公园；第二个是继续营业但是缩小规模以便缩减成本；第三个基本上是弗朗西斯的观点，照常营业。

我认为我们都已经分析过数据了，因此我想这次会议仅限于听取你们的评价和结论。哈姆特，你怎么看？

哈姆特：恐怕非常渺茫。我看不到任何公园明年能恢复盈利的迹象，或者在可预见的将来的任何时候……

弗朗西斯：我认为你没有读过……

简：弗朗西斯，待会儿你会有机会陈述你的观点。让哈姆特先说完。

哈姆特：是的，正如我刚才说的。恐怕麦格德姆是失败的。在过去的6个月中，我们已经损失将近40万美元。我们再也无法承担这样的损失了。我认为我们应当尽快关闭它以盘活资产。

弗朗西斯：盘活资产是什么意思？我们不能卖掉……

简：等一下，弗朗西斯，待会儿会轮到你。那么，让我总结一下。哈姆特支持尽快关闭公园然后出售土地和资产，对吗？

哈姆特：是的，我知道土地价格并不理想，但是再等6个月还不如现在卖，因为到时候资产价格会下跌得更厉害。

简：谢谢你，哈姆特。帕姆，你的观点呢？

帕姆：哈姆特说到的巨额损失是确实的，但是我们应该看一看整个欧洲的实际情况。我们所有在欧洲的主题公园都在经历艰难的时期，入园人数都在下降……

哈姆特：也许是，但没有像……

简：哈姆特，让我们听听帕姆要说什么。

帕姆：是的，我刚才说，由于严峻的经济环境，所有处在欧洲的主题公园都不好过。我们刚委托了一个针对全欧洲主题公园业务的第三方普查，结果显示百分之四十的主题公园在明年春天前都会关闭。

哈姆特：没错，我就是这个观点。

简：哈姆特，刚刚我们听过你的观点了。现在请听帕姆的。

帕姆：没错，因此我们可以预测明年主题公园的运营商会减少很多。同时，大多数经济学家估计明年年中全欧洲的经济会复苏。此时此刻，我们的顾客正在家里节约开支，但是我觉得我们可以预计明年年中他们会再次消费。到时候，将没有几家主题公园可去了。我认为麦格德姆会有非常有利的机会重新提高市场份额。

简：这么说，你倾向于继续开业？

帕姆：是的。但是在冬季应该缩小规模。我想让弗兰西斯起草一份在11月到3月期间限制性开放，然后在4月重拳出击迎合复活节假期的计划。

简：好的，帕姆。这么说，你倾向于第二种选择——缩小营业规模——维持 5 个月。

帕姆：是的。

简：弗朗西斯，你一直很耐心。很显然你有不同看法。

弗朗西斯：不是的。帕姆说的我都同意，但是我担心于她的结论。

简：你是说 5 个月的缩小规模经营？

弗朗西斯：是的。当然，我会考虑这个选择。但是你们要明白麦格德姆最大的运营成本是设备折旧。比如说，如果我们只在周末营业，我们必须用较少的门票收入来抵消并没有下降的折旧。

哈姆特：弗朗西斯是对的。这就是为什么我觉得唯一的选择是关掉它并卖掉设备。

弗朗西斯：你已经听到帕姆说的市场情况了吧。在目前的经济环境下，我们不可能找到设备的购买者。

简：好了，弗朗西斯，我明白你担心的是什么。我想让你回去着手作两个缩小营业规模的可选方案——比如，只在周末开业和一个更断然的方式——只在圣诞节期间开业。好的，下周一我们还要开个会，到时候你可以上交这两种方案的财务分析，我们再做决定。好了，还有一点是……

第三课 讨论与陈述观点

课文一

一个升职评估委员会正在讨论三位候选人的优势与劣势。

琼：哦，我不知道。他已经在公司 20 年了。想当然的，他应该不指望升职了吧。你同意吗，彼得？

彼得：嗯，约翰·杰弗瑞经常显示出对公司极大的忠诚。我认为是时候回报他了。

克莱夫：这不光是忠诚的问题。他会胜任这个工作吗？他将要领导一个小团队，而他还没有这方面的经验。

彼得：除非给他机会，否则他永远都不会有经验。

琼：我们不能感情用事啊。我认为他不适合这个工作。他通常是个服从者，而不是领导者。让我们看看其他候选人。丽塔·海登已经显示出非凡的人事管理技巧，我觉得，就算她……

彼得：哦，得了吧，琼！她还处在学习阶段呢！用这样一个缺乏经验的人，我们可冒不起这个风险。

克莱夫：我同意彼得的说法。丽塔还没有准备好承担重任。我倾向于苏珊·帕默尔。她很有经验。她已经在部门内的其他事项中工作了，因此她熟悉业务，并且她……

琼：但是她总给我一种小心翼翼的印象。我们这个工作需要活力四射的人。

彼得：我同意克莱夫的意见。我认为苏珊·帕默尔会做好这项工作。也许她是比较谨慎，但是她踏实可靠……我们也需要这些素质啊。

琼：好吧，如果你们俩都这么肯定，我想我不得不同意……

课文二

这是四位同事在讨论新产品的定价策略。

艾利克斯：好了，今天我们在这里要讨论一下新的计时产品，即最新系列的电子桌面记事本的定价问题。我们需要关注形成最终价格的不同因素，从制造成本开始。这个你们可以从表中看到，我们定为每台15.8美元。

海伦：抱歉，我能问个问题吗？

艾利克斯：当然，请说。

海伦：这个制造成本是基于完全生产能力计算出来的吗？

艾利克斯：我想豪斯特能很好地回答这个问题……

豪斯特：是的，当然。简单地说就是"不是的"。15.8美元是基于百分之七十的生产力计算出来的。换句话讲，就是每月生产三万台。

海伦：那么，想再问清楚些，这意味着我们的年销售任务是36万台，对吗？

豪斯特：是的，预期销售的底线。

海伦：谢谢，请继续。

艾利克斯：因此，正像我说到的，生产成本设定为15.8美元。分销成本按每台两美元计算，使得价格升高为17.8美元。

海伦：我能再打断一下吗？

艾利克斯：请讲。

海伦：我们计划只通过现有批发商分销吗？

艾利克斯：我能回答这个问题。如你所知，我们目前的分销策略是利用批发商。我们曾考虑过直接分销给零售商，但是，就目前情况，我们的渠道还是单一的。

　　海伦：我知道了。我这么问是因为，如果我们直接分销给零售商，定价当然是会变动的。

　　艾利克斯：没错。但是，我们先搁下这个选择，好吗？

　　海伦：当然可以。

　　艾利克斯：现在，接下来的因素是促销成本。这个我们定为每台3美元，这样单价就达到了20.8美元。你们都满意吗？

　　海伦：这是我们都同意的。

　　艾利克斯：那好。现在我们生产商的一般加成是百分之二十左右，就说是4.2美元吧，这意味着批发商的成本将是25美元。

　　黛博拉：我可以问明一点吗？

　　艾利克斯：当然，黛博拉。

　　黛博拉：这个数字和批发商讨论过了吗？

　　艾利克斯：我猜是的……海伦？

　　海伦：嗯，我们有过初步的讨论并透露了这个数字。

　　黛博拉：他们什么反应呢？

　　海伦：他们似乎是满意的。

　　黛博拉：好的，抱歉打断了。

　　艾利克斯：现在就剩下批发商和零售商的加成了。一般的是批发商百分之十，零售商百分之二十。

　　海伦：那么这意味着……稍等……批发价在27.5美元左右，而商店中的零售价是……33美元。

　　艾利克斯：没错。海伦，你认为如何？

　　海伦：我认为太高了。我们的目标应该是在……

课文三

　　A：如果不想让奶粉成本上升，我们就不能添加任何东西了。我们就按现在的方式销售并且加上一个警告。那么，如果某些人用了脏水，他们来承担责任而不是我们。

　　B：对不起，但是我不得不说我不同意。有三个很好的理由说明为什么这样做是错的。

　　A：你似乎很肯定啊。你能证明吗？

B：在我看来，首先，那里的大部分人都不认字，所以警告并不能帮到他们。其次，就算政府说有警告就可以了，其他利益集团并不这样认为。他们召集狗仔队，那么很多很多人会对我们感到愤怒。每个地方的销售都会下降。

C：莎拉，你刚才说有三个理由，另外一个呢？

A：是的，第三点也是最重要的，我们明明知道只要有一个人不听警告就有一个儿童会因此受到伤害而还这么做是不对的。

C：我不想辩解这些。假如我们知道事情是我们造成的，我们怎么可能会放任不管呢？只是因为我们想多赚些钱。

A：这不只是因为钱。那些人并不健康，而我们的奶粉要好于母乳。一些人可能会得病，但是我们帮助了那么多的人不是更重要吗？

第四课　访谈

访谈一

十年前，彼得·杰昆开设了自己的景观设计公司。随着他作为一流的设计师而声名远扬，他的业务发展得很快。两年前，由于经济环境的恶化，他的业务陷入了困境。他求助于市场营销顾问西蒙·克拉克，来帮助他重新提高业务。

西蒙：杰昆先生，我想我已经足够了解产品了。我能看出来您是位出色的景观设计师，在行业内的口碑很好。我想转入营销组合中的其他方面。我想最简单的方法就是考虑，首先是定价；其次是地域，即您的经营可到达的范围；最后是宣传促销，换句话说，就是您如何传播声望。因此，让我们从定价开始。您认为价格是一个重要的因素吗？

彼得：既是又不是。这要看具体的合作类型。对于大型的景观项目，你知道的，诸如新地产项目、商务区，价格很关键。另外一方面，小型的私人合约，像私人花园等，价格不是主要因素。

西蒙：在您的业务中，大型合约占有多大比例呢？

彼得：越来越少了。5年前曾经有大约百分之七十。现在，我认为不超过百分之二十。

西蒙：私人合约是对价格不敏感的。

彼得：我不会这么说。对于顾客来说，价格是重要的，但是如果他们喜欢您的设计，您能做到他们想要的，他们可以多付一些。

西蒙：我明白了。那么，让我们接着讨论地域方面的话题。基本上，您的市场在哪里？有多大？

彼得：我认为我们百分之九十的业务是在当地的，方圆50英里之内吧。偶尔，我们走得更远一些。我们最近曾做过一笔苏格兰的生意。

西蒙：有何原因使您必须局限于这一地区吗？

彼得：嗯，我觉得景观设计通常是一种当地发展的业务，当然除了大人物之外。

西蒙：您说的大人物是什么意思？

彼得：有一两家全国性的设计公司在全不列颠范围内经营，还扩展到国外。

西蒙：那就是说没有什么原因阻止您向更远的地方提供服务了？

彼得：是的，没有什么原因。纯设计方面当然可以扩展到全国。

西蒙：好的，我们待会儿再说这个。让我们转入最后一点，宣传促销。您是如何宣传业务的？

彼得：嗯，老实说，主要是靠口口相传。

西蒙：您的意思是，人际推荐？

彼得：是的，我想是的。当然这是不够的，所以我才请你来。

西蒙：但是您肯定做过广告吧？

彼得：不完全是这样，我们只是在电话簿黄页的业务栏中登记列项，就这些了。

西蒙：您认为有没有帮助呢？

彼得：很难说。我们确实接到过询价……

西蒙：您考虑过其他形式的宣传吗？

彼得：比如呢？

西蒙：嗯，在园艺杂志上做广告或其他促销宣传？

彼得：没有。这里有个年度的农业展会我们每年会参加。我不能说这为我们带来了什么业务但是我认为这是一种公共关系吧。

西蒙：那现场推销、上门推销呢？做过这些吗？

彼得：嗯，我曾经认识一位市政厅的规划官员。你知道的，这样的话我就能得知即将出现的新合约了。但是，实话说，我已经不这样做了。这样做没什么用。

西蒙：我明白了，您没做过任何直接的推销？

彼得：没有，确实没有。

西蒙：好吧，那么，让我们现在回到产品方面……

访谈二

皮特·哈里顿被评为年度青年企业家。他的公司，PH 工业生产了新一代声控电脑（VAC 系列）。在这个访谈中，他和《商务世界》的记者萨曼莎·埃文斯谈论了他的工作。

萨曼莎：皮特，你被评为了年度青年企业家。现在，这对你意味着什么呢？

皮特：嗯，我当然很高兴我在 PH 工业所做的工作得到了肯定。我不光为我自己高兴，还为每个努力过的人而高兴。但是，我不想让这一奖项使我从我的目标中分心，我的目标是使 PH 成为声控电脑市场中的主导者。

萨曼莎：PH 已经有个很好的起步了，它要向哪个方向发展呢？

皮特：嗯，如果我看一下我下周的日程安排，我们就能看出声控电脑发展的旨趣何在了。周一早晨，我将会去欣顿视察我们的新生产基地。事实上，我们需要比原计划更早一些搬过去，因为需求比我们所预计的还要高。因此，我们必须加速各方面的工作。在过去的三年里，我学到的一点就是失去的时间永远找不回。

萨曼莎：那么，现在您完全关闭旧生产基地了吗？

皮特：是的，所有的都结束了，都在欣顿进行。因此，视察欣顿之后，我将会在巴黎和我的法国团队会面。我们需要就成为很多大品牌标准型号的 VAC2000 的分销达成协议。

萨曼莎：这么说，VAC 2000 在法国成功了？

皮特：哦，是的，比我想象的还要快。当然，这是建立欣顿生产基地并运行它的压力来源之一。因此，我一明确当前法国需求的规模，下午就会动身去苏黎世与一家大型软件生产商会面。

萨曼莎：啊，是 Visitech 吗？

皮特：你很快就会知道了！也许下周吧。但是还有一些事情需要解决。嗯，那么，这就是周一的事情了。

萨曼莎：一整天吗？

皮特：嗯，我更愿意说是典型的一天。周二我要从苏黎世去布达佩斯。目前在东欧有很多振奋人心的机会。

萨曼莎：我们的信息是目前那里的市场状况是僵滞的。

皮特：嗯，罗马不是一天建成的。我们应该看得远一些，看到五年后的情况。潜力是巨大的。我的任务就是确保当障碍完全消除后我们已经准备好了。现在，我正在影响他们按照我们的方式思考和工作。时机一到，该发生的就都会发生。

萨曼莎：那么，匈牙利是你唯一感兴趣的东欧地区吗？

皮特：完全不是这样。实际上，周二上午的布达佩斯会议之后，我会去布拉格，我们在那里已经有了一家成功的合资企业的雏形。我们计划在捷克共和国北部开设一个大型生产中心。我们出一部分资，新东欧技术发展基金会出一部分资。

萨曼莎：听上去不错。

皮特：是的，周一和周二我将为 PH 工业在欧洲的经营打基础。

萨曼莎：那周三呢？

皮特：周三我会回到欣顿参加一系列内部会议。由于未预料到的销售增加了，我提议了每月召开营销会议。因此，我会在早上和营销团队浏览一下销售数字。下午有一系列的技术会议，用来研究 VAC2500 的后续系列。实际上，我只是出席一下技术会议，因为这并不是我的专长。哦，对了！在此期间我还要应邀去伦敦参加一个午餐会，就欧洲技术整合向英国—丹麦商会致辞。

萨曼莎：这是新型欧洲政治的结果吗？

皮特：不，不是的，只是巧合。周四我会待在这里。从我的日程上看，我的秘书为我安排了两个与欧洲技术专家协会的来访者的会面：一位来自德国，另一位来自日本。我很期待，应该很有意思。在会面期间，我在顾顿要处理其他一些事情。

萨曼莎：那周五呢？

皮特：一般周五我空出来处理这里需要我关注的一些事情。鉴于业务扩展得很快，如非必要，我不想让自己离开总部太远。我愿意给每个人机会定期和我聊一聊发展中的问题。你看，我强烈认为我们这里有一个成功的团队并且想要把它保持下去。

第五课　工作面试

课文一

常见面试类型

组织单位利用各种类型的面试来尽可能多地了解你和其他申请者的情况。结构型面试一般用在筛选阶段。雇主方按照事先设定好的顺序提问一系列准备好的问题，从而控制面试。虽然这样有助于搜集事实，但是总体来说结构型面试并不是一种能够很好地考察应聘者个人素质的方法。尽管如此，为了使招聘过程比较规整，一些公司仍会使用结构型面试。

与之相对应，开放型面试没那么正式也没有严格的结构，采取放松的模式。面试官问一些广泛的、开放性的问题，鼓励你随意回答。这种类型的面试有利于显示出你的个性，也有利于评判专业判断力。然而，一些候选人说的太多，侃侃而谈个人和家庭问题，这些与聘用工作所要求的素质、和同事合作的能力或任何有利于工作表现的个人兴趣都没有关系。因此要小心。你要在表现亲和和铭记这是一个商务环境之间找到平衡。

有一些组织单位实行集体面试，同时面试几个人，观察他们如何相互影响。这种类型的面试有助于评估人际交往技巧。

另外一个现代发展出的类型是情景面试或行为面试，面试官可能会描述过去你曾经怎样处理一些情况。许多公司发现，在传统的面试中，很好地回答面试问题和工作中的良好变现是没有内在联系的。情景面试是在一位需要雇员完成工作的雇主和一位必须要充分准备好工作的雇员之间的需要动手操作的、工作状态下的会面。

课文二

要想有效地操控面试，面试官需要注意一些关键的技巧。

（1）观察

如果是相关的，就要从衣着、外貌、声音、身高和体重等方面搜集信息。面试官也可以通过非言语类的线索评估候选人的情绪和适合的反应。

（2）倾听

面试官的其他证据来自倾听。不光是听回答问题的答案，还要听语调和节奏的变化、发音和重音传递的信息。两人交谈所用的时间也很重要，倾向于其中一方的不平衡现象意味着要么是候选人，要么是面试官没有足够的机会倾听对方。

（3）提问

为了可以听到对方的回答，面试官应该引导候选人。当然了，他是通过提问做到的。他的问题应该能鼓励候选人并让他能畅所欲言，以便于面试官得以观察。这样做的技巧取决于面试官的个性和风格。面试官明确地意识到他执行的面试体现了他个人的技巧。

(4) 回答问题

这是同一枚硬币的另一面。面试官需要确保候选人有足够的机会问他们想问的问题并得到满意的答案。

在结束面试之前，面试官有必要总结一下要点。最后一个步骤是面试官交代下一步的事情。

第六课 宣讲技巧之构架

宣讲一

NETCOUNT 软件公司是一家为小企业用户提供会计软件的供应商，公司总裁正在作一个发言。他勾画了公司的竞争形势。

我想讲的是勾画一个公司的 SWOT 分析，正如我们现在在做的。我很确定你们都知道，SWOT 代表优势、劣势、机遇与威胁。

那么让我们从优势开始。很显然，我们的主要竞争优势是我们产品的档次。我们的会计软件包被认为是市场上界面最友好的，与竞争者的软件包相比安装相对简单，并不需要很多的培训，更加物超所值。因此，总体来说，我们的产品很棒。我们的另一大优势是我们的人员，特别是售后服务方面。我们的售后服务团队被认为更快、素质更高、态度更好并且总体来讲比其他竞争者更有效率。这包括前台服务人员和现场维修人员。

好了，让我们转向劣势。虽然我们有拳头产品，但是我们并没有得到应有的市场渗透率。基本上这是因为我们的营销并不如竞争对手的有效。特别是，STERLING，他们在市场上无论是销售还是企业形象都更强劲。我们过于依赖产品质量，促销的力度不够。我们应该投入大量努力在广告和直销活动上。

那么，接下来要说的是机遇。我们很明显没有抓住机会占领小企业用户市场。我们的销售可以有显著的提高——我估计提高百分之五十至六十。我们还可以建立更广泛的客户群——这同时保障了更加稳定的未来。

我们主要的威胁，当然是 STERLING。他们有更加令人印象深刻的经销商网络，他们的促销比我们的更复杂化。另一方面，我们有更好的产品。我们应该利用这一点。一种方法是……

宣讲二

负责 Viscal 2000 可视电话的项目经理杰夫·布里兹正在向公司董事会就产品和营销政策进行宣讲。

杰夫：好了，这是我们期待已久的时刻。终于，我可以提供给大家一些关于我们的首款可视电话 Viscal 2000 的确实的信息，而这个产品曾经是公司的一个难于进行的项目。我今天的目的是通告大家而不是劝说，希望能充分支持这个产品。我知道大家已经有了完整的会议议程，那我就简要地就 Viscal 2000 的四个营销组合因素介绍一下，这四个因素是产品、渠道、价格和促销。如果有何问题，可以马上问我，好吗？

从产品开始。我想分为两部分讲。首先是它的组成，其次是它是如何工作的。如果大家看到这张草图，会发现它基本上是由四部分部件组成的：一个屏幕、一个摄像头、一个声频接收器和一个声频转换器。当然，从电子学的角度看，还有一些其他的复杂的部件。但是这个产品的一大优点是安装简单，因而维修也简单。再说说它是怎么工作的。理解呼叫的形成是很重要的。首先，声频信号的建立同其他普通电话是一样的。然后，只要被呼叫者也安装了可视电话装置，视频频道就会在另一条线中形成。接着，声频和视频信号会同步发出，通话的同时声音和图像就出现了。如果对方没有可视电话，那么这就是一个普通的通话，这些大家都清楚吗？

董事：啊，只有一个问题，这是否意味着接收声频信号和视频信号之间会有一个延迟？

杰夫：是的，一个很短的，大约两秒钟的延迟，但是他们开始通话时两个频道就同步了。

董事：我明白了。

杰夫：无论如何，那是一个有关产品和过程的简短描述。让我们继续说渠道，我的意思是指我们如何分销，到哪里分销产品。产品上市的时间是 2004 年 9 月 1 日，到时候全英国的注册零售直营店都会有备货。通过邮购也可以买到可视电话，我们承诺二十八天内送到。然而，影响顾客接受程度的还有一个重要的方面，我会在第三个标题下讲到。

产品零售价格大约为五百美金外加增值税。但是这一价格只适用于已经加入联合数字网络的顾客。换句话说，如果没有入网，会有额外的联网费。现在一般需要不到五百美元，但是我们同网络运营商达成了特惠联网费，只需要三百美元。因此，结论是，由于大多数顾客是还没有入网的，所以对于他们来说总价是八百美元外加增值税。我希望大家都明白了。以防万一，我会把书面的详细内容留下以便大家随时可以看一下。

最后一个因素是促销。首先，我要说我们应该预备两年的时间让产品在市场上形成显著的渗透力，这意味着要安装超过 25000 台电话终端。上市宣传广告的目标是住户，为了能打动他们，我们授权了电视广告，特别说明对于与家人与朋友相隔很远的用户，可视电话的优势。我们的目标是在全英国促销产品，但是开始主要在东南部地区。两个月之后，我会有关于促销活动的更详细的资料，到时候再向大家讲。

好了，我就说到这里。我希望大家现在对产品、分销、定价和一些促销的初步想法有了更清晰的了解。我确定大家在这里一同分享了我的信心与热情，对于 Viscal 2000，我确信不单会开启一个全新的市场，而且能确保长期的增长并能为公司带来成功与兴盛。

第七课　宣讲技巧之可视材料

宣讲一

以下是一个宣讲的节选及其可视材料。

中国内部大迁徙：原因与启示

大家下午好。请让我首先向举办此次会议的杨校长和经济学院表示感谢，向协调此次会议的赵教授表示感谢，向帮助我参加今天盛会的波特校长表示感谢。能够站在这里，我感到万分荣幸。

在人类的迁徙历史中，有一些事件总是被认为是著名的和特殊的。西方最著名的事件是"大西洋大迁徙"：在 1850 年至 1914 年间，大约 5500 万人从欧洲移民到美洲和大洋洲。美国国内最著名的迁徙事件是"黑人大迁徙"：大约 650 万非洲奴隶的后裔从美国南部向北方城市挺进。近年来，著名的事件包括：(1) 伴随欧盟扩张，东欧人向西欧的迁徙；(2) 爱尔兰多年前曾是移民净输出国，但近年来情况恰恰相反，其成为了大型的移民净输入国；(3) 几百万伊拉克难民向叙利亚和其他中东国家迁徙；(4) 大批出生和成长在前东德的人迁往现在统一德国的西部；(5) 在美国有大约 1000 万至 1100 万的来自墨西哥和中美洲的无正式记录的移民。

西方世界不太注意到的一个正在进行中的迁徙使得以上描述的迁徙全部相形见绌。这就是自20世纪80年代起在中国发生的大规模迁徙，我们称之为"中国内部大迁徙"。

如果你对照以下三个时期——1985至1990年、1995至2000和2000至2005年——的人口普查数据，你就会得出中国迁徙发生的证据。在1985至1990年，大约3300万中国人进行省内或跨省的迁徙，其中跨省的大致占三分之一。在1995至2000年，迁徙规模猛增到1.21亿人次，大约四分之三的人是在省内迁徙的。在2000至2005年，将近1.95亿人在中国内部移动，大约三分之一是在省际间发生的。

这些移民去了哪里？无论是在省内还是省际，大多数移民是从农村流向城镇，并且主要是东部沿海的核心地区。如果你核查省际迁徙，一些清晰的模式会显现出来。

这一页显示了1995至2000年每个省份的净移民数，即流入人口减去流出人口。灰色的省份是流入人口比流出多的，而浅灰色的省份是流出比流入多的。有净输入的省份是东部沿海省份，少数几个北方的省份和一些大的西部省份。有净输出的省份是中部和一些南部的省份。标有醒目柱体的省份经历了不同寻常水平的迁徙。如果左侧柱体较高，意味着该省份输入了大量的人口；如果右侧柱体较高，意味着该省份输出了大量的人口。最大的净接收地是东部沿海城市、香港和北京。同时，少数西部省份也有显著的净输入人口。

我相信，这种在过去三十年里发生的非凡的内部迁徙浪潮可以归结为两个主要原因。

1. 区域收入不平衡的加剧

经济学家一致同意在城市、地区、省份和国家之间人口流动的最重要决定因素是地理区域上的收入差别。当一个人以他的人力资本可以得到更多的回报，而迁徙成本为零，他就会迁徙。因此，中国的迁徙浪潮最根本的是收到了城乡收入差别的驱动。20世纪70年代末发生的三个大的变革主要形成了这种差别：

（1）首先是大范围的经济改革，使中国不再实行中央计划经济而是实行更像是地方分权的市场经济体制。通过把中央计划定价职权转移到地方，中国的市场竞争性和劳动力价格就更多地和劳动生产率紧密结合了。这造成了乡镇、城市、地区和省份之间收入差距的增大。

（2）技术进步（特别是信息技术）带来的全球经济繁荣、重组和私有化（特别是在全球金融产业），苏联及相关国家的解体和世界货币政策的扩张都造成了中国出口的飞速增长。全中国的劳动力需求都在增加，而东部沿海城市、香港和北京的劳动力需求增加最多。这造成进行出口产品生产的城市和地区的工资水平被推高，刺激了移民从中国其他地方，特别是中部省份，流入这些地方。

（3）一些省份接收了大量的外国直接投资资金的注入和国内融资，也促进了这些地方的劳动力需求。

2. 在过去的三十年里，在中国迁徙的成本大幅下降。这里有三个理由：

（1）正如台下中国听众所知，从20世纪50年代，中国通过"居住登记"或"户口"制度规范了国内移民。户口好比国内护照。地方和省级政府已经逐步使得人们变更当地登记容易起来。当地允许登记指标增加了，而得到城市户口的条件松动了。虽然是这样，有一点很重要的需要指出，许多移民并没有得到目的地的登记。这部分无注册的移民在中国被称为"流动人口"。无视相对严格的限制而存在的大量流动人口，本身就证明了中国迁徙浪潮中收入差异的巨大推动力。

（2）移民社区的大量增加。作出移民决定的一个重要的影响因素是从家乡到目的地是否有朋友家人的联系。在你抵达前和抵达时，移民关系网可以很大程度上帮助你降低在目的地获取信息和寻找工作的成本。由于在目的地能觉得舒适和确保能看到熟悉的面孔、听到乡音、熟悉的习惯和规则等，大的移民关系网还能减少移民的心理成本。

（3）中国的交通基础设施有了巨大的发展。得益于机票价格下降、新增航班和新航线的增加，在中国国内坐飞机比以往更普遍了。中国的铁路交通也是一样。最后，一些政府鼓励迁徙的政策也影响了迁徙模式。最突出的是"西部大开发"，这可以解释为什么那些西部省份在1999年之后净接收了人口。

在下面的三张幻灯中，我想特别强调迁徙浪潮和中国经济增长、外商直接投资和固定资产投资的相关性。

这张幻灯展示了中国1952至2006年的实际国内生产总值的增长，单位为亿美元。20世纪80年代，当迁徙开始增长的时候，也是国内生产总值开始增长的时候。20世纪90年代初至就90年代中期，国内生产总值加速增长，迁徙也加速增长……

宣讲二

杰夫·罗伯特是Aoro国际公司的财务总监。他正在向公司董事会说明年度财务结果，特别强调了一些重要的数字。

好了，让我们浏览一下这些数字并找出其中的启示。

首先，作为一种粗略测算利润率的方法，我们在损益表（你们英国人叫"损益账"）中用总销售收入减去直接成本。因此，正如你们可以看到的，我们以 300 万美元的直接成本销售了 650 万美元的产品——可以看到吗？——那么，我们的毛利是 350 万美元。这还好，基本上和我们的预算相符。但是下一个数字让人担忧——固定成本——是 185 万美元——这比去年上升了将近百分之十，太高了。这意味着我们的营业利润只有 165 万美元，比去年下降了将近 10 万美元。好了，我待会儿再说一个。在这个报表中，我还要重点提到的一个数字就是税收，很庆幸它很低——只有 12 万美元——这是我们调整海外地区利润任务的结果。无论如何，最重要的是由于税收低而使得净利润从中受益——像你们所看到的，在一两项扣除之后，净利润为 143 万美元。

不管怎样，我们先搁置这些转向资产负债表。在这里，我想让你们注意的一个关键的事情是流动比率是如何恶化的——因为它代表了公司的偿债能力，所以很重要。一般的，我们用流动资产除以流动负债来衡量。通常，我们希望看到流动资产大于流动负债的健康的指标，但是你们来看，目前公司承担着很多的短期负债——银行的和其他应付的账款——同时还有销售的下降——这意味着流动资产下的应收账款减少。我们应该马上采取行动。我建议重新规划我们的负债——如果说有什么问题的话，那就是我们的固定资产被低估了，因此我们可以通过把短期负债转变为长期负债来提高公司的财务杠杆能力。

好了，先生们，这就是我要说的了。这可能好转，另一方面，也可能变得很糟。那么，有什么问题吗？

第八课　谈　判

谈判一

　　Sohpmore 电子公司正在寻找零部件供应商。价格和装运期是很重要的条件，但是更重要的是供应商和客户都可以从中获益的长期合作关系。北方零部件公司是个新成立的公司。Sohpmore 可能成为他们的第一个大客户。Sohpmore 的采购经理凯特·娜丽甘正在和北方公司的销售经理皮特·博德曼进行最后阶段的谈判。

　　凯特：这么说，你们只是最近才成立的？
　　皮特：是的，但是公司总裁杰夫·斯坦顿在零部件供应领域已经足足有二十年了。

凯特：哦，太有意思了。他原先在哪里工作？

皮特：他和我都在标准电信公司的电子部。我们都想换一下环境，他筹措好了资金创办北方电子公司时就叫我一同加入了。

凯特：生意进行得怎么样？

皮特：嗯，逐步发展起来了。我们已经有了一些相对小规模的供应零部件的合约。你知道的，主要是专门化经营者。

凯特：是的，这是我担心的一点。你看，你们没有任何承接大订单的记录……

皮特：这是事实，但是你已经看到了我们有这个能力，我们的质量控制系统是非常精确的。

凯特：是的，你们在这方面的投资令我印象深刻。呃，现在我们能谈谈实际条款吗？

皮特：当然。嗯，我们已经讨论过了价格的细节。我想你应该要谈谈装运了？

凯特：是的，我们该谈谈了。正如你想象的，符合我们的期限很关键。

皮特：当然了。你们认为的装运期是什么？

凯特：嗯，你已经知道订单数量了，你们能做到什么水平呢？

皮特：嗯，对于AX 2000，我们肯定能……

凯特：不，我不是说单个订单。按月计算的整体装运是什么？

皮特：哦，我明白了。我没有意识到我们会谈到这个。我得回去和杰夫确认一下这个时间。

凯特：你肯定能给我一些答复。

皮特：嗯，我认为……从订单确认之日起，我们能做到15天装运。但是，正如我说的，我得确认后再答复你。

凯特：在你们的报价基础之上吗？

皮特：呃……嗯，实际上我们是按照分批来报价的。我们没有料到你们考虑的是整批的订单。

凯特：我知道了。那么我想因为是大宗订单，我们可以期待有折扣吧？

皮特：你看，我很抱歉。坦白地讲，你确实让我始料未及。我给杰夫打个电话，你介意吗？

凯特：不，当然不……通完话了吗？

皮特：是，通完话了。让你久等很抱歉。总之，我们现在可以更具体地谈一下装运条款了。

凯特：好的。

皮特：在先前报价的基础上，我们可以做到整批15天装运。这意味着从我们的仓库运出……

凯特：鉴于订单规模，我很惊讶你们不准备提供一些折扣。

皮特：嗯，我相信你能理解要完成这样一个大订单意味着增加很多加班时间——我们的价格很难降下来。

凯特：但是我们提供的是一个长期稳定的大订单啊。

皮特：这是事实。你愿意在我们讨论的基础上签订一份年度的合约吗？

凯特：嗯，有这个可能，要看质量和装运期的保证。

皮特：当然了。那么，如果在未来的十二个月内每月一份合约的话，我们可以提供百分之五的折扣。

凯特：我想的是力度再大一些。

皮特：我们恐怕只能做到这些。我们已经尽力了。

凯特：好吧，博德曼先生。我建议先签订一份在你方报价基础之上百分之五的折扣为期六个月的合约，然后我们到时候再商谈一次看看是否能进一步降低价格，好吗？

皮特：你真是个厉害的谈判手。好吧，我们成交并签订首次合约的细节吧……

谈判二

A：早上好！很高兴再次见到你！

B：今天我们将要商讨敏感的价格问题。总的来说你们的价格同其他投标者比较是很高的了

A：这个项目的价格是在我们关于发电站建设的经验而得出来的。我们已经把利润压得很低了。考虑到你们的利益，我们相信完成工作的时间以及合理价格之上的质量保证比发电延后更重要。没有人希望看到为了价格稍微低一些而出现问题。相比于从早期电力生产中得到的利益，用于土建的费用要小得多。

B：你们为什么不能给出一个更有竞争力的价格呢？

A：中国有句话说得好，你不能让马儿不吃草还要马儿跑得好。

B：现在让我们按照你们提交递交的材料回顾一下敏感的价格。分解价格将会解释你们的价格是否合理。

A：我们很愿意。总价包括9个部分。它们是：（1）劳动力成本；（2）管

理人员成本；（3）工程设备成本；（4）材料成本；（5）技术转让和培训成本；（6）调度成本；（7）税费；（8）场地费；（9）主要分包商的成本。让我们逐个处理。第一项是劳动力成本。

B：这个项目你们预计需要多少个工时？

A：最少需要大约890万个工时。因此，每天的劳动力成本只是五美元，算是很低了。几乎所有的工人都要在当地招聘。第二项是管理人员成本。大约一共需要190万美元。

B：按你们的计算，管理人员费用很高啊。每月薪金大约是1500美金，比你们国家的平均工资高很多。

A：这不是管理人员的实际工资。事实上，只有百分之六十五是他们的工资，另外百分之三十五是交通费、通信费、税费、保险和离岗工作的间接成本等。

B：你能告诉我设备的折旧率你们是怎么计算的吗？

A：我们的设备折旧使用了几种不同的折旧期。比如，大型耐用设备是十五年。一些设备是十年，一些易耗机械只有三年。对于这样一个需要大量高效机械设备严密计划的大项目来说，需要用到水泥泵、高水平生产能力的水泥生产装置、水泥搅拌车和许多种吊车，这些都在工程设备部分列出了。

B：我们理解你们应该调动足够多的设备来进行这个工程建设，但是为了控制机械成本你们最好严格结合工程进度准备设备调用计划，以避免工地上的设备空转。

A：好的。我们会检查设备的成本，看看能不能再压低。第四项是材料成本，这是最大的一部分，占总成本的百分之五十五。现在我们能讨论这一部分吗？

B：我们已经商讨了很长时间，下午再继续我们的商谈好吗？

A：我没有问题。

谈判三

A：现在，让我们讨论一下这笔交易的支付条款。

B：很好。我们作为买方，希望通过承兑交单的方式支付运费，因此我们有时间融资和再转卖商品。

A：我们作为卖方，由于参与的银行不保证付款或者像他们做信用证交易一样设想信用风险，承兑交单对我们的风险较大。承兑交单条款，代收行只根据你方凭汇票承诺稍后付款就会给你单据。承兑后，你方可以马上拿到我们发送给你的货物。在到期日，如果你方不能付款，我们损失惨重。

B：请不要这么担心我们的信用。我们保证在到期日支付汇票金额。

A：付款交单怎么样呢？我们可以更安全稳妥。这样，代收行只会凭你方全额即期付款而给你方单据。

B：这也合理吧。但是我们更愿意接受付款交单的形式。这种情况下，在我们承兑有时间限制的单据后，在到期日支付之前我们还是不能拿到货。

A：然而，这种支付条款可以给你们时间去融资来支付。同时，由于直到你方支付之后装运抬头才会交给你方，我方的安全是可以得到延续的。

B：你说得很对。那么我们达成了见票付款交单的一致意见。接下来，你方希望票据的有效期是？

A：你方是否同意今年的九月二十日到期？

B：我们没有意见。

第九课　电子邮件

邮件一

至：albert@hb.com
主题：产品信息
亲爱的格林森先生：

我们的财务代表是非常忙碌的——生活中的一半时间通常是用来在全世界拜访客户。很显然，他们在旅途中常用笔记本电脑来进入我们公司的数据库准备客户的计划书。我们的一些代表要求提供给他们便携式打印机，从而他们可以马上给客户进行打印。因此，我想要知道一些贵方便携式打印机的信息，特别是HB-340。首先，我想知道它是否是激光打印机。由于需要在旅途中打印标准尺寸的文件，我们的代表们还需要电池驱动款。

如果我需要提供给您进一步打印需求，请及时告知我。

诚挚的
卡洛琳·瑞尔森

邮件二

至：某地址
主题：替换要求（回复：Photoshop）

亲爱的先生：

  我于 6 月 23 日收到了电动剃须刀和 Photoshop 图像处理软件，我是通过在线销售网站订购的。

  我很高兴的是电动剃须刀很好用。然而，在使用图像处理软件的时候遇到了很多麻烦。在无明显原因的情况下，它经常停滞。频繁的停滞使我不能再忍受中断和由此带来的愤怒了。

  很显然，这个软件有问题。我相信我要求了更换，但是请让我知道贵方会怎么处理。

  不胜感激您的及时回复。谢谢。

greatwall@sina.com.cn

第十课　备忘录

备忘录一

发至：艾丽罗特·兰姆伯恩，副总裁
发自：杰森·彼得森，营销主管
日期：2010 年 4 月 3 日
主题：员工停车位再分配的提议

  作为支持福特汽车公司——其占有我们将近一半的年销售量——的主要方式，我提议在我们总部周边的员工停车区严格划归福特车车主使用。

  在福特公司人员频繁到访期间，他们一定会经过员工停车区。到时候他们会看到我们员工中大约百分之七十的人开的是福特竞争公司的车。事实上，上周一位福特采购代表就问过我："如果你们不支持我们，我们怎样支持你们呢？"

  那么，此备忘录的目的是寻求将周边停车区严格限定给福特汽车使用的支持。维修部门预计需要用四周的时间，五百美元的费用来制作标志牌。

我们的员工合约要求在工作环境方面的任何改变都要一致同意。然而，我们的店面主管，莎莉·马什曾经告诉我，她要考虑这个问题——特别是在行政人员停车区也要有类似的限制。

既然 5 月 8 日至 10 日将召开下一次经理会议，我期望向他们宣布这个新计划。通过了这个变革，纽顿将会给我们的到访者传递一个强有力的正面信息：我们的员工信任他们销售的产品。

备忘录二

发至：各部门主管
发自：沃特·乔布斯，培训经理
日期：2011 年 12 月 3 日
主题：秘书培训课程

公司在明年春季安排了一些秘书培训课程。

这些课程包括：
- 记账
- 打字
- 商务英语
- 信息系统

请注意这是免费对所有管理人员开放的，报名从速，先到先得。

请张贴海报。

谢谢

沃特·乔布斯

第十一课　会议记录

会议记录一

计算机应用会议
例会会议记录
2011 年 5 月 18 日

参加人：林德森（主席）、安德森—怀特、格瑞芬、金（秘书）、皮特保罗、厄

隆姆、外斯特、沃尔夫

夏农·林德森召集这次会议,在早上八点三十五分召开。按照弗兰克·格瑞芬目前记录的修改,4月14日的会议记录得以通过。

有关预算分会的报告

佐伊·皮特保罗报告了公司执行委员会已经通过了至2011年9月30日额外增加58000美元用来采购分配给分会的硬件设施。分会计划在月底提出提案要求以及在6月的会议上提出分配建议。他还分发了截至今年5月1日硬件与软件分配情况的文件（附件1）。

过去的事项

没有。

新事项

网页开发软件的标准化

詹尼·外斯特提议说:"2011年9月1日开始,CUC同意限于微软FrontPage 2003版的网页开发软件费用。"她总结了由于个人网页版主使用不同的程序而造成的协调、培训和网站维护问题并回答了基层提出的问题。吉娜·厄隆提议通过在"FrontPage 2003"后面加上"或最新版"修改这个动议。经讨论后这个修改被通过了,修改过的动议被采纳了。

语音识别软件

夏农·林德森报告称,她收到了大量询问有关购买语音识别软件的信息和相关的建议,并呼吁委员会考虑。接下来的讨论就成本、培训需要的时间,准确性、小空间内的噪声水平以及这种软件对于触碰技术的总体意义进行。丽莎·安德森—怀特的提议"主席指定一个任务组研究这一事项,下次会议报告结果"被通过了。主席指定了丽莎·安德森—怀特和弗兰克·格瑞芬成立任务组。

通告

夏农·林德森作出了以下通告:

自从3月15日她向各部门主管发出备忘录宣布新的维修政策后,她已经收到了三个正面的评论,没有负面的回馈。

她已经被要求代表CUC于6月18日参加公司执行委员会的长期计划会议,去回答有关未来三年计划中硬件与软件费用的问题。

Anthem计算机服务公司要求对CUC发表一个三十分钟的宣讲。根据委员会的政策,她拒绝了这一要求。

休会
此次会议于商务 10 点 40 分结束。下次例会定于 6 月 20 日 8 点 30 分召开。

此致

特里·金，秘书

会议记录二

董事局会议会议记录
国际拖拉机集团
总裁会议
2012 年 4 月 6 日，第四次例会

国际拖拉机集团的董事局例会在 2012 年 4 月 6 日周四召开。会议主席约翰·沃尔夫于上午 10 点在公司办公地创始人会议室召集了此次会议，地点是宾夕法尼亚州里奇伯格的吉尔斌路。

出席者　十一位董事局成员出席会议：

宝林·阿特、查尔斯·飞利浦、格兰·弗朗斯、罗伯特·海瑟、约瑟夫·拉提那、理查德·力那蒙、罗兰妮·皮尔扎、伊斯梅尔·波利兹、埃塞·兰斯姆森、伊瑞·斯坦尼克和伊丽莎白·沃顿。这些成员达到了法定人数。

缺席者　一个成员缺席：路易斯·琼斯。

会议记录　有关通过了召开董事局成员会议的 2012 年 5 月的会议记录被宣读与通过。

报告　主席报告了增长期的事项。在上个季度，特别是国际业务的销售量与上年相比增加了百分之十二。然而，他也提出面对大量强劲外国竞争者对于关键产品供应的投标遇到了更多的困难。

有关增长的组织计划提交董事会审议。

首先，将集中在总部的销售、营销和财会操作的责任下放到各营业公司。

接下来，将主席与首席行政官并行的管理职位重新制定为总裁与首席运行官。这样将保证对目前运营与未来的发展的关注不会分散。

休会　弗朗斯先生作出休会动议，斯坦尼克小姐附议。会议于上午 11 点 45 休会。

约翰·沃尔夫　主席
夏洛特·夏普耐克　秘书

会议记录三

会议记录的处理
日期：2011 年 4 月 23 日，8∶30～11∶00
地点：204 室，西萨克逊储蓄银行
参加人：撒克逊经济发展公司和西萨克逊储蓄银行的所有中层经理
会议记录人：考驰小姐，撒克逊经济发展公司秘书
以下对于下一步进程的处理是根据后续讨论作出的。

建立"经济发展者"讨论小组
将会建立有规律进行讨论的小组，遵循循环原则，每年至少两次，这被一致认为是交换信息与协调的适合方法。Breslar 地区已经提交了下次会议的邀请。在这一地区访问一些有趣的项目已经被当作扩展思维的方法而采纳了。

还有一些一致意见是应该设法使这一地区的吸引力和概貌再凸显一些。这一目标主要专注于集中于这些分支机构经济性的形成上。

简介与联系合伙人
填写合伙人的介绍文件被认为是对准备基本信息、联系合伙人和更多的核心竞争力是有利的。

所有合伙人都要求在 2011 年 6 月 14 日前将简介文件交回撒克逊经济发展公司。之后他们会向所有合伙人公开。

此次会议于上午 11 点 30 分休会。

凯瑟琳·考驰

第十二课 简历与求职信

简历

詹姆斯·阿诺德

目标

大型跨国企业中的劳工关系相关职位,要求良好劳工关系发展技巧、管理技巧和沟通技巧。

技能

劳工关系

- 主修劳工关系;辅修心理学
- 隶属于当地 463 工会国际办公室
- 曾任 WAINWEIGHT 银行第二团队主管

管理

- 在校学习的同时,每周工作三十个小时学习时间管理技巧
- 在 WAINWEIGHT 银行的三年里,升职两次
- 在处理财务事务中锻炼了判断能力,能够自信地对待所有交易

沟通能力

- 为 ALPHA KAPPA PSI 商务联谊会开发了网页
- 担任高年级副主席,经常组织活动演讲与即席演说
- 学习了报告写作与商务调研的选修课
- 擅长使用微软办公软件 2003 版和互联网搜索

教育背景

- 波士顿大学,理学学士学位,2006 年六月毕业
- 主修劳工关系,辅修心理学

工作经验

- 2003 年至今,马萨诸塞州波士顿 WAINWRIGHT 银行,银行出纳
- 2001 年夏天,内布拉斯加州若夫克 JCPENNEY,销售员

参考

可从职业信息中心得到我的信息

波士顿大学,波士顿,MA 02215,电话 617-555-2001

求职信

2011年3月13日
戴维·诺曼先生，合伙人
ROSS, RUSSELL & WESTON
第五大街452号
纽约，NY 10018
主题：EDP 专员职位

亲爱的诺曼先生：

我同时具有丰富的会计和工薪支出服务经验和财会学位，使我准备好胜任您3月9日登于《纽约时报》招聘广告中的EDP专员职位。

在纽约大学期间，除了学习了我主修财会专业的会计和管理信息系统的课程之外，我还选修了EDP审核和控制课程。在此课程中，我接受了应用、软件、系统和服务中心记录的培训，这些可以使我快速地成为您EDP顾问团中的有力一员。

作为大学学习的补充，我在一家大型会计事务所进行了实习。另外，我作为纽约市薪酬专员的两年半经验给了我非营利机构需求和运营的第一手知识。这一经验应该有助于我为您与政府部门的大型咨询事务而工作。

如果您看过了我附上的简历，能够给我机会与您讨论为什么我有适宜的能力与个性来为您与您的客户服务，我将非常感谢。每天的下午3点以后，您都能联系到我。

诚挚的
詹姆斯·怀特
AURELIA GOMEZ
纽约70大街西225
NY 10023
电话：212-555-3821
邮箱：agomez@nyu.edu

第十三课　商务书信

信函一

玛利亚·达·席尔瓦
巴西 BOTICARIO
公园路 32 号
圣保罗市

玛丽·海吉斯
客户服务
WZD 交通
Wind 路 9 号
圣保罗市

2003 年 5 月 17 日

亲爱的海吉斯女士：

　　由于我们决定运输服务外包，BOTICARIO BRASIL 与贵公司签订了一份为期四年的合同。我们这样做的最主要的原因是在这个时候我们觉得可依赖的合伙人能使我们优化分销和降低成本。

　　直到去年圣诞节，贵方的运输服务都是令人满意的。然而，自从今年 1 月份开始，我们发现贵方服务的标准绝对比我们的期望值低。今年 4 月，在我们新产品线上市中遇到困难的时候，贵公司没能给我们的三个主要零售商运货，其中的两个是处于主干道上的。毋庸讳言，这为我们的销售造成了负面的影响。我们刚刚投资了一个很有影响力的广告，当我们的顾客到商店的时候，货架上却没有商品。

　　在 4 月的时候，由于贵方给里约热内卢送货晚了二十天，又让我们面临了另一个问题。

　　我确实希望贵方优先确认这些问题，重塑贵方以往的优良服务，否则，BOTICARIO 将不得不另找其他的商务合作伙伴。

　　我期待着您的回复。

真诚的

信函二

彩虹培训学院
BRADBURN CLOSE 53 号
MUSWELL HILL
伦敦 N10

电话 0818832555
传真 0818849345
J. 费雪
人事经理
DJ 银行业务集团
史密斯登大街 54 号
伦敦 E17 6TY

1999 年 9 月 20 日
回复：国际销售工作坊 11 月 5 日

亲爱的费雪小姐：
  我写此信来通知您，非常抱歉，我们不得不取消我们 11 月的工作坊。然而，如果方便的话，我们可以将您的人员换到 10 月 8 日的工作坊。
  我很遗憾没能更早一点通知您这一变化。我希望您能参加这个稍早一些的工作坊。
  如果您能尽快地通知我参加 10 月 8 日的工作坊的人员名单，我将非常感谢。
  我保证贵方人员能在工作坊内得到有用的、信息量更大的内容。

诚挚的
J. 瑞丁
培训经理

信函三

先生：

根据您在 2008 年 6 月 3 日的 672 号订单和您今天早上的电话沟通，我很高兴地通知您集装箱目前已经装运，从南安普顿码头离岸的时间可以确认为 2008 年 9 月 15 日上午 8 点正。

如我们讨论过的，装运单（商业发票、提单、保险单和原产地证明书）连同通过中国银行办理的即期托收单据已经提交我方银行。银行会在支付即期放单。随函附上了商业发票的副本。

我相信集装箱会安全抵达，货物也会使您满意。如果在集装箱抵达上海时您能及时通知我，我将很感激。

我们当然期待着能继续接到您的订单，很希望能在未来得到您的回复。

诚挚的
汤姆·力翁斯顿
出口经理
内附：商业发票副本、2008 年 6 月 3 日签发的 672 号订单

第十四课　图表应用

1. 曲线图

这一报告描述了某国家关于制造业部门和农业部门 1991 年至 2001 年贸易平衡变化趋势。

制造业

在这一时期，进口持续增长。数字显示，在这一时期内，增长了 40 亿美元并且没有显示出什么波动。

出口从 1991 年的将近 30 亿美元增长到 2001 年的大约 70 亿美元，在此期间遭受到了小幅度的波动。总体来说，贸易平衡在我们所观测的时期保持了小幅度上涨的趋势。

农业

进口略微增长，期末达到了 10 亿美元左右。在 1992 至 1994 年期间，曾有

短暂的下降，随后出现了稳定的回升。在 1999 年达到 25 亿美元左右的高点之后，进口轻微下降到了最终的水平。

虽然出口以 40 亿美元的水平高于进口，但是出口数字显示了同样的绩效。因而，贸易平衡在这一时期保持了显著的上升趋势。

2. 柱状图

此图显示了 2000、2001 和 2002 年某公司的三种主要产品对营业额的贡献度。

总的来说，洗衣机是最强劲的产品而加热器销售势头最弱。随着洗衣机占公司营业总额从 2000 年的百分之三十上升到 2002 年的百分之三十四，而加热器的份额从 2000 年的百分之十六下降到了二零零二年的百分之七，两者之间的差别在这三年里就更明显了。第三种产品——灶具——的份额在这一时期保持得相对稳定。它在 2001 年从百分之二十二略微下降至百分之二十，但是在 2002 年又复苏了。

3. 饼形图

欧洲与亚洲的 IT 消费

这份有关明年全球计划信息技术消费的调查显示出欧洲与亚洲的巨大差别。

根据调查结果，欧洲公司将提高信息技术消费、保持今年的水平和计划下降的比例几乎是相同的。

亚洲的情况很不一样。和欧洲刚刚超过三分之一的情况相比，几乎百分之六十受调查的亚洲公司计划增加明年的信息技术花费。

进而，由于只有百分之十六的亚洲公司计划减少消费，与欧洲的百分之三十相比，亚洲公司似乎并不热衷于削减信息技术支出。

最后，虽然水平数字不同，但是计划维持信息技术支出不变的公司比例也比亚洲的底。

第十五课 （图表）趋势描述

课文一

这是奶品营销董事会主席关于奶类饮品市场趋势的宣讲。

宣讲者：我们都知道在过去的十年里我们的市场发生了一些大的变化，而我们期待在未来十年发生一些深入的变化。我将说明过去十年里的趋势以及展望未来十年可预测的趋势。

让我们从过去十年的趋势开始。在第一张幻灯片中，你可以看到两个饼形图——第一个代表年前的奶品市场，第二个代表现在的。这里有两个明显的特征：第一，市场整体规模从 2.8 亿升大幅增长为 4.4 亿升；第二，四种主要奶制品的具体份额也显著变化了。全脂奶的份额从百分之七十四大幅度的下降到了只有百分之四十二——在饼形图的这里。脱脂奶的份额飞速地从只有百分之十二上升到百分之三十五，这反映了对于低脂饮食的宣传影响力。此外两种是超长保鲜奶和奶类饮料。很有意思的是，超长保鲜奶的份额从百分之五上升到了百分之十三。考虑到最初消费者对这一品种的抵触情况，这一增长是非常有意义的。最后，奶类饮料基本保持平稳，只上升了百分之一。因此，这十年来最大的赢家是脱脂奶和超长保鲜奶，而最大的输家是全脂奶。

现在，真正重要的是这四种产品在未来十年的可能趋势。如果你看一下这张折线图，可以看到我勾画出的这四种产品的相同趋势。在这条线以上是未来十年的预测趋势。我们预计全脂奶在未来五年中会逐步下降至大约百分之四十左右，然后在十年末再继续下降百分之二。

脱脂奶份额会在未来五年继续稳步增长至百分之四十，并在接下来的五年中在这一数字上下基本保持平稳。我们期望超长保鲜奶能持续增长，并在十年期末达到意义非凡的百分之二十。最后，我们估计奶类饮料会由于消费者对于这些饮料中糖分含量的意识提高而大幅下降。我们觉得在十年期末甚至会下降到只有百分之二。

课文二

  现在是六点钟，交易员们聚集在会议室等待奥古斯特斯·法拉第。

  你们来到这里的原因是，昨天在股票市场上是不平凡的一天。因此，我们能提前做好准备是非常重要的。但是，让我先通报大家在过去的 24 小时内的最新进展。在我进入具体的几支主要股票的表现之前，我想让大家看一些上个交易日三大股票市场的图形。

  好了，我们先看看日经指数。现在，你们看到的数字是我们这里的周一下午的交易情况。开盘是 23920 点，相当的不错。在最初的两个小时里又上升到了一个高点，然后在 10 点左右逐渐回落。这一时段的表现反映了我们市场的上升势头。在这之后，日经指数保持了两个小时的平稳直到我们市场在傍晚下滑。接下来，在当地时间下午一两点钟，指数开始震动。到了下午四点左右，指数回落至早上的开盘点位。下午晚些时候，利好消息的释放暂时推高了指数，但是没有足够的利好支撑上涨，因而下行趋势继续。因此，除了在晚上有一个主要的回升之外，整体一天都是相当惨淡的，日经指数收盘于 22980 点，下降了 940 点。

  现在是周一早上金融时报指数开盘时的活跃情况。在上午 10 点钟左右，它达到了 3267 点，这是自黑色星期四以来的最高点。然而，接下来传来了建筑行业的年中报告结果。指数直线下降了 40 点，回到了开盘点位。接下来，在上午末尾有所好转，当我们开盘的时候，伦敦市场已经超过了早上开盘时的点位。除了小幅度下降，它在下午刚开始的时候一直上涨至 3412 点，反映了我们这里 11 点左右的一个小高峰。接下来，流言四起，传来低迷的电子行业的两起破产传闻，使得在余下的时间里股价下跌。到闭市的时候，伦敦几乎失掉了它一开始取得的成果。

  好了，对比一下我们自己的表现。昨天的市场是在一个震荡形式下开盘的。上周末的美元升值继续驱使市场下滑。好消息是这种下滑没有持续很长时间。在早上 10 点钟左右，我们初步看到一些市场信心。虽然有一些回落，在下午开始之前，市场还是积极的。当成交量回升，市场作出反应，我们看到持续两个小时的上涨。我就是其中一个觉得这并不能持续的人。

  然而，除了微小但剧烈的下降，市场继续在晚间一直上涨，收盘于 3742.85。至此，这就是三个主要市场的表现。现在，我想更具体地分析几支我们今天要交易的主要股票。正如我所说，我们的目标是全力保卫我们的点位，坚守我们昨天的成果。

课文三

中国外商直接投资连续六个月下滑

外商在华直接投资在全球经济困境中至 4 月份连续下滑了六个月。

外商直接投资 4 月份同比下降百分之零点七四到 840 亿美元，3 月同比下降百分之六点一，2 月份同比下降百分之零点九，1 月份同比下降百分之零点三。

在前四个月中，中国接受了 378.8 亿美元的外商直接投资，比上一年下降了百分之二点三八。

从负债累累的欧盟得到的投资在一月至四月期间同比跳水了百分之二十七点九。然而，从美国和日本得到的投资分别爬升了百分之一点九和百分之十六。

国家在前四个月批准新建 7016 家外商投资企业，同比下降百分之十三点九四。

然而，伴随着在华投资的下降，中国对外投资却有上升的势头。中国非融资性海外直接投资在前四个月总额达到 231.6 亿美元，同比上升了百分之七十二点八。

第十六课　商务报告

调查报告

上海分公司的销售业绩

依照您的指示，我们调查了上海分公司销售下滑的原因。我们走访了办公室和它们大部分的主要客户。这里是我们的调查结果。

结果

1. 在上海的一些主要客户结业了，一些搬到了其他地区。
2. 由于新苏州和无锡经济活跃并且能够从当地政府那里享受到一些优惠政策，其他一些客户计划搬到那里。
3. 上海办公室没有保留搬出的已有客户和有可能搬入的客户的即时邮件列表，以便寄出广告传单。

4. 我拜访的客户对取代目前我们供应的传统型号的更新型空调系统感兴趣。

结论
1. 需要更优惠的售后服务组合以留住客户。
2. 需要更新我们的广告宣传单。
3. 供货需要调整为用新型产品代替目前型号。

建议
1. 在上海设一名流动销售代表，与搬出上海但是依然采购我们产品的客户保持联络。
2. 上海分公司需要处理信息与数据搜索的技术支持。
3. 应该用最新型号替换我们的供货。

建议书

关于西部五针松市场销售的可行性建议书

介绍
在过去的四十多年里，在北落基山脉，大量西部五针松的死亡主要是由于受到了松疱锈病菌和山地松虫的袭击。据估计，每年的死亡率达到了3.18亿板英尺。由于五针松天然抵御松疱锈病菌的能力低，高死亡率将会蔓延下去。

问题陈述
由于商业木材市场不能接受这一问题，五针松的死亡导致木材价值的下降。这个问题主要有两个方面的影响：第一，面对木材需求的增长，大面积的林场无用武之地；第二，大量被蚕食的木材堆砌在林场，很快会形成火灾隐患。

建议解决方案
一个解决五针松死亡和浪费问题的可行性方案是寻求传统市场以外的市场。在过去的几年里，出现了大量的需求和风潮，都是有关于风化板材和带有虫蛀痕迹的市内装潢的。我国周边的一些公司正在把有瑕疵的木材当做特殊商品销售。这就有了这样一种可能性，遇到困境的五针松可能在这部分市场上找到发展空间。

方法
我的主要数据来源包括了向木材应用教授詹姆斯·希尔博士和森林经济学家史蒂文·伯格曼博士咨询后的意见，这两位都是林业及野生动物学院的老师。我还将考察几个地方的五针松枯树产地和走访加工工厂以便评估它可运营的价值。我将通过对加工者和瑕疵产品批发商的问卷或电话访谈,来进一步丰富我的研究。二手资料将包括枯树应用的出版物搜集和希尔博士关于五针松枯树应用从过去到现在的研究。

调查人资格

我随希尔博士研究五针松枯树已经有两年时间了。今年6月份,我将获得森林管理的理学学士学位。我熟悉木材加工过程并有伐木的直接经验。我与希尔博士和伯格曼博士的合作创造了深入可行性研究的良好机遇。

结论

很明显的,我们应该做点什么来降低在森林中五针松枯树的大量堆积。它们占有的土地是爱达华北部最肥沃的森林土地。通过撰写上述六个部分,我可以确定瑕疵五针松产品成产的直接资本的可行性。如您审核通过,我将立即开始我的研究。

常规报告

关于新分公司第一年情况的报告

自从我们的新分公司阿尔法在华沙成立已经有一年了。在指出其成功之处、面临的问题和来年计划之前,让我先来提醒您一下它成立的原因。

成立的原因

事实上,选择落户波兰只有一个主要原因:降低劳动力成本。实际上,作为化妆品经营商,我们需要大量人手,而劳动力成本在波兰比在瑞典低很多。

成功之处

了解了这一目标,我们再继续。我们设法按时建起了新工厂生产线运转正常!我们更大的胜利是按时开始运营以及高效生产。

经历的问题

但是,我们也遇到了两个方面的问题:
- 交通 波兰的路网不是太好,花在路上的时间比预计的多。
- 人员 我们还应多了解员工的文化与期望。

来年的计划

来年我们的计划主要是提高上述问题(在生产进行顺利的情况下)。因此,我们将研究购买少量运输车的可能性(发货配送不依赖他人)。我们还将组织面向当地员工和海外经理的恳谈会,让大家更好地相互了解。

最后,我想借此报告的机会,邀请公司管理者随时到阿尔法访问。

总经理
主管新分公司

第十七课　跨文化商务沟通

课文一

翻译问题

即使是同一语言的文化——就像美利坚合众国和大不列颠——也存在着词汇差异。不同语言的文化间，翻译就很关键——但是往往并不完美。据估计，全世界有五千种口语语言，包括变体与方言，属于大约两百个不同的语种。我们找到了五个可能会成为跨文化沟通障碍的翻译问题。

等价词汇

首先是缺少等价词汇。生活在北极地区的人们有很多不同的词来表示"雪"。如果你要一对一地翻译，你可能会把那些不同的表示"雪"的词都翻译成英语"snow"。他们那些更为具体的、描述性更强的词——比如，表示水分多、硬的或新的——其中的意思就被忽略掉了。另一个例子是，想象一下不得不将各程度的粉红、紫红、橘红等都翻译成"红色"。正如你能想象得到的，如果你习惯于使用更多具有描述性的词，如此局限是多么的让你感到挫败。

一个经常被引用的缺乏等价词汇的例子发生在"二战"期间。同盟国向日本下达波斯坦通牒，要求他们投降结束战争。在新闻发布会上，铃木首相被问到他的意见。他回答说："政府没有发现这里有什么价值。我们所能做的只有mokusatsu。"日本内阁小心措辞来传达其间含义。过了一会儿，日本内阁官员说，由于他们对于谈判投降是感兴趣的，并且需要时间讨论一下，他们当时试图表达温和的"无评价"。不幸的是，mokusatsu 一词可以含有从"忽视"到"沉默轻视对待"的不同意思。西方翻译者用了后者，随即波斯坦通牒被认为是被拒绝了。事后可靠证据说明这一翻译导致了战争的继续以及第一次核武器的使用。

等价习语

成功翻译的第二个障碍是习语的等价词汇问题。特别是英语中充满了习语。举个简单的例子是"the old man kicked the bucket"。讲母语的人知道这一习语指的是老人去世了。如果这句话被逐字翻译了，表达出的意思将会是"老人踢了水桶"——与本意完全不同。你当然还可以想到很多其他的例子。只是想一下习语"out to lunch"和"toss your cookies"就会造成沟通误解！

不理解习语会是致命的。在1993年，一位来自日本的交换生去往一个万圣节聚会找错了地址，并且因为不理解"freeze"的含义而遭到枪击。我们很容易想到一些美语中常用的习语会被误解："back off"、"ckut that out"、"get lost"、"duck"和"hands in the air"。这是为什么英语作为外语比较难学的原因之一。然而，学习文化理念是学习文化的一个有效方法。

等价语法——句法

语法——句法的等价物是第三个问题。这意味着不同语言之间并不必须有相同的语法。通常，你应该理解一种语言的语法来理解词的含义。

比如，英语中的词要视它在句子中的位置来决定它是名词、动词或形容词。在英语中，我们可以说"plan a table"和"table a plan"或者"book a place"和"place a book"或者"lift a thumb"和"thumb a lift"。

等价经验

第四个是等价经验的问题。如果一个事物或经历在你的文化中是不存在的，由于没有针对性的词存在，你就很难翻译它们。想一想在你的文化中具有的事物和经历而在其他文化中没有的。"department store"和"shopping mall"和"wind surfing"可能在一些语言中就很难翻译。

等价概念

最后，等价概念的问题指的是在不同语言中可能不存在抽象概念的相同表达形式。比如，在美利坚合众国"freedom"一词有特殊的含义，那个意思不是普遍都适用的。其他语言的使用者可能会说他们是自由的，在他们的文化中是对的，但是他们所指的自由并不是你所经历的自由的含义。

在1994年的一次访谈中，前总统卡特指出了"人权"一词的概念等价问题。对于卡特来说，每个国家都从自身来定义这个词。在美国，人权指的是《人权法案》。其他国家定义这一词为充足住房或全民医疗保险。

课文二

跨文化沟通的挑战

文化差异影响到商务信息在工作地的形成、构架、传送、接收和解释。当今日益多元化的工作团队包含有广泛的技巧、传统习惯、背景、经历、观点和对待工作的态度——所有这些可能影响到工作中员工的行为。主管们面临着与不同员工沟通的挑战，要激励他们，培养合作和谐的关系。团队面临着亲密合作的挑战，公司面临着同时面对商业合作伙伴和行业整体的挑战。

　　文化与沟通之间的相互作用是无处不在的，想要将两者分开几乎是不可能的。从你的语言和非语言信号的传递方式到你理解他人的方式，你沟通的方式都受到你成长的文化环境的影响。词汇的含义、手势的意义、时间空间的重要性、人际关系规则，这些以及其他许多沟通方面都是由文化定义的。在很大程度上，你的文化影响着你的思维，这在本质上影响着你作为发送者和接收者的沟通方式。因此，你可以看出跨文化沟通与简单语言交流相比较是多么得复杂。它超越了单一词汇而上升到信仰、价值和情感。

课文三

包容多元化，成功有保证

　　国际商业机器公司 IBM 中的 I 代表"国际的"，但是这也可以简单地理解为代表"跨文化"以证明计算机巨头长期以来包容多元化的承诺。IBM 全球员工多元化，副总裁泰德·查尔斯根据多年经验知道成功的在各文化间进行沟通不是一件简单的事情，然而——特别是在一家拥有超过 325000 名员工和在全球大约 175 个国家进行销售的公司。

　　当你考虑到 IBM 的员工讲着超过 165 种语言，你就会知道单单是语言就是沟通中一个难对付的障碍。但是语言只是跨文化沟通影响因素之一。年龄、民族背景、性别、性取向、身体素质和经济地位的差别都可以影响沟通过程。查尔斯认为这些差别既代表了挑战又代表了机遇，他主要的工作是帮助 IBM 管理层和员工在工作中将他们的文化差异转换成关键的商业实力。当他这样做的时候，多元化员工已经从道德规则转换成战略规则了。

　　IBM 的多元化努力，从吸引其能找到的最优秀的人才开始，到后来帮助这些不同文化背景的人可以有效沟通。超过一百个网络小组将不同背景、个性和专业特长的 IBM 员工结合起来并支持着他们。多元化努力也延伸到了公司以外，达到了供应商和客户那里。事实上，查尔斯看到的 IBM 的多元化努力的一个重要优势是在日益多元化的市场里更有效沟通的能力。

　　近些年随着员工多元化成为一个热门话题，对于个人的尊重已经长时间地成为了 IBM 企业文化的核心内容。比如说，1935 年公司命令女性可以得到同等的机会并且男女同工同酬——这是在同等报酬写入美国法律的 28 年之前。IBM 还是美国第一家建立保障不同种族、不同信仰人员平等就业机会政策的公司——比民权法在大陆法系中写入这样的条款早了十多年。

在其雇用并与不同文化人员合作的漫长历史中，IBM 也学到了一些刻骨明心的训诫。最具有意义的莫过于认识到由于包容多元化，避免忽视他们或假设他们对于人际沟通没有影响，管理多元化员工以及在多元化市场上竞争才能够成功。这是每一个有志向的企业应该铭记的训诫。正像查尔斯所说，"无论你是谁，你一定将会和与你不同的人一同工作……管理与你不同的人。"

课后练习参考答案

第一课

A.

1. Pan Electronics. Can I help you?
   Yes, I'd like to speak to Miss Rathbone.
   Who's calling, please?
   Peter Jones.
   Just a moment, Mr. Jones, I'll put you through.
2. Mr. Gotman here. Could I speak to Ms Fields?
   I'm afraid she's out at the moment. Can I take a message?
   Yes, could you ask her to call me back?
   Yes, of course. Could I have your number?
   She's got it, but just in case, it's 071-253-4686.
3. Just a moment, I'll get my diary … you said next week?
   Yes, could you manage Wednesday?
   I'm sorry, I'm out on Wednesday.
   What about Thursday then?
   Good, that suits me too. Shall we say 11 o'clock?
   Yes, Thursday morning would suit me fine.

B.

1. Could you spell it, please?
2. Is it 24 Tunnyside Lane?
3. 0432

No, it is
Oh, I see. It is 04325686.
4. Could you tell me what it is in connection with, please?
5. Of course.
6. I see. It is 3.56 metres.
7. Would you repeat the hotel name
Could you spell it, please

C.
1. l   2. h   3. j   4. m   5. k   6. a   7. c   8. c
9. g   10. d   11. l   12. m   13. f   14. i   15. e   16. d

D. 略

第二课

略

第三课

略

第四课

1. Could I start by asking about the full company name?

2. Where is your company? Where is your company based?

3. How many employees do you have at the moment? What is the scale of your workforce?

4. Is it a limited company or not? Do partners have limited responsibility for the company or not?

5. When did the company set up? What is the starting year of your company?

6. How is your business? What are your secrets of success?

7. Your delivery time is perceived as one of the best in this city, what is the critical step about it?

8. After-sales service is an important segment in your business, how do you train your staff in that?

9. Right, let's leave that open and move to the financial area.

10. Under the current economic climate, what is the major problem of your finances?

11. What is the exactly figure of your liabilities by the end of last month?

12. Would you mind telling us the bank's name that you loan from?

13. Thank you for your time and information. Could you help us contact more customers so that we can make the interview more relevant and informative?

第五课

A. 招聘要求：
学士学位
在战略策划、投资银行或相关企业一至三年相关工作经验优先。
较强的分析能力
出色的口语与书面沟通能力
同时管理多个项目的演示能力
具备作为团队成员的幽默感

B. 略

第六课

A. 1. g 2. c 3. I 4. a 5. f 6. I 7. c 8. a
9. d 10. e 11. f 12. h 13. j 14. e 15. b 16. g

B. at last/finally/next/last of all/lastly
In fact/Actually
Obviously/Clearly/of Course
In brief/In short

namely
such as/for example/for instance
Of course/Clearly/Obviously
Therefore/So/As a result
In addition/Also
particularly/especially
However/But
in other words/that means

C. 参考译文

英语宣讲技巧

很多时候，我们大多数人不得不发表一次宣讲。就算英语是你的母语，在公开场合讲话也会让人害怕，更别说英语只是你的第二语言。

本文是有关宣讲技巧的，我们展示给你如何用八个步骤甩掉宣讲中的压力，帮助你准备好出色的宣讲。

1. 了解你的听众

为了宣讲的有效性，你需要了解你的听众。他们的英语水平如何？他们对于你要宣讲的主题了解多少？为什么他们会有兴趣听你的宣讲？找出到底是谁会参加你的宣讲是个不错的主意，以便你可以准备与他们有关的、有趣的内容。比如，面向财务分析师的有关你公司财务结果的宣讲就应该重点是结果、原因与分析。有关新的审计软件的宣讲应该把重点放在软件的优点与特性上。

还要问一问自己，通过宣讲你要达到什么目的。比如销售宣讲与信息传达宣讲就不同。由于可以帮助你专注于宣讲的语言和内容，明确你想要听众如何思考或在宣讲结束时做什么通常是明智的。

2. 强有力的开场白或问题使听众感兴趣

宣讲的第一分钟是至关紧要的。在这段时间里，你要取悦你的听众，给他们一个理由听下去。在第一分钟里说什么取决于你的听众和他们的兴趣，但一定是他们觉得重要的。也许是一个你知道如何解决的问题，或者他们需要知道的事实或数据。

3. 不要忘记硬件条件

你需要确保场地能满足参加的人数，并且有你需要的所有设备。在宣讲的时候你会发现，如果恰好在午饭前或周末，参加的人数会减少。如果宣讲会发生在不利的时间，你需要确保宣讲很有意思。

4. 准备宣讲目录

计划有助于你专注于宣讲的目标，尽量减少出错的几率。

如果你知道你的听众是谁以及你为什么要对他们宣讲，你要站在他们的角度想一想。你可以决定一下要包含什么内容和如何组织这些内容。

宣讲不要超过三十分钟，在最后留出提问和回答的时间。请记住：听众很难吸收很多的新信息，所以不要面面俱到。

许多宣讲分为五部分：

a. 介绍（请别人向听众介绍你。这样可以提高你的可信度并传递出你并不需要浪费时间告诉大家你是谁、你为什在这里的信息。）

b. 概述

c. 宣讲主体

d. 总结

e. 提问与回答的部分

把你在宣讲中所要说的内容整理为要点，做一个计划。按照主要观点加支持论据的模式整理你的宣讲。

在宣讲中，切记重述你在开场白中的内容是提醒听众为什么要听你的宣讲的好方法。

5. 使用索引卡片

把要点写在你个人的索引卡片上，在你的宣讲中是有帮助的。把关键词写在卡片上（一张卡片上一个关键词或要点），如果忘记你可以随时看到。

任何你觉得难记、难读的词都可以写在卡片上。

你还可以用卡片来写两个要点之间的连接，比如："这使我……"，"现在我要进行到……"，"好了……"。

6. 保持可视材料的简洁

在可视材料上不要放太多的信息，只是用它们来说明信息而避免了过多的解释。

一些图表可视材料，比如饼形图和柱状图，比那些文字和标注要好。可以使用不同的颜色和字体使信息突出。

7. 多练习效果好

用索引卡片尽可能多地练习你的宣讲。通过练习，你会知道需要多长时间，哪些部分是困难的。练习得越多，你会感觉更自信！

8. 准备问题与回答

在宣讲的最后，你很可能面临很多提问。因此试着预先设想一下以及可行的回答。这些你准备得越多,你就更有信心去面对和处理。

第七课

A. 参考译文

宣讲一

……我认为,在大多数公司中的大多数经理都不能完全信任。当然,所有这些公司都已经进行了重组,因此没有那么多的管理层;当然,所有这些公司已经把他们的资历较浅者,甚至中层管理人员放入了团队建设项目。但是我问你——在你的公司有多少高管经历了这种培训?一个都没有!权力欲望强烈的、妄自尊大的、工作狂般的和极端自私的高管依然在大多数公司盛行。当然了,这些公司在 80 年代需要这样的经理——这些无情的人是为跨国公司开疆拓土的人。但是问题在于,他们还适合当今吗?就算你能说服他们参加团队建设项目,他们也不会改变……

宣讲二

……我想占用你们的一点时间来揭示一些管理发展的新途径。如果需要,你可以随时打断我。好了,那么管理发展……这个词表示什么?我不认为这需要花很多时间来下定义,但是仅仅为了让我们基本上统一认识,我把自己定义为中层以上管理者——我不想谈论毕业生发展项目或者资历尚浅的员工的管理课程……(一些人起身离开)是的,这是离开的好时机……那么我们定义自己为中层以上管理者。我要从我们最近运行的一个为设在布鲁塞尔的国际团队进行的领导力项目谈起……

宣讲三

……女士们,先生们,主席先生。我很荣幸今天在这里代表欧利根管理研究院。我的发言是关于我们的长期管理项目的,我的目的在发言中包括以下几个大的方面:首先,典型新生的简要描述;其次,课程与主要管理规程;最后,我们自己的内部评估与毕业生的安排记录。那么大多数新生都是在九年级之后加入这个项目的。他们没有或有很少的工作经验,在之前的教育经历中没有涉及过任何的商务管理内容。然而,他们是受过良好教育的,计算能力强的人,我们计划把他们打造成明日的经理……

B. 略

第八课

A. 1.d　2.e　3.b　4.g　5.c　6.a　7.h　8.f
B. 1.d　2.g　3.e　4.c　5.c　6.d　7.a　8.f
C. 美国商人与日本商人的区别是什么？以下信息可供参考：

美国人的谈判风格

- 快速进入主题
- 独立处理谈判情形，除非发生不可预见的、谈判员权力以外的事情，一般不用经过总部确认即可全权达成协议。
- 对于人际关系中的不拘礼节和平等性很看重，强调个人平等高于社会地位。
- 将真实信息和直接的回答视作相互合作的关键。
- 将复杂的谈判分割成为小的部分，一次只处理一件事。
- 依赖法律而不是友情。
- 连贯性与可预测性强，以行动为导向的处理每个人与事，风格直率。

日本人的谈判风格

- 强调人际和商务中的上下级关系
- 强调长期关系的重要性
- 相比较真诚程度，更重视人际间的和谐关系，很难从日本人口中得到"是"或"不是"的回答。
- 在一致同意的基础上作出决策。
- 用语调、眼神、沉默和肢体语言等方式交流。

第九课

A. 略
B. 略

第十课

A. short, inform, persuade, setting, policy, increase, attend, little, deadline, Change

B. I would like to let you submit … files to me.

I want to know what has happened exactly.

According to your requestment in memo on March 2nd, I have investigated …

Shall we get together and discuss … later this week?

C. 3,5,1,4,2

D. 喂？威廉姆斯先生？我是丹尼斯·唐。是的，高级财务主管。您看，威廉姆斯先生，我恐怕在最近发送给您的数字中出了一点小错误。是的，嗯嗯，并不是我的问题。计算机死机了。您也知道事情是怎么回事……我可以给您发一份修改后的数字吗？可以啊，好的。

E. 略

第十一课

A. 参考译文

雪拉：好了，我今天召开这个会议是要确定一下年度欧洲销售大会的细节。基本上，我们需要决定三个方面的问题：首先是日期，其次是地点，最后是会议设施。让我们从日期开始。罗伊，你有什么想法？

罗伊：我想我们只能安排在9月——很可能是最后一个周末。我刚看了一下日程表。在7月即将有个大型的交易会，大多数推销员都会参加。8月也不行——大部分销售人员那个时候会休假。9月的前两周……

特瑞希：抱歉打断一下，罗伊。雪拉，我刚查看了你的日程安排。9月的最后一周你将飞往日本……

雪拉：我什么时候回来？

特瑞希：嗯，你订的是周五晚上返回迈阿密的航班。周末再奔赴伦敦很困难。

雪拉：是啊。罗伊，我们为什么不能安排在 9 月的第二个周末呢？那是……

特瑞希：15 和 16 日。

罗伊：那不好办。正如我所说，9 月的前两个周末都会很忙。团队中的大多数人会参与到新型 XION 产品的上市中。

雪拉：确实，我忘记了。第三个周末呢？特瑞希，我什么时候动身去东京？

特瑞希：嗯，稍等，你将在周一早上从肯尼迪机场起飞。

雪拉：可不可以我改从伦敦走呢？

特瑞希：我觉得没有问题？

雪拉：好的，罗伊，第三个周末怎么样？也就是 22 和 23 日。

罗伊：好像可以。当然，我需要再和皮特确认一下。

雪拉：当然。一确定好马上告诉我们。现在，地点呢？罗伊，有什么主意？

罗伊：是的，我想我找到了一个理想的地点——就在伦敦郊外，离希思罗机场不远，叫作 SWALLOW 酒店。

雪拉：听起来不错啊。价格如何？

罗伊：嗯，我们现在可以得到周末每个参会代表两百五十美元的优惠，我认为还可以更少些。

雪拉：好的。全部包括吗？

罗伊：是的，全都有。

雪拉：太好了。看，我现在必须离开了。两个小时内我的飞机就要起飞了。我能留下你和特瑞希把这些细节整理一下吗？

B.

background

On the 23 of this month at 6:30 in the morning, a security guard discovered that a fire had broken out on the roof of the Shafesbury Building. The fire had burnt the outside surfaces of Cooling Tower 14. In particular, the wooden topping and part of the cooling tower's upper casting were completely burnt.

Discussion

JC moved the fire started outside, lighting has problem. HF moved lighting is not to blame as the building is completely sheltered under the lighting protection system and it is routinely checked and serviced. And they agreed on vandalism.

Solution

JC and PK agreed on tougher security, extra patrol points around the building perimeter and dead corners.

PK moved the timber of the cooling towers should be protected with flam-retardant paint.

Summary

JC summarized the most likely cause of the fire was vandalism and increased security is needed to combat in the future. Kuen Wah has carried out the necessary remedial work on Wednesday May 1, and undertaken the repainting with flame retardant paint.

第十二课

A. 8, 3, 2, 4, 1, 7, 6, 5
B. 略
C. 略
D. 略

第十三课

A.
Dear Mr. Matthews

With reference to your letter of 25 May, I am pleased to confirm my participation at this year's conference in July.

I would be grateful if you could send me further details about the programme.

Unfortunately, I will not be able to give an update on last year's talk. I am afraid that pressure of work will not allow time to prepare a talk.

However, I look forward to attending the conference again.

B. 1. A　　2. B　　3. A　　4. C　　5. D　　6. B
　　7. A　　8. C　　9. B　　10. B　　11. C

C. 略

D. Extract 1　letter of enquiry
　　Extract 2　chase-up letter threatening legal action if ignored
　　Extract 3　cover letter for an invoice

Extract 4　apology

Extract 5　congratulations

第十四课

A. 1. 折线图、柱形图、示意图等

 2. 地图、示意图等

 3. 组织结构图等

 4. 循环图、示意图等

 5. 直线图、柱形图、示意图等

 6. 组织结构图、示意图等

 7. 饼形图、示意图等

 8. 折线图、柱形图等

B. 略

C. At the first stage

 start/begin

 complete/finish

 While/Whilst

 once

 having finished/After finishing

 next step/stage

 finally/then

 After/Once

 start/begin

 has been completed/finished

 once/after

 At the same time as

 As soon as

 Finally

第十五课

A. Note the modifiers used below are not the only correct version

1. substantially
2. rapidly
3. fairly
4. by
5. slowly
6. markedly, from, to
7. significant
8. considerably
9. rocketed, plummeted.
10. modest

B. increased/risen

To

Slight

Going down

Slight/moderate

Increase/rise

Significant/ substantial/ considerable

Drop/fall

Push up

By

Remained constant

Drop/dip/slide/fall

Of

Push … up

to

C. 略

第十六课

A. 参考译文

艾莉森：你好，皮埃尔。这里是艾莉森。事情进行的怎么样？

皮埃尔：不太顺利。市场很不活跃。

艾莉森：哦，是吗？我们在欧洲其他地区的反响很好。

皮埃尔：我知道。但是法国的情况不同。

艾莉森：当然。好的，嗯… 我们先来浏览一下你那里产品的季度结果。新四氯乙烯系列销售得如何？

皮埃尔：嗯，上个季度我们销售了价值45万法国法郎的商品。

艾莉森：哦，计划不是60万吗？

皮埃尔：是的。我本来希望从连锁超市那里拿到一个大订单。

艾莉森：是的，我记得你告诉过我。发生了什么事？

皮埃尔：他们削减了香水的上架量，我们只拿到了15万法郎的订单。

艾莉森：哦，这很让人失望。其他系列呢？

皮埃尔：阿耳特弥斯系列销售的很好——达到了88万——比预计高很多。

艾莉森：哦，很好。其他地方没有这么好，很明显它更受法国人喜爱。

皮埃尔：可能吧。恐怕我要说，我们的两款主要产品没有如此成功——赫顿须后水和迈诺斯面霜。这两种产品的市场竞争激烈。

艾莉森：嗯。那么季度数据是？

皮埃尔：须后水只有80万，迈诺斯达到了55万。

艾莉森：哦，我这里有预测数据。我们当初认为须后水可以达到150万，麦诺斯达到75万。那么它们都比预计的低。

皮埃尔：我知道。我显然是过于乐观了。我以为我们会很快走出经济低迷。同去年相比，消费者在奢侈品上的消费下降了。

艾莉森：我能理解这些，但是所有地方的经济都不好。我们一定是漏掉了你们市场上的其他一些因素。

皮埃尔：嗯，我不认为是这样的。经济不景气有所好转但是预计的消费复苏还没有到来。

B. 略

第十七课

A. 1. b 2. f 3. d 4. a 5. g 6. e 7. c 8. h

B. 1. well-balanced
   2. random
   3. cohesive
   4. commitment
   5. evolves
   6. productive
   7. individuals
   8. foster
   9. multinational
   10. empowers
   11. incremental
   12. dimensions

综合练习

略

主要参考文献

1. Nick Brieger, Jeremy Comfort：《中级商务英语》，外语教学与研究出版社，2004 年。
2. Nick Brieger, Jeremy Comfort：《高级商务英语》，外语教学与研究出版社，2004 年。
3. John Thill, Courtland Bovee：《卓越的商务沟通》，北京大学出版社，2012 年。
4. Jeff Madura：《商学导论》，人民邮电出版社，2009 年。
5. Scot Ober：《现代商务沟通（第二版）》，中国人民大学出版社，2009 年。
6. Ian Mckinnon：《商务英语专题发言》，华东理工大学出版社，2011 年。
7. 陈准民：《工商导论》，高等教育出版社，2009 年。
8. 董洪兰：《商务会议与电话英语口语》，大连理工大学出版社，2011 年。
9. 金利：《600 词搞定英文 E-mail & 电话》，机械工业出版社，2010 年。
10. 庄恩平：《跨文化商务沟通案例教程》，上海外语教育出版社，2008 年。
11. 安秀梅：《现代商务英语写作》，清华大学出版社/北京交通大学出版社，2012 年。
12. 朱文忠、周杏英：《实用商务谈判英语》，对外经济贸易大学出版社，2008 年。
13. 朱梅萍：《商务英语阅读》，外语教学与研究出版社，2012 年。
14. 陈准民、陈建平：《商务英语写作（第二版）》，高等教育出版社，2009 年。

南开大学出版社网址：http://www.nkup.com.cn

投稿电话及邮箱：　022-23504636　　QQ：1760493289
　　　　　　　　　　　　　　　　　　QQ：2046170045(对外合作)
邮购部：　　　　　022-23507092
发行部：　　　　　022-23508339　　Fax：022-23508542

南开教育云：http://www.nkcloud.org

App：南开书店 app

　　南开教育云由南开大学出版社、国家数字出版基地、天津市多媒体教育技术研究会共同开发，主要包括数字出版、数字书店、数字图书馆、数字课堂及数字虚拟校园等内容平台。数字书店提供图书、电子音像产品的在线销售；虚拟校园提供 360 校园实景；数字课堂提供网络多媒体课程及课件、远程双向互动教室和网络会议系统。在线购书可免费使用学习平台，视频教室等扩展功能。